The birds of Mount Nimba, Liberia

Peter R. Colston & Kai Curry-Lindahl

with a section on the biogeographic context by
Malcolm Coe

British Museum (Natural History)
(1986)

Peter R. Colston
Subdepartment of Ornithology
British Museum (Natural History)
Tring, Herts, HP23 6AP

Kai Curry-Lindahl
Grenstigen 3
18133 Lidingo (Stockholm), Sweden
or
United Nations Environment Programme
Box 30552, Nairobi, Kenya

Malcolm Coe
Department of Zoology
Animal Ecology Research Group
South Parks Road, Oxford OX1 3PS

© British Museum (Natural History) 1986
Publication Number 982
ISBN 0–565–00982–6

Filmset by Gem Publishing Company, Wallingford
Printed by Henry Ling Ltd, The Dorset Press, Dorchester

First Published 1986
British Museum (Natural History)
Cromwell Road, London SW7 5BD

British Library Cataloguing in Publication Data

Colston, Peter R.
   The birds of Mount Nimba, Liberia.
   1. Birds—Nimba, Mount
   I. Title   II. Curry-Lindahl, Kai
   III. Coe, Malcolm
   598.29666'2   QL692.W4

The birds of Mount Nimba, Liberia

Contents

Mount Nimba
  Introduction: *Kai Curry-Lindahl*   3
  Mount Nimba: structure, climate and vegetation: *Kai Curry-Lindahl*   7
  The vertebrate fauna except birds: *Kai Curry-Lindahl*   13
  The biogeographic context: *Malcolm Coe*   13
  Man-made changes and their effects on the birds: *Kai Curry-Lindahl*   18

The Birds
  Introduction: *Peter R. Colston & Kai Curry-Lindahl*   21
  Breeding and moulting seasons: *Peter R. Colston*   21
  List of families   26
  Systematic section: *Peter R. Colston & Kai Curry-Lindahl*   27

References   104

Appendix
  Biometrics of Nimba birds: *Peter R. Colston*   107

Index   126

Acknowledgements

The Nimba Research Committee wishes to express its deep gratitude to the Liberian-American-Swedish Minerals Company (LAMCO) for its continuous financial and logistic support during a period of 20 years (1962–1982) of field and laboratory activities at Nimba.

The Nimba Research Committee is also indebted to the British Museum (Natural History) for publishing this report. It is also with great pleasure that we acknowledge Mr Peter R. Colston's willingness to undertake the writing up of the Nimba Bird collection, and the good cooperation I have had with him in sharing the authorship of this report. The pencil sketches of the birds (pp27–103) were drawn by Peter Colston.

In Liberia Mr Edward S. Yallah has worked with the Nimba Research Laboratory since 1964, and during this long period he has collected and prepared the great majority of the specimens on which this report is based. I am pleased to acknowledge the always excellent collaboration we have had with Mr Yallah. His intimate field knowledge of Liberian birds and other vertebrates has been a great help to zoologists working at Nimba under the auspices of the Nimba Research Laboratory.

Our indebtedness to the National Museums of Kenya, Nairobi, and to their former and present Directors, the late Robert H. Carcasson and Richard E. Leakey, cannot be adequately expressed. They generously made it possible for us to use the services of staff members of the Museums for several terms of field work in Liberia, and later on for them to work exclusively for a whole year on the Nimba bird collection after it had been brought to Nairobi. Moreover, the National Museums of Kenya and the East Africa Natural History Society gave me special permission to borrow a number of books and journals from their joint library to be used for writing my part of the present report. I am also under great obligation to Mr Donald Turner, Nairobi, who kindly assisted me with the loan of books and journals for the same purpose, and to Dr David Snow, who helped in the preparation of the final MS and was largely responsible for the section on breeding and moulting seasons.

Dr Malcolm Coe, Dr James R. Karr, Mr Stuart Keith, Mr Donald Turner and Robert J. Wolton (on behalf of the Oxford University Expedition) have kindly assisted me with notes and data from their ornithological field work at Nimba.

Last but not least I would like to express my gratitude to Professors Maxime Lamotte and Théodore Monod, who from the inception of the establishment of the Nimba Research Committee and Laboratory have helped by offering ideas and advice for research at Nimba and for the recruitment of scientists for the field work.

Kai Curry-Lindahl
Chairman
Nimba Research Committee and Laboratory
Nairobi, March 1982

The northern part of Mount Nimba in Guinea. Piedmont secondary vegetation in the foreground. Rain forest covers the lower slopes and grassland savannas the upper ones including the ridge. Photograph Kai Curry-Lindahl.

The main ridge of Mount Nimba in Liberia has virtually been carved away. The debris from the surface mining is thrown down the slope, destroying the forest; then erosion continues the destruction. 2 March 1981. Photograph Kai Curry-Lindahl.

Mount Nimba

The main mine site in 1978. The surface overburden has been dumped onthe left slope, which has led to severe siltation of streams at the mountain's foot. In the middle ground rows of shot holes lie ready for blasting, which will break up the iron rich itabirite. While on the terraces of old mine workings above a little secondary vegetation has begun to develop. In the background the extensive grassland patches, which lie beyond the Guinea border can be seen through the mist filled valleys. Photograph Malcolm Coe.

Rain forest around the bed of a perennial stream in Mount Nimba's Iti Valley during the dry season. 1 March 1976. Photograph Kai Curry-Lindahl.

Andropogon-Loudetia grassland established on shallow lateritic soils 1 km from New Camp on the Mount Bele road, here the laterite has been undermined by water and the cap has broken up allowing small patches of forest to develop. This forest is dominated by *Albizia*, *Ficus* and *Musanga cecropioides*. Once the grassland reaches its full height this area provided a large nesting site for a colony of the Red-headed Quelea (*Quelea erythrops*). Photograph Malcolm Coe.

Introduction

Liberia lies in West Africa between 4°13' and 8°35' north of the equator. It is almost entirely located within the tropical lowland rain forest belt of Africa. Only its northernmost part extends into the belt of Guinean savanna woodland, which stretches across Africa from Senegal to Sudan. Coastal mangrove swamps and lagoons, river marshes, and man-made savannas and bushlands are scattered within the high forest and concentrated along the coast. Far into the interior, on Liberia's northeastern border, an isolated mountain range, 40 km long and 12 km wide at its broadest point, rises above the lowland rain forest; Mount Nimba. It lies at the meeting point of three countries: Liberia, Guinea and Ivory Coast, the last two both former French territories. In 1942 the French initiated investigations into the natural history of their part of the mountain, and discovered its extraordinary biological interest, and the very high number of endemic species. In 1944 they declared their part of the Nimba Range as a strict nature reserve, and as a result of numerous publications it soon became known as one of the most important in Africa. However, on Liberian Nimba nothing was known about the plants and animals. Fortunately, the governments of Guinea and Ivory Coast have continued to maintain their parts of the Nimba Range as strict nature reserves.

The discovery in 1955 of high-grade iron ore in Liberian Nimba led to the formation of the Liberian-American-Swedish Minerals Company (LAMCO), which soon began to open up the rain forest area on and around Mount Nimba in order to mine. That meant the creation of a town for about 15 000 inhabitants, and the construction of industrial plant, roads, and a 275 km long railway linking Nimba to the Atlantic coast at Buchanan. Mining operations began in 1963.

All these industrial activities, in a rain forest area that from the human point of view had been almost dormant for millennia, were disastrous for the ecosystem of the Nimba Range and the surrounding country. The surface mining stripped the mountain of its vegetation and carved away its crest and slopes, so that the mountain's profile changed rapidly from year to year. The exposed soils and tons of mineral waste washed downwards, silting the rivers which became transformed from crystal clear streams to reddish muddy waters. It is not difficult to imagine what this change meant to all living organisms.

In order to document for science, if not to save, what existed of the plants and animals of Liberian Nimba and to investigate their ecology, I proposed in 1958, to the General Manager of LAMCO, that long-term botanical, zoological and ecological investigations should be carried out at Nimba without delay and before the destructive exploitation had been initiated. The initial response to this suggestion was unfortunately negative, but in 1961, Mr Erland Waldenström, President of LAMCO, realising what was at stake, accepted the proposal and this led to generous grants for research, a laboratory, houses for scientists, vehicles and other equipment.

LAMCO wished that the scientific investigations at Nimba should come under the aegis of an international organization. Therefore, in 1962 at a meeting in Seattle, U.S.A. of the Executive Board of the International Union for Conservation of Nature and Natural Resources (IUCN), I proposed that the Nimba Research Committee should be set up as an arm of IUCN responsible for the Nimba Research Laboratory plus the organization, administration and supervision of the scientific research at Liberian Nimba. This was accepted, and the Nimba Research Committee has since consisted of three persons: Professors Maxime Lamotte (France & Ivory Coast), Théodore Monod (France & Senegal), Kai Curry-Lindahl (Kenya, Liberia & Sweden – Chairman). The arrangement was approved by the Liberian government.

The Nimba Research Laboratory has been in operation from 1963 to 1982. The first team of scientists, led by Dr Malcolm Coe (Great Britain & Kenya), arrived at Nimba in 1964. Since then a number of scientists from 13 countries, chiefly botanists and zoologists, have worked at Nimba for varying periods, many of them returning for repeated visits. In this way all seasons at Nimba have been covered by botanical and zoological investigations.

Previous publications on the fauna and flora of Nimba

Project descriptions for the programme of research and preliminary accounts of the first seasons' studies of the vegetation and vertebrate fauna have been published by Coe & Curry-Lindahl (1965), and by Curry-Lindahl (1965, 1968, 1969*b*).

Since then, major works on the results have been published and others are in progress. Jacques-Georges Adam (France and Senegal) for many years carried out an extensive survey of the vegetation of Liberian Nimba. The results of this task have been published in a monumental work consisting of six volumes (Adam, 1971–1983), three were published after Adam's death in 1980. Almost all of the 1096 drawings of plant species were made by Adam. We are grateful to the author for his magnificent contribution. Other important publications on the fauna of Liberian Nimba are by Coe (1975), Misonne & Verschuren (1976), Verschuren (1976), Verschuren & Meester (1977), Hill (1982), Wolton *et al.* (1982*a*), and Wolton *et al.* (1982*b*) on mammals; Forbes-Watson (1969), Karr (1975, 1976*a, b*, 1980); Karr & James (1975), and Verschuren (1979) on birds; Curry-Lindahl (1972) and Xavier (1978) on amphibians; and Carcasson (1971) on butterflies. The moth collection from Nimba consists of some 8 000 specimens, mostly in excellent condition, and includes a large number of undescribed species (Carcasson, *in litt.*). It is located in

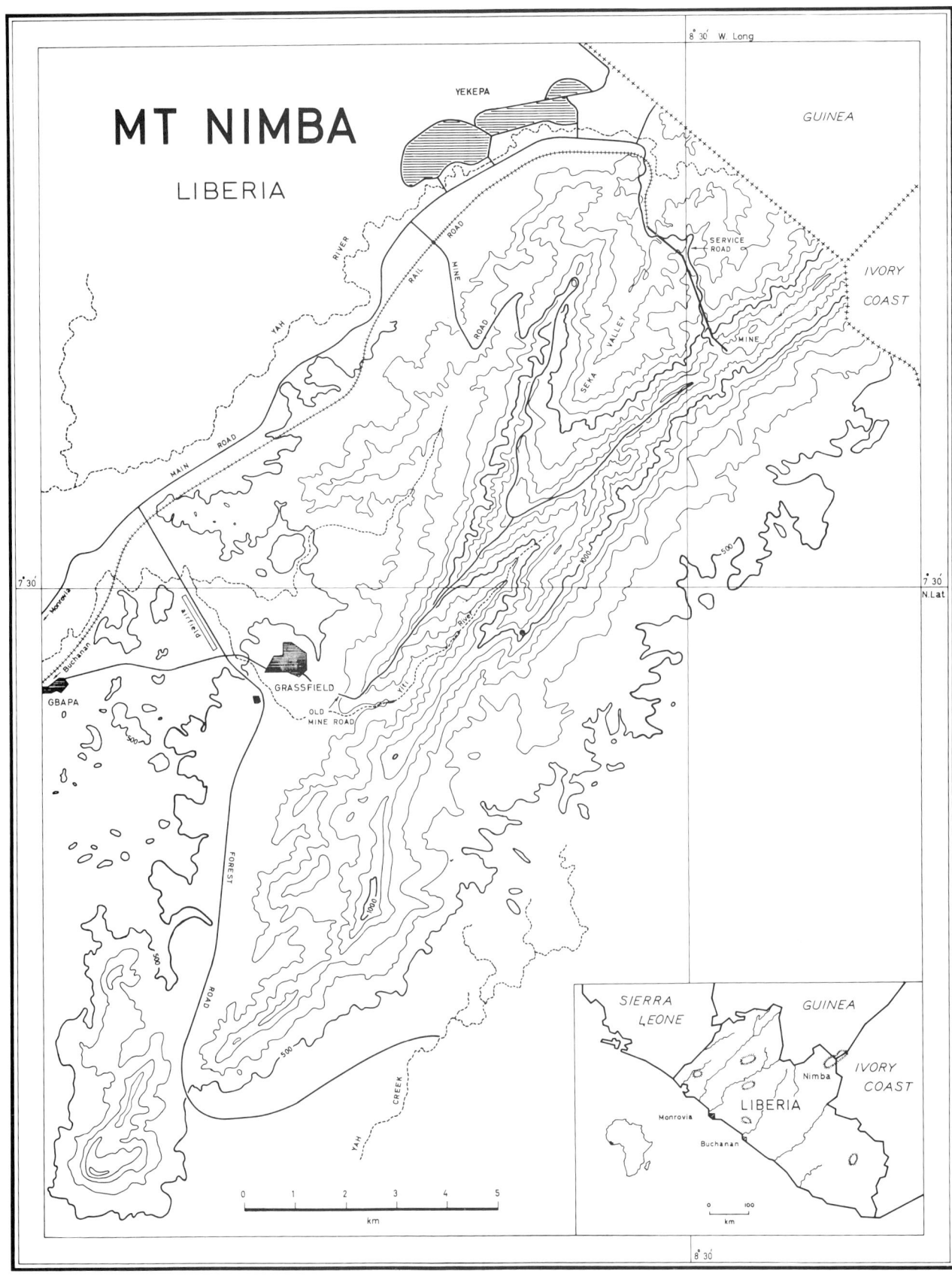

the National Museums of Kenya in Nairobi. Unfortunately the major part of this collection has not been worked on systematically. The material on reptiles will soon be published by Lamotte and Xavier. Other published papers have dealt with orchids, bats, fishes and shrimps.

The Guinea and Ivory Coast parts of Nimba are well-known through a number of publications. The major works are by Schnell (1952), Angel, Guibé & Lamotte (1954), Angel et al. (1954), Leclerc et al. (1955), Heim de Balsac (1958), Heim de Balsac & Lamotte (1958), Guibé & Lamotte (1958, 1963), Laurent (1958), Lamotte (1959), Aellen (1963), and Lamotte & Xavier (1972).

A summarized account of the natural history of the Nimba Range in Guinea, Ivory Coast and Liberia is given by Curry-Lindahl & Harroy (1972).

The ornithological programme

In planning the investigations on the vegetation and fauna of the Liberian part of Mount Nimba special attention was paid to the birds. There were good reasons for doing so. While all other vertebrate classes had been studied in the Guinea and Ivory Coast parts of Mount Nimba by French scientists of the Institut Fondamental d'Afrique Noire (IFAN), Dakar, no one had so far investigated the avifauna of the Nimba range or its surrounding lowland areas. The Nimba Research Committee was naturally anxious that this gap in our knowledge of West African ornithology should be eliminated. To this end Mr Alec Forbes-Watson of the National Museums of Kenya, Nairobi, was engaged for the task of making a representative collection of birds from the Nimba region, and at the same time carrying out detailed studies on avian biology, ecology, vertical distribution and zonation, migratory movements and so forth.

Forbes-Watson spent several periods of work at Nimba. He first worked for some 18 months in the field from May 1967 to December 1968. Another period of field work followed in January–April 1971, during which he was joined from 6 February to 2 April by Professor J. R. Karr (University of Illinois, Champaign) and Mr Stuart Keith (American Museum of Natural History, New York). In July 1976 Forbes-Watson returned to Nimba together with Mr Donald Turner (East Africa Natural History Society, Nairobi) for a week of observations. Between October 1964 and November 1966 Dr Malcolm Coe (University of Oxford) was Director of the Nimba Research Laboratory. He also worked on the birds and made collections. Dr Martin Moynihan (Smithsonian Tropical Research Institute, Balboa, Panama) worked for a period at Nimba on the ethology of some groups of birds. In July–September 1978 the Oxford University Expedition (R. J. Wolton (leader), P. A. Arak, H. C. J. Godfray and R. P. Wilson) worked at the Nimba Research Laboratory. Its main study was the fruit bats of Nimba through a programme of intensive mistnetting. Also 62 species of birds were caught in the nets, more or less by accident. In addition, the members of the Oxford Expedition observed and identified about 20 species of birds. These netted and recorded species have been communicated to us. They are taken into the account of this report.

During the period 1963–1982 I visited Nimba almost annually for month-long periods of field work. These visits were timed in such a way that each month of the year has been covered by field observations. However, it was not until after 1978, when it became clear that Alec Forbes-Watson would be unable to produce a manuscript on the birds, that I began to concentrate my field studies on birds in a more systematic way.

During the years 1964–1979 some 3400 study skins of 313 species of birds were collected and prepared at the Nimba Research Laboratory, Grassfield. Most of them were collected and beautifully prepared by Mr Edward S. Yallah and other members of the Laboratory, under the supervision of Malcolm Coe and Alec Forbes-Watson. For a period in 1968 Mr Joseph Mwaki, Taxidermist of the National Museums of Kenya, also worked with the 'bird team' at Nimba. The greater part of the collection consisting of 3070 study skins of 305 species, was presented to the British Museum (Natural History) by the Nimba Research Laboratory in April 1977. A further 63 study skins of 28 species, collected between 1971 and 1978 by Edward S. Yallah and other staff members of the Nimba Research Laboratory, were sent to the British Museum (Natural History) for confirmation of identifications. In November 1979 a third and final lot, consisting of 112 skins of 70 species, was likewise despatched to the British Museum (Natural History).

A collection of about 150 study skins representing 73 species was kept at the Nimba Research Laboratory, Grassfield. The material in this collection was checked and determined as to species by me in 1980 and 1981. A few of these species are not represented in the collections sent to the British Museum (Natural History), but they have been included in this report. Unfortunately, the collection kept at the Nimba Research Laboratory was destroyed or stolen in May 1981, when the laboratory was ransacked. It has been impossible to trace where this lost material (including mammals, reptiles, amphibians and fishes as well as invertebrates) has gone.

These collections made at Nimba have added very considerably to our knowledge of West African birds, and especially to knowledge of the avifauna of the Upper Guinea forest and of Liberia. Two species new to science were discovered: a flycatcher, *Melaenornis annamarulae* Forbes-Watson, 1970; and a honeyguide, *Melignomon eisentrauti* Louette, 1981; also a new race of

Fig 1 Map showing Liberian Nimba. The mining area is close to the borders of Guinea and Ivory Coast. Both slopes of this long ridge are steep and abrupt, mostly forest covered. Mining operations began in 1963.

Gradual elimination of the *Parinari* forest on the ridge of Mount Nimba is the first step for further mining activities. At this stage the forest is rapidly replaced by bushes, but soon this vegetation will be removed and the soil denuded. Photograph Kai Curry-Lindahl.

the flycatcher, *Muscicapa olivascens*. The studies at Nimba have added 117 species to the known Liberian avifauna and the ranges of 23 have been extended by anything up to 2 000 km west (Tables 2 & 3, prepared by P. R. Colston). Previously Allen (1930) listed 278 species for Liberia; Bouet (1931) added 12 more; and Rand (1951) a further 16. Louette's (1974) revised list included 347 species. The new total now stands at about 477 species.

Preparation of the report

Originally Alec Forbes-Watson was to have followed up his field work by writing a full report, that is, a description of the collection and a detailed account of the biology, ecology and vertical distribution of the Nimba birds. After some years it became apparent that for various reasons Forbes-Watson was unable to meet this commitment. Additionally, detailed data on localities, habitats, altitudes and other ecological information on the birds collected by Forbes-Watson, and his field observation records on breeding, behaviour and migrations are unavailable, and this has seriously handicapped the present report. In spite of these problems Mr Peter R. Colston undertook to write the major part of this work, while I have tried to cover ecology, behaviour and related topics, so far as my field data from Nimba allowed me to do so. Thus, the text of this report is the combined work of two authors, with an additional section on the biogeographic context by Malcolm Coe. The list of contents indicates which authors are concerned with the introductory chapters and tables. With regard to the 386 species accounts, Peter R. Colston is responsible for the sections on specimens, impermanent colours, stomach contents, annual cycle, geographical variation, status and distribution; while I have taken care of the sections on habits, migration and field notes, and of the entire entry in the case of species which were not collected. Sometimes there are deviations from this system, in which case the authors' initials indicate who is responsible for what. A full set of tabulated measurements and weights of the bird specimens are housed at the Sub-department of Ornithology at Tring, and are included here in an Appendix.

The conservation of Mount Nimba

During 20 years of work at Nimba we have constantly tried to make the Liberian Heads of State and governments aware of the great scientific, educational, recreational and scenic values of the Nimba area and the necessity for conservation measures in Liberia in general. Reports on these issues, requested by the government, were submitted in 1969 and 1979 (Curry-Lindahl, 1969a, 1979). Already in 1969 the President of

Liberia and his government approved the proposals to set aside a considerable part of Mount Nimba and surrounding lowland forests as a national park. As a first step two forest reserves were established. The governments of Guinea and Ivory Coast welcomed the idea of creating a combined international park covering the Nimba range in all three countries. As a step in that direction the government of Guinea submitted in 1980 to UNESCO a proposal that the Mount Nimba Strict Nature Reserve should become a World Heritage Site under the 1972 Convention concerning the Protection of the World Cultural and Natural Heritage. In October 1981 the UNESCO World Heritage Committee elected the Guinean Mount Nimba Strict Nature Reserve as a World Heritage Site. However, Liberia failed to take any action despite the constant efforts of conservation organizations including UNEP, UNESCO, IUCN and the Nimba Research Committee. Instead the destruction continued. So as far as conservation is concerned our work at Liberian Nimba has regrettably been a total failure.

Mount Nimba: structure, climate and vegetation

In the rain forest region of tropical West Africa are several isolated mountains, separated from one another by lowland forests and savannas. Only a few exceed 1500 m. The highest, Mount Cameroon on the coast, is 4070 m, the neighbouring island of Fernando Po rises to 2850 m, and the Loma massif in Sierra Leone reaches about 2000 m. After these comes Nimba, some 170 km from the Atlantic coast. Its highest point is 1752 m. The general orientation of the Nimba range is SW.-NE. The southern end of Mount Nimba in Liberia gradually drops and narrows, giving the impression from the air of gradually diving down into the lowland forest canopy. Both slopes of this long ridge are steep and abrupt, mostly forest-covered but in Guinea with scattered savannas on the highest parts extending down the slopes. There are also some isolated patches of grassland in the lowland forest. At the foot of the western side of central Nimba there is a large grassland savanna, mainly in Guinea but stretching into Liberia. The geology of the mountain is complex. It is a syncline consisting chiefly of ferrugineous quartzites and gneisses dating from the Precambrian period. A general description is given by Adam (1971) and briefly by Coe (1975).

The isolated situation of Mount Nimba gives it the character of a great Inselberg, with types of habitats quite different from the surrounding lowland forests and savannas, and an astonishingly high number of endemics almost entirely at the specific level. This is particularly the case for the animals of which about 200 endemic species are known.

At present there are among vertebrates 15 endemic species and 5 endemic subspecies known from Nimba. Moreover, one of the endemic species (a toad) exists exclusively on Liberian Nimba. These endemic vertebrates are divided as follows: mammals 4 species and 2 subspecies (1 bat species and insectivores); birds 1 subspecies (passerine); reptiles 4 species (3 lizards, 1 snake); amphibians 4 species and 1 subspecies; and fishes 3 species and 1 subspecies. The number of endemics will presumably be reduced when the surrounding lowlands and other isolated mountains in West Africa have been explored, although further explorations at Nimba will probably yield more biological surprises. At present it is difficult to say whether the high number of endemic species is due to the fact that Mount Nimba has functioned as a refuge for animals, which during previous pluvial periods were more widely distributed than today, or whether these animals, through geographical isolation have evolved from their ancestral forms into local races and species. Probably many factors have played a part. In any way Mount Nimba is important for speciation studies and it must be regarded as a key area for evolutionary and biogeographic research.

Climate

The typical climate at Nimba is humid, but the humidity decreases in the dry season from December to February–March. When the desert wind, the *Harmattan*, blows for several consecutive days humidity may drop to 12%, which K C-L experienced at an elevation of 1200 m on 10 January 1982, the lowest he had ever recorded at Nimba during a period of 20 years. Normally the maxima of relative humidity in the mornings vary throughout the year between 99 and 94%, and in the afternoons between 93 and 18%. The average minima of 18% are valid only for January and February during *Harmattan* periods. All the other months have much higher minima. The recording of only 12% on a '*Harmattan* morning' was indeed exceptional, but it indicates the tremendous climatic effect of air masses blown southwards by *Harmattan* winds, even in a rain forest area far away from the Sahara and the Sahel. This wind is not only dry, it is also so dust-laden that it reduces the visibility from 20–30 miles to less than one mile. This dry air can descend to ground level and persist there for several days until it is forced upwards by incoming moist air from the Atlantic Ocean.

A dense cloud cover hangs over Mount Nimba above about 850 m for much of the year but less during the dry season. Conflicting air currents create tornados in March–April. Since 1957 precipitation and temperature have been recorded at the Geologists' Camp on Liberian Nimba. As the Camp shifted sites several times, due to mining operations and the gradual disappearance of the mountain, readings were made at different altitudes from 1343 m in the 1950s and 1960s to 965 m in the 1970s and 1980s. Hence the statistics for the entire period of readings are not comparable. The annual rainfall at

Mount Nimba before the mining operations. The slope and the crest in the foreground are in Liberia, the farther part with natural montane savannas in Guinea. The Ivory Coast is located on the other side of the ridge. The boundary point between the three countries is situated in the cloudy part of the crest. 30 September 1963. Photograph Kai Curry-Lindahl.

these elevations has varied from 3825 mm to 1818 mm. The average is about 3000 mm. At Yekepa at the foot of Mount Nimba, located at 475 m, the precipitation is less than half that of Mount Nimba. The wettest months are usually May–October up in the mountain and April–October at its base, but there is a pronounced variation of rainfall within these periods, though the maxima normally fall in August–September. January is the driest month with 20 mm as an average.

The mean maxima and minima temperatures recorded on Mount Nimba give an amplitude of 16°C, from 30°C to 14°C.

There are detailed data on the climate of Mount Nimba in the works by Schnell (1952) and Adam (1971). There is also a good summary by Coe (1975).

The forests and their destruction

Liberian Nimba is entirely located within the rain forest biome, from the lowland plain to the highest ridge. In 1963, when Curry-Lindahl visited Nimba for the first time, the massif's slopes, crests, gorges and valleys were clad in magnificent primary forests, while the surrounding lowland rain forest on the Liberian side was essentially secondary in all stages of regeneration and with rather few plots opened by shifting cultivation. However, numerous patches of virgin lowland rain forest were at that time scattered here and there in the secondary forest as relicts. These natural forests were mainly found on hills or in marshy areas. In clear weather the view from the ridge of Mount Nimba over the lowland rain forest in Ivory Coast was spectacular. An unbroken leafy canopy stretched to the horizon in all directions.

This grand view is now only a memory. In the 1970s, and thereafter, a very different scene met the eye. Smoke from hundreds of fires now hangs over the forest, clearings can be seen in many places, and where formerly only rivers broke the dense high forest now roads cut frightful scars in it, and along the roads the forest is quickly destroyed.

On the Liberian side the forest destruction during the last 20 years has been even worse. The felling of forest has had profound effects on the birds. Some species have reacted negatively, others in a positive way. In addition to habitat alteration there have been other pressures. The human avalanche during two decades at Nimba has subjected the birds to tremendous persecution from the omnipresent gunbearers, who shoot for meat to eat or sell. The larger birds in particular have been victims of this shooting.

The habitats

In the following sections, brief descriptions are given of all habitats of significance to birds. This terminology is also used in the species accounts (pp. 27–103).

A detailed description of the vegetation and the flora of Mount Nimba has been given by Adam (1971–1983), from whom the following data have been summarized with some modifications. There is also a useful summary on the vegetation by Coe (1975), though readers of it may be confused by his terminology, since he refers to tropical rain forest as 'deciduous high forest'.

Primary and secondary lowland rain forest at the foot of Mount Nimba in Liberia. In the foreground *Musanga cecropioides* is a characteristic species of the secondary vegetation. 9 January 1982. Photograph Kai Curry-Lindahl.

THE MAIN FOREST TYPES. The marked increase in rainfall with altitude is reflected in the zonation of vegetation. The lower slopes of Liberian Nimba consist of mixed rain forest grading at 800–900 m into *Parinari* forest. This point of change also marks the cloud line, so that the capping *Parinari* forest associations may be regarded as 'mist' forest. *Parinari excelsa*, the dominant tree in this vegetation, has its trunk completely covered with a thick layer of filmy ferns, mosses and to a lesser extent lichens.

Rain forest between 450 and 850 m is very mixed but contains a large number of trees of commercial importance which have been exploited by LAMCO for construction purposes. The common genera are *Bussea*, *Chlorophora*, *Entandophragma*, *Lophira*, *Parkia*, *Piptadenia* and *Terminalia*. With the introduction of forest roads much shifting rice cultivation is taking place within this forest, and below an altitude of 550 m much of the high forest habitat is already in an advanced state of destruction and degeneration. Valley bottoms contain small areas of wet ground that support small stands of *Raphia* palm, while river courses associated mostly with the Ya River drainage support interesting riverine forests.

The main part of the lowland rain forest is located on a gently undulating and hilly plain at an elevation of 450–500/600 m. Secondary forests dominate. Primary forests have been greatly reduced during the last 20 years due to increased human population pressure through farming and other tree felling activities, but isolated patches of virgin lowland high forests are still present, though they are doomed to disappear soon. These primary forests vary from 1.5 ha to about 30 ha but are mostly only 5–10 ha.

PRIMARY LOWLAND RAIN FOREST. The remaining patches of dense high forest consist of up to 64 species of large trees (up to a height of 50 m and a diameter of 2.5 m) which form a closed canopy. Below it there are other strata composed of lower trees and larger bushes of up to 47 species. All these strata are characterized by numerous lianas (at least 28 species) and epiphytes (at least 13 species). Among the largest trees *Uapaca guineensis* is usually the commonest, *Piptadeniastrum africanum* the tallest and *Ceiba pentandra* the widest. (The latter species is not necessarily an indication of previous human activities.) Other characteristic larger trees are *Lophira alata* (up to 45 m), *Bussea occidentalis*, 4 species of *Entandrophragma*, and 2 species of *Terminalia*. Where the sun penetrates the canopy, there is a rich herbaceous growth, with at least 48 species, including 4 species of *Afromomum* and 3 of *Dracaena*.

The primary lowland rain forests around Nimba, and in Liberia, Guinea and Ivory Coast in general, are not as moist and luxuriant as those of the Congo Basin in Zaire and Gabon. They are nevertheless impressive enough and contain a very rich resident avifauna.

SECONDARY LOWLAND RAIN FOREST. As mentioned earlier, these forests around Nimba are in all stages of regeneration. It is impossible to describe all these stages, as it is a slow process, taking about 100–200 years, for the forest to restore itself to its former glory. Moreover, the regeneration takes a different course depending on the

Young saplings of *Terminalia* regenerate in a straight line in a gully alongside a forest track. The winged seeds of these trees are washed into these germination sites by heavy rain. Photograph Malcolm Coe.

soil, drainage and so forth. In areas which have been cleared and, or, burned and later abandoned, after only 2–7 years there is regeneration of young forest, covered by lianas, provided that there has been no subsequent disturbance and there is high forest near at hand. It is at this point that trees like *Musanga*, *Harungana* and *Trema* invade the area, become dominant and shade out the pioneering herbs and bushes. At this stage one may distinguish up to 48 species of young trees forming a kind of thicket which is later succeeded by other trees including 2 species of *Albizia*, *Anthonota*, *Fagara*, 2 species of *Terminalia*, *Elaeis* and 11 others. Then, gradually larger trees like *Ceiba*, *Celtis*, *Chlorophora*, *Ficus*, *Lophira*, *Piptadeniastrum* and several species of *Terminalia* take over. Later they are joined by others.

All these stages of secondary forests are important to the birds. A number of true forest bird species have adapted to these habitats. Apparently, clearings and areas of secondary growth surrounded by mature forest are optimal habitats for many true forest birds.

SWAMP FORESTS. There are very few primary swamp forests left in the lowland area around Mount Nimba, and on the mountain itself there are hardly any forested wetlands. However, in the lowlands there are several areas of secondary swamp vegetation, chiefly consisting of *Raphia vinifera* mixed with *Mitragyne ciliata*, that are remnants of the original forest. A few species of birds make permanent use of these habitats.

PLANTED FORESTS. At several places where the rain forests have been eliminated, LAMCO has planted exotic trees for timber production, mainly *Gmelina*, which now locally form deciduous or semi-deciduous forests. They are of little value to birds, but are visited occasionally by some species.

SLOPE AND RIDGE RAIN FORESTS AT 500/600–1200 m. The 'slope forests' on Mount Nimba are a type of forest transitional between lowland and montane rain forest. The Nimba Range is not sufficiently high for the development of true montane rain forest of the type existing on the high mountains of Zaire and East Africa, where such forests extend up to 2400 m or higher.

For Mount Cameroon, Serle (1981) draws a dividing line between the lowland and montane forest at approximately the 1050 m contour. From Curry-Lindahl's experiences of Mount Cameroon the upper limit of the montane forest runs at 1500–1600 m (Curry-Lindahl & Lamotte, 1964). This is much lower than is the case for the higher mountains and volcanoes of Eastern Zaire, Rwanda and East Africa. The upper Nimba forest has no similarity with the Zairese and East African montane forests, which even at their upper levels are much more luxuriant and much richer in birds and other vertebrates. For example, on the western slope of Mount Ruwenzori in Zaire there is, at about 1000–1300 m, a dense transitional rain forest (Watalinga Forest), with a very rich flora and vertebrate fauna, located between the lowland and montane rain forests (Curry-Lindahl, 1961). This level corresponds to the upper parts of Liberian Nimba. Thus the vegetation belts and zonation on Mount Nimba are in no way comparable either in structure or in altitudes with those in Zaire and eastern Africa, though both complexes share many species of plants and animals.

A Raphia palm swamp developing along a track side at 500 m where the drainage has been impeded and standing water accumulates through and beyond the wet season. In the background the secondary forest is festooned with lianes. This is an important habitat for birds, especially in the insectivorous species. Photograph Malcolm Coe.

The secondary forest below the main mine site rapidly gives way to anthropogenically derived grassland. Photograph Malcolm Coe.

The Nimba slopes are nevertheless covered by dense forests of a large number of species representing no fewer than 84 genera of trees and bushes. The altitudinal succession of the various types of forest from 500 m to 1200 m differs on different slopes depending on soils, rocks, steepness, exposure and drainage. In general one finds the following altitudinal succession:

> 500–700 m. *Piptadeniastrum, Lophira, Drypetes* and *Geophila* are dominant genera.
> 700–900 m. *Parinari excelsa* becomes increasingly common, with *Parkia, Amanoa, Schizoclea* and *Leptaspis*.
> 900–1000 m. At about the 900 m contour there is an important ecological boundary line. From here upwards a dense layer of clouds and mists usually covers the upper slopes and summits except during the dry months. This phenomenon is reflected in the vegetation. *Parinari excelsa* dominates with *Rinorea djalonensis* and *Dicranolepis laciniata*. Birds are less common in these forests, both in species and numbers, than at lower levels.
> 1000–1200 m. This is the 'ridge forest'. *Parinari excelsa* dominates with *Amanoa bracteosa* and *Ochna membranacea*, but *Parinari* may often form pure stands.

All these transitional montane habitats are important in maintaining a high diversity of birds. Some species seem to be very faithful to certain of these habitats while others move between all of them. A number of species living in the lowland forests also frequent the forests on the slopes of Mount Nimba. In general the number of vertebrate species on African mountains diminishes with altitude. This is also the case at Nimba (Curry-Lindahl & Lamotte, 1964).

At many places along an abandoned mine road there are secondary forests in all stages of regeneration, mainly with *Musanga cecropioides* and 3 different species of *Vernonia*. Along this road there are 38 species of larger trees, and 48 species of smaller trees and large bushes. Such successional habitats on disturbed ground, both in 'slope' and lowland forests, are seasonally important for several species of birds.

At altitudes up to 900 m the Umbrella Tree (*Musanga cecropioides*) occurs. At Nimba it grows in the wet season within a few months of the ground being cleared, and becomes the dominant tree within about three years. Its succulent fruits attract many frugivorous birds and mammals. Cleared tracks and made-up roads leave strips of vegetation on either side after the forest trees have been taken out and *Musanga* develops as a belt with an understorey of *Macaranga* and *Vernonia*. Along the outer edge of this association there develops a dense stand of *Harungana madagascariensis* (Dragon's Blood Tree) which reaches up to some 3–4 m in height. Where gullying occurs along the sides of the tracks, seedlings of *Terminalia* rapidly establish themselves together with lianas, climbing shrubs and fruit- and seed-bearing plants which provide food for birds and small arboreal mammals. Brambles and razor grass are common at any level on cleared ground. Above 900 m clearings and tracks become completely covered with dense *Dissotis* scrub up to 1 m high although *Harungana* still forms an important component of the forest-edge colonisers.

Lianas are extremely common in both primary and secondary forests of Mount Nimba. Adam (1971) lists 86 species, which indicates that their diversity is higher than in the lowland rain forests.

Almost daily mist in the summit forest favours the profuse growth of mosses and filmy ferns on all the tree trunks. This forest is poor in species and stature, and is dominated by *Parinari, Eugenia* and *Gaertnera* in the canopy, while the ground vegetation is often dense. Photograph Malcolm Coe.

A dense patch of the tree fern – *Cyathea manniana* lies shrouded in mist at the head of the Iti Valley, below the main mine site. These habitats have been badly disturbed by clearance and drainage. Photograph Malcolm Coe.

MONTANE FORESTS ABOVE 1200 m. Before the mining operation the highest point of Liberian Nimba was Mount Alpha, 1385 m. There are now only small remnants left in Liberia of forests above 1200 m, but they still exist intact in the Guinean and Ivory Coast part of the mountain.

These forests are dominated by *Parinari excelsa* and *Garginia polyantha*. This is a real mist or cloud forest, saturated with moisture for most of the year and with a great abundance of epiphytes such as filmy ferns, selaginellas, lycopods, orchids and dense mosses from ground level to the canopy. On peaks and ridges this mist forest is gnarled and stunted, the trees rarely exceeding 9–10 m in height. The mist forest is visited by a number of birds, but only a few species breed in it.

TREE FERN FOREST. In moist places in the upper part of the Iti Valley, at about 1000 m, there are several small areas with almost pure stands of *Cyathea manniana*, which forms a forest-like association with an understorey of *Afromomum*. Reptiles, particularly lizards, are abundant here, and their abundance seems to attract birds of prey. Other birds do not seem to be particularly attracted to this habitat.

SAVANNAS. As mentioned earlier, the only natural savannas in Liberia close to the Nimba range are located at the foot of the mountain and along the border with Guinea. In the latter country, this lowland grassland is extensive.

Hyparrhenia diplandra is the predominant grass. Old termitaries are colonized by *Andropogon macrophyllus*. Some Palaearctic migrants winter here year after year, for example *Saxicola rubetra* and *Motacilla flava*. This habitat is also favoured by snakes of several species, at least they are more visible here than in the forest; and this may be the reason for the occurrence here of several species of reptile-eating birds of prey.

Dense *Parinari excelsa* forest on the wall of the main Nimba ridge at 1200 m. In the foreground the pioneer *Musanga cecropioides* has established itself along the side of the main mine road. Photograph Malcolm Coe.

Thickets have become an important habitat at Nimba in many areas with scrub and vegetation degraded by man's activities. They may often hold a number of bird species for feeding, roosting and even breeding.

MARSHES AND SWAMPS. There are only a few small marshes on Mount Nimba. At lower levels around the massif there are several, but unfortunately most of them have been silted up by debris from the mine or destroyed in other ways. They no longer serve as habitats for waterfowl, but if there are trees alongside the water the Black and Chestnut Weaver (*Ploceus castaneofuscus*) may use them for breeding. If there is other vegetation than trees around these marshes some finches are usually found there. However, frogs and toads persist in these dying aquatic habitats, and perform their nightly concerts as in the good old times before the devastation.

RIVERS, STREAMS AND MUDFLATS. There is only one important river in Liberian Nimba, the Yah River, but it has now lost almost all its importance for plant and animal life, being nothing more than a liquid sludge of sediments from the mine area.

Still full of life, however, is the Iti River, a mountain stream running between the two main ridges of Liberian Nimba. Its gorge and surrounding steep slopes are still covered by rain forests in which Chimpanzees (*Pan troglodytes*) may regularly be seen feeding. Tree ferns (*Cyathea manniana*) and at least 20 other species of 12 genera of ferns grow here, among them *Osmunda regalis*.

The densely forested shores of the Iti River may be visited by Tiger Bitterns (*Tigriornis leucolophus*) and Hamerkops (*Scopus umbretta*). Even a Palaearctic wader, the Green Sandpiper (*Tringa ochropus*), has found its way to this well-hidden forest stream.

Rivulet flowing in the bottom of the Iti Valley, Mount Nimba. Lianas hang down to the water. 18 February 1966. Photograph Kai Curry-Lindahl.

The vertebrate fauna except birds

The Nimba forests in their original state were rich in large mammals. The Forest Elephant (*Loxodonta africana cyclotis*), Forest Buffalo (*Syncerus nanus*), Bongo (*Boocercus euryceros*), Royal Antelope (*Neotragus pygmaeus*), and Pygmy Hippopotamus (*Choeropsis liberiensis*) are known to have been in the area. The Forest Buffalo still occurred in the 1960s but has now disappeared. The Leopard was observed in 1963 (KC-L) and is still occasionally seen. The Mano tribesmen have repeatedly assured us that the Golden Cat (*Felis aurata*) occurs at Nimba but there has been no evidence of it. So far five viverrids have been recorded as well as the Three-cusped Pangolin (*Manis tricuspis*). We have already mentioned the Chimpanzee, and four more species of primates (genera *Colobus* and *Cercopithecus*) are to be found. Jentink's Duiker *Cephalophus jentinki* (Curry-Lindahl, 1974) was observed in 1971. Other antelopes occurring are three species of Duikers and the Bushbuck (*Tragelaphus scriptus*). There are also Water Chevrotains (*Hyemoschus aquaticus*), Bushpig (*Potamochoerus porcus*) and Tree Hyraxes (*Dendrohyrax dorsalis sylvestris*), and in January 1982 colonies of Rock Hyraxes (*Procavia rufescens*) were discovered in abandoned parts of the mine area (KC-L). This species was previously unknown at Nimba except for an isolated record of an animal secured on the forest floor in 1967 (Coe, 1975).

Bats are numerous in both individuals and species; 39 species are known for Mount Nimba (Brosset, 1984). An endemic Otter Shrew (*Potamogale lamottei*) occurs at Nimba and adjacently in the Ivory Coast. Shrews are numerous: there are no fewer than 11 species of *Crocidura* and 13 species of Soricidae within a restricted area of Nimba, a wealth of species which is exceptional for Africa. We know this thanks to the cooperation of a Barn Owl (*Tyto alba*), whose pellets revealed that it had caught all these shrews (Heim de Balsac, 1958). There are about 30 species of rodents, representing at least 10 genera, belonging to the Nimba fauna, of which 7 are squirrels and 3 flying squirrels. The largest rodent is the Brush-tailed Porcupine (*Atherurus africanus*).

Reptiles are common, snakes more numerous in species than lizards. Amphibians abound, frogs and toads being represented by 13 genera. Only a few species of fish exist at present after the destruction of the Yah River.

As prey for birds, the mammals and reptiles of Nimba provide a relatively good source of food despite the tremendous competition from trapping and shooting by human beings.

The biogeographic context

In relation to the other high mountains of Equatorial Africa, the eroded quartzites of Mount Nimba (1752 m) on the Guinea-Ivory Coast-Liberian border, and the Loma mountains (2000 m) in Sierra Leone may seem insignificant. They do, however, represent important terrestrial islands which protrude above the surrounding areas of lowland forest. Today Mount Nimba lies within the rain forest belt, but close to the southern boundary of the Guinea savanna biome, while the Loma Mountains rise above the surrounding Guinea moist grassland and woodland savannas. The ecotone between rain forest and Guinea savanna has undoubtedly been strongly influenced by the anthropogenic agencies of fire, agriculture and forestry in historic times.

During the Miocene period (27 million to 7 million years ago), the gently undulating land surface was drastically altered as a result of tectonic activity, which led to the formation, through uplifting of the Ethiopian and East African highland plateaus (Carcasson, 1964; Moreau, 1966). These activities were accompanied by intense rifting and the raising of the Lake Victoria basin, which had a profound effect on the continent's drainage, in the late Miocene. Alongside these dramatic events, intense volcanicity gave rise to Mount Cameroon on the west coast and most of the great ice capped peaks of East Africa. Further activity which pre-dated the formation of the larger volcanoes, resulted in the uplifting of the great igneous blocks of Ruwenzori on the Zaire-Uganda border, and the Usambaras in northern Tanzania. These events extended from the late Miocene into the Pliocene period (7–2.5 million years BP), though volcanicity has continued to the present time on a less dramatic scale, and led to the formation of the Chyulu Range (2170 m) in eastern Kenya, little more than 40 000 years ago (Hamilton, 1974).

These profound changes in the continent's surface were also accompanied by dramatic variations in climate, which resulted in a mild extra tropical belt which extended from 55°N to 40°S during the mid Miocene, while Aubréville (1949) has suggested that the Equator lay further north than its present position during Tertiary times, and has only moved to its present position since the Pliocene. These presumed climatic variations were accompanied, if not caused by intense periods of glaciation, that have influenced the African biota throughout these periods, resulting in the vegetation undergoing profound distributional changes. Carcasson (1964) and Moreau (1966) have both independently predicted that during wet periods the lowland and montane forests were much more widespread than they are today, while during the dry periods the forests contracted until all that remained were small forest refuges isolated in the far west and in west central Africa. When the 25 000 plant species that comprise the African forests is compared with the 40 000 species found in South American forests, it seems probable that the relative species paucity is to a large degree associated with these profound climatic perturbations (Carcasson, 1964). Monod (1966) has proposed the hypothesis that a hot, humid climate forest covered much of the Sahara until about 40 000 years ago.

Our knowledge of these dramatic events is rather fragmentary for the Miocene and Pliocene periods, but advances in the study of palynology (pollen analysis) have provided us with a detailed picture of the effect of the Pleistocene glaciations on montane vegetation over the past 30 000 years. These have confirmed that the well studied glaciations of northern latitudes have been temporally synonymous with those on the montane environments of Africa and South America (Hamilton, 1974). Studies on Mount Kenya, Ruwenzori, and Mount Elgon (Livingstone, 1962; Coetzee, 1967; Morrison, 1968; Hamilton, 1970) have demonstrated that the movement of vegetation zones, reflected in dated pollen profiles from montane lakes, may predict the scale of temperature changes that may be expected as a result of variations in the degree of glacial activity. Thus they suggest that temperatures 2–4°C lower than those of the present would have been experienced between 30 000 and 26 000 years ago, and after the termination of a cold period 12 500 years ago, when the glaciers were in full retreat, the temperature has slowly increased to the present, except for a slightly warmer interval about 4000 years ago. These changes are of course only montane events, although it seems likely that their influence extended into the lowlands. Such an inference is confirmed by the studies of Kendall (1969) on the history of the Lake Victoria basin, who has demonstrated that prior to 12 000 years BP forest was either completely absent, or at least of very limited extent in the region of the lake, when it must have dried up and completely lost its outlet. Subsequently he records a wet period till 10 500 years BP, followed by a dry interval until 9 500 years BP, a wet period until 6 500 years BP, succeeded by a more seasonal rainfall pattern after 6000 years BP. Kukla (1977) has concluded that there have been eight glacial and interglacial periods in the last 700 000 years and no less than 17 in the last 1.7 million years (Curry-Lindahl, 1981). Thus there appears to be good evidence to suggest that periods of alternate forest extension and contraction have had a profound effect on the distribution of the major biomes, especially with regard to that of the humid forests. During the Miocene period when the forests extended their limits, the presence of a large lake in the centre of the Congo basin would have excluded it from that region. During the Pliocene however it is unclear whether it became occupied before the advent of period of increased aridity and forest retreat. The present location of the Congo forest on oligotrophic Kalahari sand suggests that the forest invasion post dates the translocation of these sands, but the timing of these events is unclear (Curry-Lindahl, 1981).

These, now well documented climatic changes have been reflected not only in vegetation distribution patterns but also on the speciation patterns exhibited by the fauna. Since, however, the fauna is almost entirely dependent on the habitats they occupy, it is important to first examine the patterns of endemism exhibited by the flora. Numerous authors have recognised the importance of the Guinea-Congolian region, as forest areas in which there are located a high percentage of endemic species (Monod, 1957; Lebrun, 1961; Aubréville, 1962; Leonard, 1965; Troupin, 1966; and White, 1979), and where they have identified three important sub-centres: one in Upper Guinea that is isolated by the Dahomey Gap; Lower Guinea – a region close to the west coast between the Sanaga and Ogoue Rivers; and the Congolian region to the east of the Congo River and west of the Ruwenzori, Virunga and other mountain massifs in the Kivu. White (*op. cit.*) has examined the relationship of the Guinea-Congolian region to other phytochoria and has identified the main montane areas in West Africa. These include the plateau of Fouta Djallon, the Loma Mountains and Nimba in Upper Guinea, and Mount Cameroon and the Bamenda-Adamawa Highlands east of the Dahomey Gap at the western margin of the Lower Guinea region. In this study he examined the distribution of 288 Guinea-Congolian species, belonging to 11 plant families. Of this total he observes that 179 species (62.1%) were strict endemics confined to the Guinea-Congolian region, while 82 species (28.5%) extend into the adjacent transient regions, and only 16 species (5.5%) are widespread beyond the boundaries of the transient regions. He identifies the Guinea-Congolian region as a major centre of specific endemism, while the Upper Guinea, Lower Guinea, and Congolian areas are termed sub-regions of endemism. Bearing in mind the possibility of the sub-regions having been isolated from one another during past periods of forest contraction, it is of interest to examine the distribution of the sample of 288 species. White (*op. cit.*) found that 110 of these species are found in Upper Guinea, of which 30% (33 sp.) are endemic, 210 species are recorded in Lower Guinea, of which 33.8% (71 sp.) are endemics, and 146 species are located in the Congolian sub-region, of which 23.3% (34 sp.) are endemics. It is interesting to also note that the distant forests of the East African coastal belt only contain 7 (2.4%) of the Guinea-Congolian sample, but the fact that 40% of the tree flora of that region is endemic, illustrates the importance of isolation as a profound factor in speciation. The comparative levels of shared species between the three sub-regions of the Guinea-Congolian belt strongly indicate the likelihood of past connections between them, while the strong representation of local sub-region endemics, indicates that they have been isolated, may be repeatedly, from one another, in the past.

When we come to compare the distributional patterns exhibited by the faunal elements of these regions, we observe the strong influence that periodic isolation has had on them, which to a large degree parallels that observed above for the flora. These connections however differ depending on whether we are observing mobile (birds) or comparatively static groups (amphibians). An excellent example of the latter is that observed in the viviparous toads *Nectophrynoides* (Anura, Bufonidae) which occur on Mount Nimba. Prior to the studies on Liberian Nimba, a single species, *Nectophrynoides occidentalis* Angel, 1943, was known from Guinea Nimba, but in 1964 Malcolm Coe discovered a population isolated on the Nimba (*c.*1200 m) ridge in Liberia (Coe & Curry-Lindahl, 1965), which is now known as *N. liberiensis* Xavier, 1978. Remarkably these two species are only separated by a narrow belt of forest about 10 km wide, and a natural saddle where the laterite cap occupied by these amphibians has been eroded away. This genus was believed to be separated from other species by 2000 km, for *N. viviparus* and *N. tornieri* are isolated on the Usambara and Uluguru mountains of Tanzania. Recently however Grandison (1978) has studied the genus and has drawn attention to two further species in Tanzania, (*N. cryptus* and *N. minutus*), and two further species in Ethiopia, (*N. osgoodi* and *N. malcolmi*). This newly revealed distributional pattern still leaves a large geographical gap from the Nimba species, but Grandison (*op. cit.*) points out that *Didynamipus sjoestedti*, which occurs on Fernando Po, and Mount Cameroon is very closely related to *Nectophrynoides*, indicating that at some time in the past these amphibians have had connections with both the northern highlands of Kenya and Ethiopia and those to the south in Tanzania. Indeed these observations on the distribution of highly specialised montane vertebrates encourages us to look at the Equatorial mountains both in respect of endemism and shared species. White (1978) in a study of the afro-alpine region of southern Africa has pointed out that of 91 tree species in the South African montane system 37% occur in Ethiopia, and 58% in the Kivu Highlands-Ruwenzori area, demonstrating a distinct distance effect in their distribution. Additionally it is clear that there are few endemics, for up to 62% of a large sample studied by White (*op. cit.*) appear to have their origins in the forests of the lowland tropics.

A considerably more mobile, but specialised animal group are the butterflies, which Carcasson (1964) has studied in relation to their distribution and species abundance. He divides the Guinea-Congolian region into three subdivisions which he terms Western (Upper Guinea), Central (Lower Guinea), and Congolese (Congolian). These three divisions contain respectively 750, 1150, and 1000 species. Arguing that the richness of the Central and Congolese divisions indicates that at times of forest contraction they remained more or less intact even if they were smaller than they are today, an observation supported by the fact that these rich areas mainly differ at the sub-specific level. The Western division however, though less rich, has evolved a considerable degree of subspeciation. While at the furthest extremity of the lowland forest extension to the east, in the Kakamega forest (Kenya), there is considerable impoverishment. In the East African coastal forests the number of butterfly species is reduced to 100, but these are either endemic or very distinct subspecies, a picture very similar to that observed in the flora (White, 1979). Similarly the highland species show distinct affinities between the western and eastern continental highlands, and between species of the montane and lowland forests. Any impoverishment observed in the eastern montane forests might be further explained by the fact that they are surrounded by lowland and savanna woodlands rather than the lowland forests that are associated with the Kivu-Ruwenzori and Cameroon massifs.

Booth (1958) in a review of the West African Primates

also recognised similar divisions of the Guinea-Congolian region, but introduced a further terminology to deal with the area between the Volta and Niger rivers, especially in respect of the High Forest *Cercopithecidae* and *Colobidae*. Grubb (1978) in a more wide ranging review of the distribution of African mammals recognised a Western region (Upper Guinea); a West Central region (Lower Guinea) as a centre between the Sanaga and Ogoue rivers; and an East Central region (Congolian), to the west of the Zaire-Uganda-Rwanda mountain chain, and bounded in the west by the Congo River. As major refugia for 'larger' mammalian super species, he records totals of 58 in Upper Guinea, 68 in Lower Guinea, and 71 in the Congolian region. Of these totals, endemics were represented by 23 (39.6%), 17 (24.6%), and 16 (22.5%) respectively, in each of these areas. As with the butterflies, we once more observe a slightly higher level of endemism in the Upper Guinea region.

The above authors place emphasis on the endemic forms, although it is necessary to remember that many of the Guinea-Congolian forms are represented as far east as western Kenya, where they still exist in the otherwise species impoverished environments of the Kaimosi-Mau forests (Kingdon, 1981). In discussing these mammalian isolates this author postulates that during periods of forest extension there would have been two forest connections between West and East Africa. A northerly route from Ruwenzori via Elgon and the western Kenya highlands to Kilimanjaro, and a southerly route from Ruwenzori via the Virunga Volcanoes, the southern Tanzania highlands and north to Kilimanjaro and Mt Meru. Interestingly he predicts that this route is the one which provides the distant connection with the East African coastal region rather than that to the north, although both routes appear to have had a connection at their origin in the Ruwenzori region and Kilimanjaro in the east.

The present study of the avifauna of Liberian Nimba has yielded a surprising total of 385 species, which now allows a more detailed examination of the zoogeographical affinities of this part of West Africa than has hitherto been possible. Tables 2 and 3 summarise the statistics of species additions and range extensions for comparison with Louette's 1974 list. It will be noted that collections, and reliable field observations have added a further 117 bird species to the known Liberian avifauna (Table 2). These are represented by 56 (48%) forest species, 33 (28%) non-forest species, 23 (19%) Palaearctic migrants, and a small residual of 5 species which fall between migrant and non-forest species. From a biogeographic standpoint, however, it is far more interesting to look at the details of range extensions listed in Table 3, for they indicate the degree of connection between the forests of Upper Guinea, and the Lower Guinea and Congolian regions. The range extensions of the 23 species listed may be broken down into 10 species with extensions to East Africa, 7 species that extend to the Congolian region and the Ituri forest in Zaire, and 6 species limited to the Upper Guinea-Niger-Cameroon area. It will be noted that none of these species so listed are limited to Upper Guinea. The discovery of two new species of a flycatcher (*Melaenornis annamarulae*) and a honeyguide (*Melignomon eisentrauti*) add two new Upper Guinea elements to the Nimba avifauna, the former only known from Nimba and the Ivory Coast, and the latter now known from Nimba, Ghana and Cameroon. The new race of the flycatcher, *Muscicapa olivascens nimbae*, indicates an important extension of a species previously known, but uncommon in dense forest from Ghana to eastern Zaire.

Moreau (1966) has examined in detail the distribution of birds in the Guinea-Congolian region, and has pointed out that we may recognise 182 species which occur in the lowland forests of Upper Guinea. Of this total, however, only 9 (5%) of these species are endemic, although we may now add the two further species enumerated above. Indeed the fact that 86% of the 212 sp. recorded for Lower Guinea (NE. Congo) are shared with Upper Guinea (Moreau *op. cit.*) indicates that the levels of endemicity are less obvious in the avifauna than in the flora and less mobile elements of the fauna. The same author compared the avifauna of the distant NE. Congo with that of Upper Guinea and drew attention to the fact that 24 species occurred in each of these two regions but not in the intermediate areas of dense forest. Of the 7 species whose distribution is detailed, four of them have now been recorded at Nimba. It would be unwise though to describe the Nimba avifauna as unique, for few other areas in West Africa have been submitted to such detailed collections and observations as have been carried out at this station. A fact which illustrates the necessity of long term study, observation and collection in these fast disappearing rain forest habitats, for, since so many of the species recorded appear to be exceedingly rare, it is not difficult to imagine how many species have already become extinct before they have even been observed or named.

These collections provide a detailed description of what is present in wet forest not far away from the Guinea savanna mosaic, but they fail to add more than locality records for zoogeographic studies. It is, however, worthwhile looking at the distribution of a single well represented family, the Pycnonotidae (bulbuls), for they are mainly fruit and berry eaters which are largely limited to forest and forest edge habitats. The collections at Nimba have yielded 23 species, a richness that may be favourably compared with the 33 species recorded for the whole of West Africa (Serle, Morel & Hartwig, 1977), and 38 for East Africa (Forbes-Watson, 1971; Britton, 1980). In order to examine their distribution from Upper Guinea, through the Lower Guinea-Congolian region to the East African coastal forests we have recorded the number of the Nimba species which are also found in Lower Guinea (Serle, Morel & Hartwig, *op. cit.*), the Congo forest region in eastern Zaire (Chapin, 1953), the Bwamba (Forbes-Watson, pers. comm.) and Budongo

Another forest giant falls to the forester's axe in the mature secondary forest near Mount Bele south-west of the Grassfield township. Photograph Malcolm Coe.

(Friedmann & Williams, 1975) forests in Uganda, the Kakamega forest in western Kenya (Ripley & Bond, 1971; and Forbes-Watson, pers. comm.), riverine forest in the Tsavo (east) National Park, Kenya (Lack, Leuthold & Smeenk, 1980), and the Arabuko-Sokoke forest on the Kenya coast (Ripley & Bond, 1971). These figures reveal a steady fall with latitudes east of Nimba (which is classified as zero) as follows: Cameroon 22 sp., Congo 13 sp., Bwamba 12 sp., Budongo 13 sp., Kakamega 10 sp., Tsavo 2 sp., and Arabuko-Sokoke 3 sp. If we calculate a linear regression of latitudes east of Nimba against the number of Nimba bulbul species present at each of the 8 localities we obtain a highly significant correlation coefficient (r) of -0.92 (p = <0.001; intercept = 26.17; slope = -0.43). Although this result indicates that there is a steady linear (negative) fall in the number of species present at the hypothetical 'source', we obtain a rather different picture if we examine the total number of bulbul species at each locality, for we then find that the 23 species at Nimba rises to 33 or 34 species in the Lower Guinea-Congolian region before it falls to 15 and 16 at Bwamba and Budongo, and finally to 5 in Tsavo and 9 in the Arabuko-Sokoke forest. Thus although there is undoubtedly a distance effect on dispersal, the Upper Guinea region is distinctly impoverished in species, a conclusion that accords with that of other authors who have observed similar effects for elements of both the flora and fauna. Clearly, once more the periodic isolation of Upper Guinea has led to the loss (or lack of arrival) of several species, although its isolation has led to the evolution of two species (*Andropadus ansorgei* and *Bleda canicapilla*) which are endemic to the region. The extension of the range of species which seem to have evolved in the Guinea-Congolian region has been limited by narrow corridors of forest whose existence may have been transient in the east. The fact that the montane species show a disruptive distribution on widely isolated montane masses in the east and west supports the contention of Carcasson (1964) and Moreau (1966) that there has been a montane forest connection between them. This is supported by the observation that 63% of the Cameroon montane species occur in the eastern Zaire mountains, while of the remainder, which appear to be endemics, up to 50% of these are shared super species. The ability of the bulbuls to have spread across the continent must in part be due to the fact that most of these species are occupants of secondary forest and thickets, which must have represented ecotones that persisted along the edges of advancing and retreating forest during periods of climatic change. The appearance of 3 species of bulbul in the East African coastal forests (*c.*13%) is not at great variance from the overall figure of 14 species (7%) that Moreau (*op. cit.*) records as being shared with those of the Guinea-Congolian region.

Much needs to be done before we can fully understand the relationship of climatic change, vegetation movement, speciation and dispersal. The present study has indicated the groups that would reward further investigation. Mount Nimba does not provide truly montane conditions, as is evidenced by the absence of species that would be found at higher altitudes in the Cameroon-Bamenda highlands, but local geological and climatic conditions do provide a range of habitats that are occupied by one of the most diverse birds faunas observed in West Africa. This small mountain, with its mist forest, fern forest, and laterite grassland summits, and its altitudinal zonation of vegetation on its slopes is an ornithological 'jewel' that must be preserved for future generations to marvel at the diversity of bird life that must once have existed throughout the region.

A track disappears into the forest on the Mount Bele road south-west of the Grassfield village, where forestry operations have just started. Secondary pioneers will colonise this site with dense vegetation within 12 months of the operation ceasing. Photograph Malcolm Coe.

The burn and slash phase of shifting cultivation in the 'slope forest' c Liberian Nimba inside the 'Nimba National Forest Reserve', where logging, farming, burning, tree felling and hunting are 'strictly prohibited'. 26 March 1972. Photograph Kai Curry-Lindahl.

Man-made changes and their effects on the birds

Many kinds of man-made habitats have suddenly been created at Nimba and have changed the rain forest into a number of different habitats previously unknown to the birds of the area – cultivation, villages, gardens, habitations, roads, airstrips and a golf course. Some species have quickly taken advantage of this situation, particularly bulbuls, sunbirds and weavers. Among Palaearctic birds Yellow Wagtails (*Motacilla flava*) have become increasingly abundant during the last 20 years, occupying lawns in Yekepa and Grassfield, the airstrip, the golf course and several paved mountain roads surrounded by high forest.

The most dramatic environmental change at Nimba has been the metamorphosis of the forest-covered mountain to an industrial, denuded rocky landscape, where dynamite and bulldozers have literally eaten down the mountain from the top ridges downwards. Of course all the forest birds disappeared except for raptors, bee-eaters, swifts and swallows, which constantly visit the mine area. Impressive concentrations of birds of prey, from falcons to buzzards and eagles, perch on the rocky outcrops of the mine or soar above. Swallows (mostly *Hirundo griseopyga*) hunt daily throughout the year over the remaining ridges. More surprising is the fact that almost immediately after Liberian Nimba became denuded, Palaearctic birds like Yellow Wagtails and two species of rock thrushes (*Monticola*) took up 'winter' quarters there (Curry-Lindahl, 1964, 1981).

At the present time the remaining forests of the Nimba region contain only a fraction of the rich and diverse animal life that 10–20 years ago was characteristic for the area. Mammals, birds and reptiles have become seriously depleted by a ruthless and illegal over-exploitation by Liberian hunters, who have operated freely in the two forest reserves without any control by local authorities. People are found everywhere walking with guns, which can be bought over the counter without any formalities. Through this constant persecution most animals have fortunately developed an extreme shyness in relation to human beings, and several species of birds have shifted from forest edges to the interior of the forest during the period under observation.

Other species have been favoured by the opening up of the forests, for example the Bat Hawk (*Macheirhamphus alcinus*), which requires open space to hunt forest bats at dusk. The Black Bee-eater (*Merops gularis*) and Long-billed Pipit (*Anthus similis*) have established themselves in open parts of the montane forest at about 1100 m during the last decade. Before 1976 they were not seen at all in this forest.

The most spectacular increase in number and vertical range of any bird at Nimba is the extraordinary expansion of the White-vented Bulbul (*Pycnonotus barbatus*), which in the course of 20 years has colonized all habitats where there are trees or bushes from the lowlands up to 1300 m. It has increased enormously and is now the commonest bird at Nimba.

The birds

This is the only photograph in existence of a living specimen of Coe's Honeyguide (*Melignomon eisentrauti*) a new species to science which was first observed within the compound of Nimba Research Laboratory in 1964. The species is confined to Upper Guinea. Photograph Malcolm Coe.

The rare forest lemon dove (*Aplopelia larvata*) perches on a branch at the Nimba Research Laboratory. This species was widespread but uncommon in the low altitude forest but virtually nothing is known of its habits. The specimens taken at Nimba are similar to the ones at Cameroon, but there are no records of this bird between there and Liberia. Photograph Malcolm Coe.

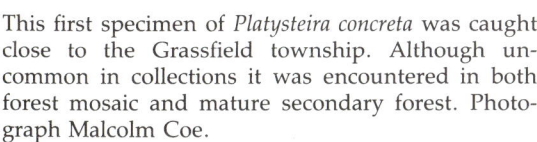

This first specimen of *Platysteira concreta* was caught close to the Grassfield township. Although uncommon in collections it was encountered in both forest mosaic and mature secondary forest. Photograph Malcolm Coe.

New species from Mount Nimba. Upper: *Melaenornis annamarulae* (Anna's Forest-flycatcher). Lower: *Melignomon eisentrauti* (Coe's Honeyguide). (Painted by Philip Burton.)

Introduction

The sequence of orders and families used in this section is the same as in White (1965), except that for the passerines we follow Morony, Bock & Farrand (1975). The sequence of species within the families follows White (1965) throughout. The nomenclature and taxonomy generally follow Snow (1978) for the non-passerines and Hall & Moreau (1970) for the passerines.

For all species for which there are specimens, the information is given under more or less standardised headings, beginning with a list of the specimens with dates of collection. Measurements and weights of all species are tabulated in an Appendix (p. 107). In the case of polytypic species, the following treatment has been adopted. If the Nimba specimens are indistinguishable from the subspecies which is already known from Liberia or, on the basis of its known distribution, would be expected to occur in Liberia, the appropriate trinomial, with a brief statement of the range of the subspecies, follows the list of specimens. If the Nimba specimens differ from the expected subspecies or show variation of interest in other ways, this is mentioned under a separate heading 'Geographical variation'.

For species of which no specimens were collected, the field data are presented without subheadings. These species are mostly admitted to the Nimba list on the basis of sight records by the following observers, whose initials are used in the text: Malcolm Coe (MC), Kai Curry-Lindahl (KC-L), Alec Forbes-Watson (AF-W), James Karr (JK), Stuart Keith (SK), Donald Turner (DT), Robert J. Wolton (RW), Edward Yallah (EY).

For a better understanding of the general distribution of Liberian birds over Africa, the atlases of Hall & Moreau (1970) and Snow (1978) are indispensable and should be used in conjunction with the present publication. The atlas of African passerine birds (Hall & Moreau, 1970) was prepared before all the Nimba records were available and only a small minority of them were included. When the non-passerine atlas (Snow, 1978) was prepared, the available list of Nimba birds was still incomplete, and this was used in the distribution maps, which are, therefore, inconsistent in their mapping of the Nimba avifauna.

Breeding and moulting seasons

Although there is a regrettable lack of field data on breeding (see p.22), the considerable number of specimens collected, some in all months of the year, enables a rough analysis to be made of the annual cycles of Nimba birds. Added interest is given to such an analysis by the recent paper by Serle (1981) on the breeding seasons of forest birds in West Cameroon at 4°–5°N, the only other West African rain forest area north of the Equator for which such data are available. The area studied by Serle has a climatic regime broadly similar to that of Nimba, with a wet season from April to October and a comparatively drier season from November to March; but the total annual precipitation in West Cameroon, though locally variable, tends to be higher than at Nimba.

For the breeding seasons we have used data from ovaries of females which, when collected, showed that they were shortly about to lay or had recently laid eggs. The testis size of males has not been used, as the testes of tropical birds may be enlarged and apparently in breeding condition for much longer than the female's egg-laying period (e.g. Moreau, 1936; Snow & Snow, 1964). A few nest records have also been used, and juvenile specimens that were young enough when collected (e.g. wings and tail not fully grown) to give information on their approximate date of hatching. In all cases records have been back-dated, when necessary, to the estimated egg-laying date, and are grouped by calendar months.

For moult seasons we have used adult specimens which when collected were undergoing a complete moult, involving the flight feathers. Birds in post-juvenal moult, which may involve the inner secondaries and tail in addition to the body plumage, are not included. As the moult is a slow process, taking some 3–4 months in small or medium-sized tropical passerine birds, it is comparatively uninformative to record simply that a bird is in moult. We have accordingly used 10 stages, from stage 1 (innermost primary growing, the rest old) to stage 10 (all primaries new, the outermost still growing), and have calculated the month when the moult began on the basis of known durations of moult in related species in the tropics. Further details are given in the footnote to Figure 2.

For all the non-passerine families and some passerine families, little breeding and moult data are available and quantitative treatment is not possible. For several of the most important passerine families, however, the number of records is sufficient to indicate the broad seasonal pattern. We have taken the following groups, as forming a reasonably homogeneous assemblage of insectivorous and frugivorous (in one case also nectarivorous) small to medium-sized passerine birds: Pycnonotidae, Laniidae, Turdidae, Timaliidae, Sylviidae, Muscicapidae, Nectariniidae, *Parmoptila* and *Nigrita* in the Estrildidae, *Malimbus* in the Ploceidae (See Table 1). Taken separately, on the data available they do not show any marked differences one from another in breeding and moult seasons (though more complete records would surely show some differences), and the data from all of them are combined in Figure 2.

Figure 2 shows the seasonal pattern of breeding and moulting in the above-mentioned groups. It is apparent that, although there is some breeding in each month, there is a main breeding period round the middle of the year. The low figure for May is undoubtedly misleading,

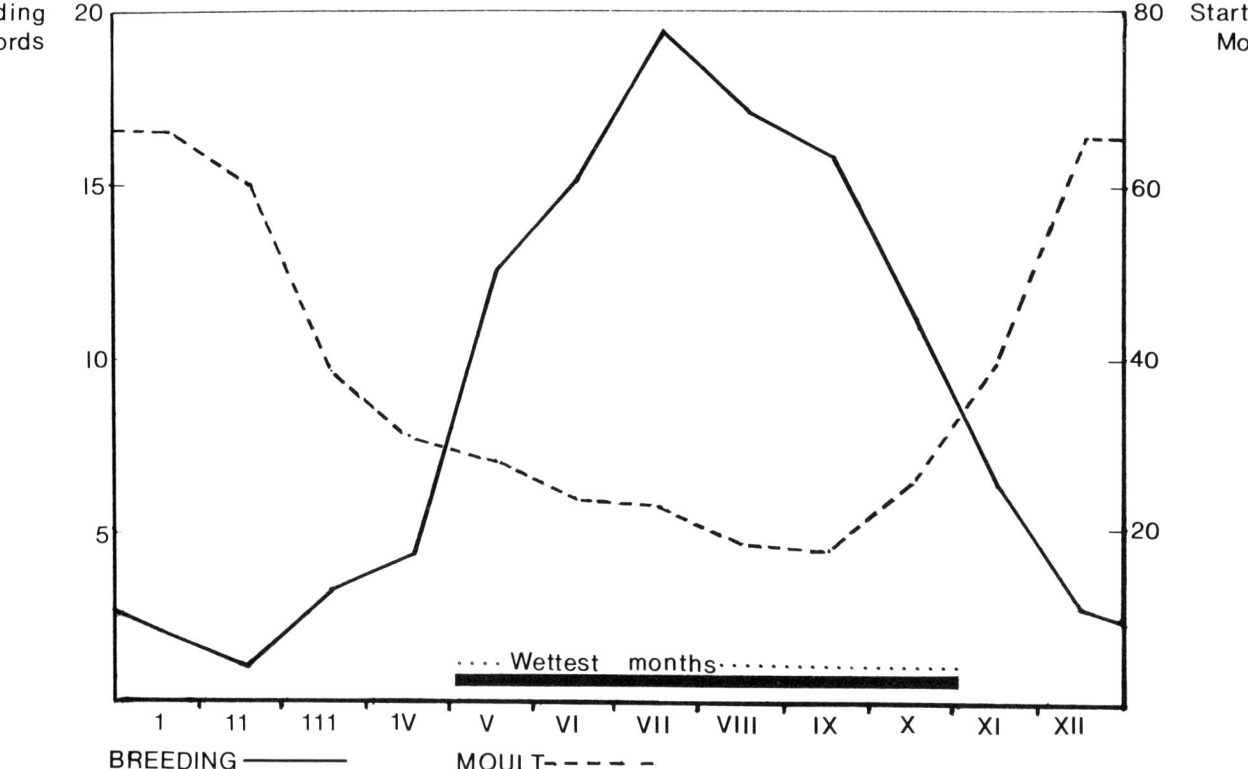

Fig 2 Breeding and moulting seasons of insectivorous and frugivorous passerine birds at Nimba (see Table 1, p.23, for families included). Breeding: month of egg-laying, derived from females in breeding condition and young birds recently fledged. Moulting: month of start of complete moult, calculated from specimens in all stages of wing-moult. The following durations of complete moult were used in the calculations: Pycnonotidae, 130 days; Laniidae, Turdidae, Muscicapidae, Sylviidae, 120 days; Nectariniidae, Estrildidae, Ploceidae, 100 days. In order to compensate for irregularities in numbers of specimens collected in different months, monthly moult totals have been adjusted by the method described in Snow (1976), and monthly totals for both breeding and moult have been smoothed, e.g. January figure = Dec + Jan + Feb/3.

being attributable to the fact that few birds were collected in that month. Likewise the high figure for June is attributable to the large number of specimens collected in that month. An unbiassed histogram would probably show a more evenly rounded peak. As mentioned above, there are no obvious differences between the patterns shown by individual families, but there is some indication that the Pycnonotidae and Laniidae may have more extended breeding seasons than the others.

In relation to climate, the data show that breeding is at a low level during the first four months of the year, the dry season, and is at its height during the first part of the wet season. The end of the wet season, when the rainfall is highest, is accompanied by an apparently steady decline in breeding activity. A similar relationship between breeding activity and the rainfall regime has been found in other tropical areas with well-marked single wet and dry seasons (e.g. the Nyika plateau of Zambia/Malawi at 10°–11°S (Dowsett & Dowsett-Lemaire, unpubl.), much of tropical South America (Snow, 1976)). The seasonal pattern in West Cameroon, nearer the Equator and with a wetter climate, is markedly different. Serle's data show that in lowland forest, below about 1050 m, the groups of birds used in the analysis for Nimba breed throughout the year with no obvious peak. In montane forest, above 1050 m, where the humidity is very high, breeding is concentrated into the drier part of the year, with a virtual cessation of breeding during the months of heavy rains and mist, May–September.

The seasonal pattern of onset of moult is almost the exact reverse of the pattern of breeding (Fig. 2). There is a sharp rise in the onset of moult in November, when the main breeding season has ended, reaching a peak in January (perhaps too abrupt a peak in Figure 2, since there is some uncertainty as to the exact month of moult onset for records back-dated from a late moult-stage). The data are in good agreement with what has been found elsewhere in tropical areas with moderately well-marked single wet and dry seasons, where the main moult period follows immediately after the end of the main breeding season.

Table 1
Records of breeding (egg-laying) and moult (calculated month of start of full moult) of some passerine families at Nimba

		Jan.	Feb.	Mar.	Apr.	May	Jun.	Jul.	Aug.	Sep.	Oct.	Nov.	Dec.
Breeding	Pycnonotidae	1	1				3	1	2	3	3	1	
	Laniidae			1				1			1	1	
	Turdidae						10	7	3	5		1	1
	Timaliidae				1		1	1	2		1		1
	Sylviidae				4	2	5	1	4	6	3		1
	Muscicapidae				2		1	4	1	2			
	Nectariniidae					2	6		2	1	2		
	Estrildidae				1			1	3	2	1		
	Ploceidae										1		
Start of moult	Pycnonotidae	15	9	7	4	2	6	1		1	1	3	5
	Laniidae	2	6	3	2	2		1		2		5	4
	Turdidae			3		3	4	3	2			1	
	Timaliidae	2	3	4	2		1	1			1		
	Sylviidae	3	5	5	6	5	4	2	2	2	3	2	6
	Muscicapidae	1	1	1	7	9	5	6					
	Nectariniidae	3	1	3	2		1	1	7				3
	Estrildidae		1	2	4	2	5				1		
	Ploceidae	2	1	2	2					1	1	2	

NOTES. The data are for the main passerine families that are primarily insectivorous (in some cases also frugivorous or nectarivorous); for the Estrildidae and Ploceidae, only the insectivorous genera *Parmoptila*, *Nigrita* and *Malimbus* are included. It should be noted that the unevenness of collecting in different months of the year biasses these figures, which cannot be taken as necessarily indicating the actual peaks of breeding and moulting at Nimba. An attempt has been made to correct the biasses in Figure 2.

Coastal forest between a freshwater lake and the sea shore. Buchanan, Liberia. Photograph Kai Curry-Lindahl.

Table 2

Bird species new to Liberia recorded from Nimba

The bold italic species have been collected

| Palaearctic | Afrotropical | |
Migrants	Non-forest	Forest
	Tachybaptus ruficollis	
	Egretta intermedia	
Ardea cinerea		
	A. goliath	
A. purpurea		
	Scopus umbretta	
	Ciconia abdimii	
Anas querquedula		
Circus aeruginosus	*Circaetus gallicus*	
	Accipiter badius	*Accipiter melanoleucus*
Buteo buteo		*Lophaetus occipitalis*
		Spizaetus africanus
Hieraaetus pennatus		*Hieraaetus ayresii*
	Chelictinia riocourii	
Falco subbuteo		*Falco cuvierii*
F. peregrinus		
F. biarmicus		
F. tinnunculus		
F. naumanni		
	Coturnix delegorguei	
Tringa ochropus		
		Cuculus solitarius
		Pachycoccyx audeberti
		Cercococcyx olivinus
Otus scops		*Otus icterorhynchus*
		Bubo poensis
		B. lacteus
		Glaucidium tephronotum
		G. capense
	Caprimulgus tristigma	*Caprimulgus binotatus*
Apus melba		*Apus batesi*
		Raphidura sabini
		Telacanthura ussheri
		T. melanopygia
		Neafrapus cassini
		Ispidina lecontei
Merops apiaster		*Merops muelleri*
	Coracias abyssinica	
		Phoeniculus bollei
		P. castaneiceps
	Lybius vieilloti	
		Indicator exilis
		I. willcocksi

Table 2 (cont.)

| Palaearctic | Afrotropical | |
Migrants	Non-forest	Forest
		Melichneutes **robustus**
		Melignomon **eisentrauti**
		Prodotiscus **regulus**
Jynx **torquilla**		
	Mirafra **africana**	
	Pinarocorys **erythropygia**	
Riparia **riparia**	Hirundo **fuligula**	Psalidoprocne **nitens**
Anthus **trivialis**	Anthus **similis**	
		Campephaga **lobata**
		Phyllastrephus **scandens**
		Criniger **olivaceus**
	Tchagra **minuta**	Malaconotus **lagdeni**
Monticola **saxatilis**	Myrmecocichla nigra	Cossypha **polioptera**
Luscinia **megarhynchos**		
		Trichastoma **rufipennis**
Acrocephalus schoenobaenus		T. **puveli**
A. **scirpaceus**	Cisticola **erythrops**	Apalis **nigriceps**
Hippolais **polyglotta**	C. cantans	A. **sharpii**
H. icterina	C. **natalensis**	Bathmocercus **cerviniventris**
Sylvia **atricapilla**	Prinia **leontica**	Sylvietta **denti**
Phylloscopus **sibilatrix**		
Ficedula **hypoleuca**	Muscicapa gambagae	Muscicapa **epulata**
	M. aquatica	M. **olivascens**
		M. **griseigularis**
		Melaenornis **annamarulae**
		Hyliota **violacea**
		Batis (**poensis**) **occultus**
		Platysteira **concreta**
		Trochocercus **nigromitratus**
		Terpsiphone **viridis**
		Anthoscopus **flavifrons**
		Parus **funereus**
	Nectarinia **cuprea**	Nectarinia **minulla**
	Emberiza tahapisi	
	Serinus **mozambicus**	
	Estrilda caerulescens	Nigrita **fusconota**
	Lagonosticta rara	Parmoptila **jamesoni**
	Amandava **subflava**	
	Amblyospiza **albifrons**	
	Ploceus **superciliosus**	Ploceus **preussi**
		Poeoptera **lugubris**
Oriolus oriolus	Oriolus auratus	
Total 23 (19%)	5 (4%) 33 (28%)	56 (48%)

Table 3
Important range extensions in West Africa to Nimba

Species	Nearest locality to Nimba previously known
Cercococcyx olivinus	Ghana (*c.*750 km)
Otus icterorhynchus	Ghana (*c.*750 km)
Glaucidium tephronotum	Ghana (*c.*650 km)
Glaucidium capense	Ivory Coast (*c.*350 km)
Caprimulgus binotatus	Ghana (*c.*700 km)
Apus batesi	Cameroon, Nigeria (*c.*2000 km), but sight records from Ghana, Sierra Leone and Guinea (Macdonald & Taylor, 1977)
Telacanthura melanopygia	Ivory Coast (*c.*250 km)
Neafrapus cassini	Ghana (*c.*800 km)
Melichneutes robustus	Nigeria (*c.*1700 km)
Melignomon eisentrauti	Cameroon, Ghana (*c.*900 km)
Prodotiscus regulus	Togo (*c.*1000 km)
Campephaga lobata	Ghana (*c.*800 km)
Malaconotus lagdeni	Ghana (*c.*800 km)
Muscicapa gambagae	Ghana (*c.*900 km)
Muscicapa epulata	Ghana (*c.*700 km)
Muscicapa olivascens	Ghana (*c.*800 km)
Muscicapa griseigularis	Ivory Coast (*c.*150 km) and Nigeria
Trochocercus nigromitratus	Nigeria (*c.*1700 km)
Anthoscopus flavifrons	Ghana (*c.*700 km)
Parus funereus	Ghana (*c.*800 km)
Nectarinia minulla	Ghana (*c.*800 km)
Parmoptila jamesoni	Ghana (*c.*800 km)
Estrilda caerulescens	Mali (*c.*600 km)

List of families

Family	Pages	Family	Pages
Podicipedidae	27	Indicatoridae	56–59
Ardeidae	27–28	Picidae	59–60
Scopidae	28	Eurylaemidae	60–61
Ciconiidae	28	Pittidae	61
Threskiornithidae	28	Alaudidae	61
Anatidae	28	Hirundinidae	62–63
Accipitridae	28–33	Motacillidae	63–65
Falconidae	33–34	Campephagidae	65–66
Phasianidae	34–35	Pycnonotidae	66–70
Rallidae	35–36	Laniidae	70–72
Heliornithidae	36	Turdidae	72–76
Jacanidae	36	Timaliidae	76–77
Charadriidae	36–37	Picathartidae	77–78
Recurvirostridae	37	Sylviidae	78–84
Columbidae	37–39	Muscicapidae	84–90
Psittacidae	39	Remizidae	90
Musophagidae	39–40	Paridae	90
Cuculidae	40–42	Nectariniidae	90–93
Strigidae	42–45	Zosteropidae	93–94
Caprimulgidae	45–46	Emberizidae	94
Apodidae	46–48	Fringillidae	94
Trogonidae	48	Estrildidae	94–98
Alcedinidae	48–50	Ploceidae	98–101
Meropidae	50–52	Sturnidae	101–102
Coraciidae	52	Oriolidae	102–103
Phoeniculidae	52–53	Dicruridae	103
Bucerotidae	53–54	Corvidae	103
Capitonidae	55–56		

A large emergent specimen of *Piptadeniastrum africanum* rises above the secondary forest on the edge of the laterite grassland of Grassfield village. Photograph Malcolm Coe.

Systematic section

Family Podicipedidae

Tachybaptus ruficollis Little Grebe

Observed at Yekepa by Forbes-Watson in February or March 1971; new for Liberia.

Family Ardeidae

Ixobrychus sturmii Dwarf Bittern

SPECIMEN. 1 ♀, January 1968; moderately enlarged ovary, fresh plumage.

IMPERMANENT COLOURS. Legs dull greyish-green, yellow behind; soles orange-yellow. Iris red-brown. Bare skin round eye yellowish-green. Bill brown, yellowish-green below.

STATUS. An intra-African migrant that probably visits Nimba only occasionally; also observed on 16 February 1971 (JK).

Tigriornis leucolophus African Tiger-heron

Observed (KC-L) at the Iti River in 1964 and several times along the same stream in subsequent years up to 1981; also seen (MC & AF-W) near Grassfield in 1968, and (JK) in 1971. Seen feeding along the shores of forest streams, very shy. Each time (KC-L) has come upon this bird it has quickly flown up to hide in dense vegetation. Not seen in the cryptic upright posture adopted by bitterns.

Gorsachius leuconotus White-backed Night-heron

An immature was observed at a forest stream at Nimba on 2 March 1971 (SK).

Ardeola ibis Cattle Egret

Four birds were observed at Grassfield in October 1963 (KC-L) on a newly opened grassy area. Local Europeans said that they had not seen this conspicuous species there before. Since then the Cattle Egret has developed a regular pattern of movement at Nimba, which it visits mainly in the wet season. Apparently it migrates south from Nimba to coastal areas where it is locally abundant all year round. At Buchanan there is an increase in numbers in December, roughly corresponding to the departure from Nimba. Despite the relative scarcity of cattle in Liberia the Cattle Egret has increased during the last 20 years in both range and numbers.

Butorides striatus Green-backed Heron

SPECIMENS. 1 ♂, June 1968; gonads small, fresh plumage. 1 ♀, July 1970; fresh plumage. — *B. s. atricapillus* (widespread in Africa south of 17°N).

IMPERMANENT COLOURS. Legs yellow, dusky in front. Iris bright yellow, tinged green. Bill black, greenish-yellow below. Bare skin round eye dull greenish-yellow.

STOMACH CONTENTS. Small fish.

Egretta garzetta Little Egret

Observed at Yekepa (AF-W, JK & SK). The nearest breeding colony is in river marshes close to the coast near Monrovia (KC-L). The species is common around Monrovia and in suitable habitats along the coastal marshes eastwards to Abidjan in the Ivory Coast. This is a resident as well as a Palaearctic winter visitor.

Egretta intermedia — Yellow-billed Egret

Observed at Yekepa on 10 February 1971 (AF-W, JK & SK), and on 4 March 1979 (KC-L); apparently the first records for Liberia.

Ardea cinerea — Grey Heron

Observed at Yekepa in 1971 (AF-W). Previously seen at Buchanan in February 1966 (KC-L) and later many times in different years around Monrovia. These are the first records for Liberia.

Ardea melanocephala — Black-headed Heron

Observed at Nimba several times (KC-L) during the wet season (Aug.–Nov.), with the exception of one record on 4 March; also seen (JK & SK) on 28 February 1971. This species is migratory in many areas of West Africa.

Ardea goliath — Goliath Heron

Observed at Yekepa in July 1976 (AF-W & DT); new for Liberia.

Ardea purpurea — Purple Heron

Observed at Yekepa in 1968 (AF-W) and in February 1971 (JK & SK); in 1966 seen on the coast at Buchanan (KC-L). These are the first records for Liberia.

Family Scopidae

Scopus umbretta — Hamerkop

Observed (KC-L) in 1965 in the Iti Valley, and several times in later years in the same valley, where it seems to be resident along the shores of the river in high forest; not seen elsewhere. These are the first records for Liberia.

Family Ciconiidae

Ciconia abdimii — Abdim's Stork

On 2 March 1966 a few individuals arrived in Grassfield at the foot of Nimba. They rested there, but were immediately killed by the local people (Verschuren, 1979). This is the first record for Liberia. A year or two later Dr Dick Johanson photographed this stork at Yekepa. Abdim's Stork is one of the most pronounced transequatorial migrants among African birds, breeding during the rains in a wide belt north of the Sahara and wintering mainly in the southeast of the continent.

Ciconia episcopus — Woolly-necked Stork

Observed at Nimba in 1967 or 1968 (AF-W).

Mycteria ibis — Yellow-billed Stork

Observed at Yekepa on 28 February 1971 (AF-W & SK). Previous records in Liberia have been from the coast.

Family Threskiornithidae

Bostrychia rara — Spot-breasted Ibis

This little known forest ibis was observed at Nimba in 1967 or 1968 (AF-W).

Family Anatidae

Pteronetta hartlaubi — Hartlaub's Duck

Observed several times at Nimba (KC-L & EY). Previous records have been from coastal regions in Liberia. Although not migratory this species does not appear to be resident at Nimba, because many years have passed between each record.

Anas querquedula — Garganey

SPECIMEN. 1 ♂, Feb. 1973; gonads small, moult into breeding plumage almost completed.

IMPERMANENT COLOURS. Legs grey. Iris brown. Bill blue.

STATUS. A Palaearctic winter visitor to tropical Africa. Liberia is just south of the Garganey's winter range; normally it does not visit rain forest areas. As this is the only record at Nimba over a period of 20 years the bird was obviously a straggler. This is the first record for Liberia.

Family Accipitridae

Gypohierax angolensis — Palm-nut Vulture

This is one of the most common birds of prey, which is to be expected as the oil palm *Elaeis guineensis*, whose fruits are its staple diet, is widespread in the Nimba forests. Since 1963 (KC-L) it has been seen every year, in every month, and of raptors only the Harrier Hawk (*Polyboroides typus*) has been observed more frequently at Nimba. Both species are resident, though *Gypohierax* is partially migratory in West Africa.

Palm-nut Vultures are often seen soaring over or flying above the forests, or inside them. They also fly over the lowland savanna in Liberia and Guinea and have twice been seen perching on the ground there. It has often been seen (KC-L) crossing the Nimba ridge and commuting between Liberia and the Ivory Coast, indicating that their home range may be large despite the abundance of food. The Palm-nut Vulture does not, however, feed exclusively on oil palm fruits. On four occasions, it was seen feeding along the Iti River, picking up crustaceans and molluscs at the water's edge.

A large nest in a tall tree (*Anthonotha fragrans*) was used for several years. Only once, in March, was an almost half-grown nestling in it, but the adults often perched on it.

Circus aeruginosus — Marsh Harrier

This species, a common Palaearctic migrant to West Africa, was observed at Grassfield on 11 and 19 February 1971 (AF-W, JK & SK); new for Liberia.

Polyboroides typus — Harrier Hawk

SPECIMENS. 1 ♀, Dec. 1972. 1 imm. ♀, Jul. 1968. — *P. t. pectoralis* (Gambia to Gabon and Zaire).

IMPERMANENT COLOURS. Legs yellow. Iris brown. Bill dark blue-grey. Cere yellowish. Imm, bare skin round face pale yellowish-green.

STOMACH CONTENTS. Insects and the remains of a palm nut.

FIELD OBSERVATIONS. This is a common bird at Nimba. It was observed (KC-L) in 1963 and in the following years, in all months. The number of observations made on the Harrier Hawk during 20 visits to Nimba (KC-L) exceeded the sight records of all other birds of prey within the area, although this does not necessarily mean that it is the most common raptor.

It has been observed in various kinds of activity: soaring or flying above the forest canopy, flying below the tree crowns searching for food, perching on branches or hanging from them in various positions, including upside down, often with flapping wings. Feeds extensively by pillaging weaver colonies, ripping the bottom out of pendant nests. It can also attach itself vertically or diagonally to a tree trunk, often with outstretched wings, while searching for or feeding on insects, or working on a hard fruit which it has anchored in a crevice in the bark. It feeds on all sorts of fruits including those of the oil palm, insects, and smaller vertebrates such as reptiles or birds including their eggs. It has also been seen (KC-L) chasing a tree squirrel but without success. It frequently moves about on the ground searching for food and digs out insect nests; at least twice it was seen digging out wasps' nests. In this respect and as a fruit-eater it may compete with the Honey Buzzard (*Pernis apivorus*) which shares the same forest during the European winter.

Terathopius ecaudatus — Bateleur

Observed at Nimba (KC-L) in October 1963, November 1965, and in several subsequent years, and also (AF-W) in 1971. This raptor patrols over the lowland savanna in Liberia-Guinea, and has also been observed flying over the closed canopy of the rain forests. The only other Liberian locality from where it has been recorded is near the coast.

Circaetus gallicus — Snake Eagle

This medium-sized eagle (West African form, *C. g. beaudouini*) was observed at Nimba (AF-W) in 1967 or 1968; new for Liberia.

Dryotriorchis spectabilis — Congo Serpent Eagle

SPECIMENS. 2 ♀♀, Jun. 1970, Aug. 1968. 1 imm. ♀, Apr. 1969. — *D. s. spectabilis* (Sierra Leone to Cameroon).

IMPERMANENT COLOURS. Legs creamy-yellow. Iris dark brown. Bill black, yellow at the base of the lower mandible. Cere and gape yellow.

STOMACH CONTENTS. Insects and reptilian remains.

ANNUAL CYCLE. The adults were in non-breeding condition and in slightly worn plumage. The imm. was in fresh plumage, with white margins to the back and wing feathers and the underparts creamy-white with few markings.

HABITAT. All 14 observations made at Nimba (KC-L) have been of birds in the forest between 600–900 m. The birds were observed perched in trees, on exposed branches 6–10 m from the ground, on five occasions directly beside a mountain road.

Accipiter melanoleucus   Black Sparrowhawk

This species was observed at Nimba in 1971 (AF-W). It frequents well-grown forest of all types, up to 3100 m in East Africa, but is rare west of the Ivory Coast. This is the first record for Liberia.

The West African race, *A. m. temminckii*, is at least a partial migrant in southern Nigeria. The Nimba bird may have been a straggler.

Accipiter tachiro   African Goshawk

SPECIMENS. 5 ♂♂, Jan. 1969, Apr. 1968, Jun. (2) 1967, Oct. 1964. 4 imm. ♂♂, Jun. 1968, Jul. 1965, Aug. 1967, Oct. 1968. 3 ♀♀, Jan., Mar., Apr. 1968. 2 imm. ♀♀, Mar., May. 1968. 1 imm. o, Feb. 1972. — *A. t. macroscelides* (Senegal to Cameroon).

IMPERMANENT COLOURS. Legs yellow. Iris yellow. Bill black, yellowish-green below. Lores, cere and gape yellowish-green.

STOMACH CONTENTS. Small rodents, birds, lizards and a small snake; also grasshoppers and crickets.

The Grassfield village, site of the Nimba Research Laboratory, lies on a patch of laterite grassland which provides a rich breeding site for frogs and toads, and the mature grassland attracts a rich avifauna of seed eating birds. In the distance the main Nimba ridge rises steeply and is clothed by mature secondary forest. Photograph Malcolm Coe.

ANNUAL CYCLE. The April ♂ was in breeding condition with enlarged gonads. March and April ♀♀ had slightly enlarged ovaries and were probably approaching breeding condition. The January ♀ was in very worn condition and was replacing old brown juvenile tail-feathers with new adult ones. The other two adult ♀♀ were in moult. Curry-Lindahl observed aerial displays from January to March, and in March saw a nest with the ♀ incubating.

HABITAT. Generally found in dense secondary-growth forest in the lowland or in primary montane forest up to about 1000 m, but also seen in more open shrub habitats such as at Grassfield and Yekepa. In frequency, related to the number of observations made (KC-L) this is the most common *Accipiter* at Nimba. The nest mentioned above was in dense forest at about 750 m.

Accipiter badius   Shikra

SPECIMEN. 1 ♀, Jan. 1968, ovary small, worn plumage. — *A. b. sphenurus* (Senegal to Somalia, south to Tanzania).

IMPERMANENT COLOURS. Legs yellow. Iris bright orange. Eye-rim yellow. Bill black, yellow at the base of the lower mandible. Cere and gape yellow.

STOMACH CONTENTS. Lizards.

STATUS. This species is a pronounced migrant in West Africa, spending January to May at 6°–13°N and July to December at 12°–18°N. Presumably the Nimba bird was resting during migration; a new record for Liberia.

Accipiter erythropus   Western Little Sparrowhawk

SPECIMENS. 3 ♂♂, Apr. 1968, Jun., Jul. 1967. 1 imm. ♂, Jun. 1967. 1 juv. ♂, Apr. 1968. — *A. e. erythropus* (Gambia to southern Nigeria).

IMPERMANENT COLOURS. Legs bright orange. Iris red. Eye-rim orange. Bill black, paler below. Cere and gape orange.

STOMACH CONTENTS. Small birds, insects and grasshoppers.

ANNUAL CYCLE. The April male had moderately enlarged gonads and was approaching breeding condition. Gonads of the other two adults were small. The July male was in fresh plumage and the other two adults were in worn condition. The tail of the juvenile, which was found sitting near the nest, was very short, about one-third grown.

HABITAT. Most observations (KC-L) of this species have been in secondary growth and thickets beside roads, but this may be due to the better visibility than in dense forest.

Urotriorchis macrourus   Long-tailed Hawk

SPECIMENS. 4 ♂♂, Apr. 1974, May, Jun. (2) 1968. 2 ♀♀, Aug., Nov. 1968. 1 imm. ♀, Jun. 1970.

IMPERMANENT COLOURS. Legs yellow. Iris yellow. Bill black, yellowish at the base below. Cere dark greyish-green.

STOMACH CONTENTS. One large rodent recorded.

ANNUAL CYCLE. The males were in non-breeding condition. The November female was approaching breeding condition with an enlarged ovary. The April male was in moult and the remainder were in worn plumage.

HABITAT. All observations made (KC-L) have been of birds in the forest undergrowth, often flying like a coucal from one thicket to another, sometimes rapidly crossing a clearing or a road.

Kaupifalco monogrammicus   Lizard Buzzard

SPECIMENS. 2 ♂♂, Jan. 1968, Dec. 1967. 3 ♀♀, Mar. 1969, Jul., Nov. 1967. — *K. m. monogrammicus* (Senegal to Ethiopia and Kenya).

IMPERMANENT COLOURS. Legs dull orange. Iris orange-brown. Eye-rim pale orange. Bill black, orange at the base. Cere and gape orange.

STOMACH CONTENTS. Lizards and grasshoppers.

ANNUAL CYCLE. None of the birds were in a breeding condition. The January male was in very worn plumage and the December male was in moult. The July female was in moult and the other two females were in worn plumage.

HABITAT. In most parts of its wide range over Africa the Lizard Buzzard is considered to be a bird of rather open woodlands, but it is surprisingly found in the Nimba rain forests, both in the lowland and on slopes, up to about 1000 m. It is often seen perched beside a mountain road in the forest where skinks like to bask and hunt.

Buteo auguralis   Red-necked Buzzard

This species has been observed (KC-L) every year from 1963 to 1982, between October and May; in frequency it has been recorded as the third most common raptor. At Nimba it is a forest bird, often seen soaring just above the canopy of the montane forests. When searching for prey, however, it does so from a tree perch, or from a rocky outcrop in the mine landscape. It preys on mammals and insects which are caught on the ground or on branches; insects may also be scratched up from the soil. The species has twice been found nesting at Nimba in trees in the montane rain forest, on both occasions in the same area (about 900 m). One nest contained 2 eggs in January and the other 2 half-grown nestlings in February. Observations elsewhere in West Africa show that after breeding in the forest the Red-necked Buzzard migrates northwards in May-June to the Sudan and Sahel zones, returning to the south in September-November.

Buteo buteo   Common or Steppe Buzzard

SPECIMENS. 3 ♂♂, Jan. (2), Oct. 1968; gonads small — one *B. b. buteo*, two matching BM specimens of *B. b. vulpinus* (Scandinavia–Central Russian Asia).

IMPERMANENT COLOURS. Legs yellow. Iris brown. Bill black. Cere and gape yellow.

STOMACH CONTENTS. Rats, young birds, a skink, large grasshoppers and an earwig.

STATUS. Winter visitor from the Palaearctic; first seen at Nimba (KC-L) in October 1963 and then over many years up to 1982; most records January–February, first and last dates of *B. b. vulpinus* 21 October and 23 March. A new species for Liberia.

FIELD CHARACTERS. The Common Buzzards observed at Nimba (KC-L) were often difficult to separate from the similar migratory afrotropical *B. auguralis*. *Buteo oreophilus* also presents similar problems and has to be separated from the similar *B. b. vulpinus*. All three species are variable in colouration, especially *B. buteo*. One useful field character for separating these three buzzards in tropical Africa is that both the two afrotropical species are much more vocal than *B. b. vulpinus*. All have similar calls, but KC-L has never heard *B. b. vulpinus* calling in Africa, while it does so frequently on the breeding grounds in Eurasia.

HABITAT. Primary and secondary, lowland and montane forests. Common Buzzards were seen in the interior of these forests or soaring above them as well as in clearings, along their edges and in woodlands. Often the birds crossed over the Nimba ridge in both directions. The species was also observed soaring over cultivated land and grasslands.

MIGRATION. *Buteo b. vulpinus* is a Palaearctic migrant to tropical and southern Africa with the main wintering areas in the drier parts of central and western southern Africa. It has also been recorded in Mauretania, Senegal, Gambia, Mali, Ivory Coast, Ghana, Gabon, Zaire, Angola and South West Africa (Curry-Lindahl, 1981). There is a recovery recorded from Ghana in September of an adult that had previously been banded in Tunisia (Thiollay, 1977).

Buteo b. buteo may migrate to western Africa. One bird from Lapland has been recovered in Morocco (Haftorn, 1971), and one was found poisoned in Mauretania on 1 November 1973 (Morel & Browne, 1981).

Lophaetus occipitalis — Long-crested Hawk-Eagle

This eagle was observed at Nimba in 1964, 1972, 1977, 1979 and 1980 (KC-L), in 1965–66 by Verschuren (1979), and in 1967 or 1968 (AF-W). These are the first records for Liberia. It had previously been recorded on the Guinean side of Nimba. The species is partially migratory in parts of West Africa and this may explain its irregular occurrence at Nimba. All observations (KC-L) have been of birds flying over the montane forest canopy, or perching in trees close to small clearings in the lowland forest.

Stephanoaetus coronatus — Crowned Hawk-Eagle

This powerful forest eagle was observed at Nimba (AF-W) in 1967 or 1968 and in 1969 and 1971 (KC-L). An eagle of high forest, feeding largely on mammals, it appears to be rare at Nimba, probably due to the scarcity of both monkeys and duikers, which have greatly decreased as a result of hunting pressures in which the raptor itself has presumably also become a victim.

Spizaetus africanus — Cassin's Hawk-Eagle

SPECIMENS. 2 ♀♀, Jun., Sept. 1968; fresh plumage, ovaries slightly enlarged.

IMPERMANENT COLOURS. Legs creamy-yellow. Iris brownish-yellow. Eye-rim and below dull greenish-grey. Bill dark grey. Cere yellow.

STOMACH CONTENTS. Unidentified rodents.

STATUS. This is a new record for Liberia. It is probably rare at Nimba, as KC-L has never seen it despite his annual visits there. It may be difficult to observe in dense forest, although in other rain-forest areas it is known to soar above the canopy.

Hieraaetus pennatus — Booted Eagle

On 2 March 1981 a Booted Eagle (dark phase) was observed perched rather low in an isolated tree on the golf course at Yekepa, 50 m from the edge of lowland forest. Curry-Lindahl was able to drive up to the bird and watch it closely. The main wintering area of this Palaearctic eagle seems to be in eastern Africa but it is also recorded in West Africa, from Rio de Oro and Senegal to Nigeria. This is the first record for Liberia.

Hieraaetus ayresii — Ayres' Hawk-Eagle

SPECIMEN. 1 ♂, Oct. 1968; gonads small, very fat, in fresh plumage.

IMPERMANENT COLOURS. Legs lemon-yellow. Iris clear yellow. Eye rim and brow greenish. Bill dark grey, paler and bluer basally. Cere and gape greenish-yellow.

STATUS. In addition to the specimen collected, this eagle was observed (KC-L) in 1963, 1966 and several subsequent years in the same area at Nimba, namely the tree savanna close to the Guinea border. A new species for Liberia.

Milvus migrans — Black Kite

Although Black Kites are not common at Nimba they have been observed every year since 1963 mainly October to April, occasionally in other months, chiefly in the more open areas around the township of Yekepa. Their racial identity is hard to tell. Probably three subspecies are involved: *migrans*, *tenebrosus* and *parasitus*, coming from both north and east.

Pernis apivorus — Honey Buzzard

SPECIMENS. 2 ♂♂, Sept. 1977, Nov. 1968. 2 ♀♀, Apr., Oct. 1968.

IMPERMANENT COLOURS. Legs yellow. Iris yellow. Bill black, creamy-yellow at the base. Cere yellow.

STOMACH CONTENTS. Many hymenopterous larvae.

ANNUAL CYCLE. The three specimens collected September–November were in worn condition. The April female had moulted into fresh plumage.

FIELD NOTES. This Palaearctic migrant and winter visitor was observed at Nimba in 1966 (KC-L) and has since then been seen in most years between September and April. One of the seven most frequently observed birds of prey at Nimba in terms of sight records made during the period 1963–1982 (KC-L). It is found in primary and secondary forests at all altitudes, both in the interior and at edges. Whilst often active in digging for wasps or other insects on the ground of the forest floor, it has also been noted beside roads and has several times been seen even amongst the rocks in the denuded mine landscape. Twice it has been seen eating figs.

Aviceda cuculoides — Cuckoo Falcon

Observed on several occasions in different months of the year (KC-L), twice in 1971 (JK) and also in July 1976 (AF-W & DT). The birds seen (KC-L) have been of different colours, which suggests that the two West African races may overlap in the Nimba area. *Aviceda c. cuculoides* ranges from Gambia to Nigeria and the northern edge of Zaire; *A. c. batesi*, a darker form, occurs in the more humid and forested belt south of *cuculoides*, from Sierra Leone east to the Congo basin. At Nimba the Cuckoo Falcon occurs in primary and secondary forests at various elevations, and is occasionally seen soaring above the forest canopy.

Chelictinia riocourii — Swallow-tailed Kite

This little kite visited the savanna area at the foot of Liberian Nimba on 10 January 1982 (KC-L), after *Harmattan* winds had been blowing for several consecutive days. This is the first record for Liberia. The Swallow-tailed Kite is a migrant, moving southwards during October–December to areas between 12°N and 8°N, where it remains until March, then migrating northwards back to the Sahel, where it breeds. Thus its southern quarters are not far from Nimba.

Macheirhamphus alcinus — Bat Hawk

SPECIMEN. 1 ♂, Jul. 1968; gonads small, fresh plumage. — *M. a. anderssoni* (wide-spread in sub-Saharan Africa).

IMPERMANENT COLOURS. Legs very pale bluish-grey. Iris bright yellow. Bill black, blue-grey basally.

STOMACH CONTENTS. Small amount of fine hair (? bat).

HABITAT. Occurs in lowland as well as montane forest, with a preference for clearings or the vicinity of roads or other open sites close to the forests. Observed both at Yekepa and Grassfield.

Family Falconidae

Falco biarmicus — Lanner

An adult Lanner was observed on 13 January 1982 (KC-L) perched in an isolated dead tree on one of the bare ridges in the mine area of Mount Nimba. The bird was watched at close range for several minutes and flew away when KC-L tried to photograph it.

This is a new record for Liberia. Presumably the observed bird represented *F. b. abyssinicus* which breeds in the Guinean savanna belt of the nearby Ivory Coast north of Liberia. This race is at least partially migratory, moving between the Guinean savanna and the Sahelian belts. In Nigeria there is an influx of birds to the Guinean savannas in December–January. The North African Lanner (*F. b. erlangeri*) occasionally migrates to Senegal and movements in eastern Morocco are reported November–February. It is possible that the bird seen at Nimba could have been a straggler of this race.

Falco peregrinus — Peregrine Falcon

This falcon has been seen a number of times on and around the ridge of Mount Nimba during the period November to March. Most records are from the mining area, and the fact that Peregrines were never seen there in the 1960s may indicate that they did not visit Nimba prior to the industrial alteration of the mountain top. The first records are from February–March 1971 (AF-W, JK & SK). Subsequently, the Peregrine was observed every 'winter' between 1978 and 1982 (KC-L). These are the first records for Liberia. In the past it has been recorded at Nimba on the Ivory Coast side (Brunel & Thiollay, 1969).

Falco peregrinus occurs throughout much of Africa, but is very sparse in its distribution in West Africa. Main wintering race in Africa is *F. p. calidus*. In addition, several Eurasian races migrate to Africa.

Falco cuvierii — African Hobby

This small falcon was observed at Nimba in 1967 or 1968 (AF-W) and on 7 July 1978 (RW). These are the first records for Liberia. It is a non-migratory species found in woodlands, but avoiding heavily forested areas, and is widespread in sub-Saharan Africa.

Falco subbuteo — Hobby

This species was observed at Yekepa in February 1971 (AF-W, JK & SK). This is the first record for Liberia. Serle *et al.* (1977) list it as an uncommon Palaearctic migrant to West Africa, but Brunel & Thiollay (1969) recorded it regularly in small numbers at Lamto, Ivory Coast, September to April. The main wintering area seems to be south of the equator.

Falco tinnunculus — Kestrel

SPECIMENS. 2 ♀♀, Jan., Feb. 1968; ovaries small, worn plumage. — *F. t. tinnunculus* (breeds western Palaearctic).

IMPERMANENT COLOURS. Legs yellow. Iris dark brown. Bill dark grey, yellowish basally. Gape and cere pale yellow.

STOMACH CONTENTS. A rat; also insects, including grasshoppers.

STATUS. In addition to the two specimens, Kestrels were observed at Nimba in 1965 (KC-L) and many times in subsequent years, frequenting savannas, short grassy meadows and lawns, cultivated land, and the open parts of the mine area. The local race is *F. t. rufescens*, but subspecific determinations were not made in the field. The records of *F. t. tinnunculus* are the first for Liberia. Subsequently, a Swiss bird ringed in Europe has been recovered in Liberia (Moreau, 1972).

Falco naumanni — Lesser Kestrel

This species, a Palaearctic migrant and a rather rare winter visitor to West Africa, was observed at Nimba on 19 February 1966 (KC-L). This is the first record for Liberia. The observation was of four birds which pursued and captured insects close to a fire front sweeping across the Liberian grassland near the Guinean border. At least a dozen other Lesser Kestrels were seen the same day on a visit into Guinea.

Family Phasianidae

Francolinus lathami — Forest Francolin

SPECIMENS. 4 ♂♂, May 1968, Jun. 1970, Dec. 1968, 1971. 3 ♀♀, Jan. 1972, Mar., May 1968. 1 o juv., Apr. 1968. 1 o chick, Mar. 1968. — *F. l. lathami* (Sierra Leone to Cameroon and the lower Congo).

IMPERMANENT COLOURS. Legs bright yellow. Iris brown. Eyelid pale greenish. Bill black.

STOMACH CONTENTS. Mostly small termites and a few worms.

ANNUAL CYCLE. The chick had just hatched (12 March) and still retained the egg tooth. The juvenile was half-grown (24 April) and retained some down around the head and lower belly. The adults provided little information. None had fully enlarged gonads; the June specimen was in worn, the others in more or less fresh plumage.

FIELD NOTES. This is a rather common francolin at Nimba and is found in dense forest where it is difficult to observe and almost impossible to flush. It has invariably been seen on the ground, usually singly or in pairs, up to about 800 m.

Francolinus bicalcaratus — Double-spurred Francolin

SPECIMEN. 1 ♀, Nov. 1964; fresh plumage. — *F. b. thornei* (Sierra Leone to Benin).

IMPERMANENT COLOURS. Legs pale yellow-green. Iris brown. Bill dark brown, greenish-yellow below.

HABITAT. Valleys and lower slopes of Mount Nimba.

Francolinus ahantensis — Ahanta Francolin

SPECIMENS. 3 ♂♂, Sept. 1967, Nov. 1968, Dec. 1972. 6 ♀♀, Jan. 1971, Jun. 1977, Jul. (2) 1968, Aug., Sept. 1967. — *F. a. ahantensis* (Sierra Leone to Nigeria).

IMPERMANENT COLOURS. Legs orange. Iris brown. Bare patch behind eye, dull pale orange. Bill dark orange with a blackish culmen.

STOMACH CONTENTS. Vegetable matter, including seeds, cassava pulp and large fruits; insects, including termites; also one white gastropod.

ANNUAL CYCLE. The specimens give clear evidence of a moult ending about September: the June bird was just over half way through the wing moult (4 outer primaries old), the July–August birds were all in late stages of primary moult, and the two September birds had completed their moult but retained sheaths at the base of the outermost primaries. The November–December birds were in fresh plumage and the January bird in moderately worn plumage. Gonad data give no definite information on breeding. The July–September females had ovaries measuring 10–14 mm, and the September and November males testes of 10 and 14 mm, respectively.

FIELD NOTES. Most observations (KC-L) made on this bird were close to cultivation, on abandoned farms and in shrub and secondary growth. It is mainly in such habitats that one hears their characteristic calls in the early morning and late evening. This species appears to be social, keeping in groups of 5–7 birds.

Coturnix delegorguei — Harlequin Quail

On the misty night of 28 November 1975, a ♀ collided with a lighted house in the mine area of Mount Nimba at about 1000 m, apparently on migration (KC-L). This is the first record for Liberia. This species is a trans-equatorial migrant that occasionally may reach Liberia on extended southward migration.

Guttera edouardi   Crested Guineafowl

This species was observed at Nimba (AF-W) and on the Guinean side of the border (KC-L). It is found in gallery forest and forest edges. The form *G. e. verreauxi* occurs in Liberia.

Agelastes meleagrides
     White-breasted Guineafowl

According to Edward Yallah this species used to occur at Nimba, but it rapidly became extinct there with the opening of the area in the later 1950s and early 1960s. It is a forest species, usually found in small vulnerable flocks (AF-W). This species has died out in most of its West African range and is in severe danger of extinction. An adult male was collected (EY) from the Cavally River in eastern Liberia on 4 December 1978, which was included with the Nimba collection (PRC).

Family Rallidae

Canirallus oculeus   Grey-throated Rail

SPECIMENS. 1 ♂, Jun. 1968. 2 ♀♀, Jan. 1967, May 1971. — *C. o. oculeus* (Liberia to southwestern Nigeria).

IMPERMANENT COLOURS. Legs polished brown. Iris orange; eye-rim yellowish-green. Bill black, greenish below.

STOMACH CONTENTS. Ants.

ANNUAL CYCLE. Gonads of the male were small. The size of the females' ovaries was not recorded. The birds were in fresh plumage.

HABITAT. The species was observed in dense vegetation along a slow-running rivulet in lowland secondary forest.

Amaurornis flavirostris   Black Crake

SPECIMENS. 1 ♀, Feb. 1973; fresh plumage.

IMPERMANENT COLOURS. Legs red. Iris red. Bill olive-green.

STATUS. At Nimba this is a rare species. In West Africa it is widely distributed south of 17°N wherever there are lakes or pools fringed with aquatic vegetation.

Sarothrura elegans   Buff-spotted Crake

This small rail's mournful but musical, far-carrying whistle was heard at about 1000 m on Mount Nimba (AF-W) in 1971. The bird inhabits low dense second-growth in forest clearings and is widespread in Africa, but with few records west of Cameroon.

Sarothrura pulchra   White-spotted Crake

SPECIMENS. 4 ♂♂, Mar. 1968, 1975, Nov., Dec. 1967. 4 ♀♀, Feb. 1967, 1968, Sept. 1968, Nov. 1967. In addition one individual was trapped at Grassfield on 10 Aug. 1978 (RW) — *S. p. pulchra* (Senegal to Cameroon).

IMPERMANENT COLOURS. Legs grey. Iris orange-brown. Bill blackish, paler horn below.

STOMACH CONTENTS. Adult insects, spiders and a caterpillar; also seeds and two small gastropods.

ANNUAL CYCLE. Only the September female was in breeding condition (ovary 15 mm, ova to 3.5 mm). All were in fresh plumage except for one February female which was moulting out the last stages of immaturity.

HABITAT. Repeatedly seen (KC-L) in or near a degraded and polluted swamp, full of debris from a felled forest.

Himantornis haematopus   Nkulengu Rail

SPECIMENS. 3 ♂♂, Apr. 1970, Jul. 1967, Dec. 1968. 1 ♀, Sept. 1976. — *H. h. haematopus* (Sierra Leone to western Uganda).

IMPERMANENT COLOURS. Legs bright pink. Iris orange-brown to chestnut-brown. Bill black tipped pale grey, grading to pea-green at the base of the lower mandible. Facial skin dark grey.

STOMACH CONTENTS. Black ants and large seeds.

ANNUAL CYCLE. Gonad data (incomplete) gave no information on breeding. The September and December birds were undergoing a wing-moult; in both, the 5th primary was incompletely grown (6th in order of replacement, the primary moult being ascendent in this genus).

HABITAT. Only observed on relatively dry ground in lowland secondary forest (KC-L).

Family Heliornithidae

Podica senegalensis — Finfoot

SPECIMENS. 2 ♂♂, May 1970, Nov. 1968. 1 imm. ♀, Nov. 1970. 1 o juv., Dec. 1965. — *P. s. senegalensis* (Senegal to Zaire).

IMPERMANENT COLOURS. Legs bright pale orange. Iris pale brownish-grey. Bill black, whitish below.

STOMACH CONTENTS. Small shrimps.

ANNUAL CYCLE. Gonad data gave no information on breeding. The juvenile was in down and about one-third grown. The immature female had all flight-feathers about half-grown. The November male had evidently just completed a moult (fresh plumage, and traces of sheaths still present at base of primaries).

Family Jacanidae

Actophilornis africanus — African Jacana

SPECIMEN. 1 ♀, Jan. 1973; body moult.

IMPERMANENT COLOURS. Legs greyish-green. Iris dark brown. Bill grey with a paler tip.

STATUS. In the early and middle 1960s the African Jacana was absent at Nimba, but after the opening up of the swamp forests for maize cultivation it occasionally began to be seen in the 1970s.

Family Charadriidae

Vanellus senegallus — Senegal Wattled Plover

SPECIMEN. 1 ♂, May 1968; gonads small, worn plumage. — *V. s. senegallus* (Senegal to Uganda and Sudan).

IMPERMANENT COLOURS. Legs bright pale yellow. Iris pale blue-grey. Eye-rim bright yellow. Bill bright yellow with a dusky tip. Wattle bright yellow, dark dull red above the eye.

STOMACH CONTENTS. Insects.

HABITAT AND STATUS. Five individuals, apparently on migration, were observed in October 1963 (KC-L) on the savanna close to the border of Guinea. This species undertakes local migrations; in the nearby Ivory Coast it occurs in November–April.

Charadrius forbesi — Forbes's Banded Plover

SPECIMENS. 1 ♂, Feb. 1968. 3 ♀♀, Nov. (2) 1964, Dec. 1967.

IMPERMANENT COLOURS. Legs pale pink. Iris brown. Eye-rim orange-red. Bill blackish with a pink base.

STOMACH CONTENTS. Insects.

ANNUAL CYCLE. Gonad data (incomplete) gave no evidence of breeding. One of the November ♀♀ was in a late stage of wing-moult (9th and 10th primaries growing).

HABITAT AND STATUS. This species was observed twice during January–February in the 1970s on the golf course at the foot of Nimba, and has also been seen at Grassfield. In West Africa it makes local movements. It is present only during November to April in southern Ivory Coast, which fits with the dates of its appearance at Nimba.

Tringa nebularia — Greenshank

This Palaearctic visitor to Africa was observed at Yekepa (AF-W). In West Africa it is widely distributed in winter in suitable localities.

Tringa glareola — Wood Sandpiper

This common Palaearctic migrant and winter visitor to Africa was observed at Nimba (KC-L) in 1964 and (AF-W) in 1967 or 1968. The birds seen in 1964 were a group of three individuals visiting a partly inundated ricefield.

Tringa ochropus — Green Sandpiper

SPECIMENS. 2 ♀♀, Feb., Nov. 1968.

IMPERMANENT COLOURS. Legs pale greyish-green. Iris brown. Bill black tinged olive-green.

STOMACH CONTENTS. Insects.

HABITAT AND STATUS. A Palaearctic migrant, wintering in northern, tropical and southern Africa. Single birds were observed (KC-L) in 1964 and 1966 at small, shallow pools and puddles along roads. Since then it has been seen on four occasions along the forested stream in the Iti valley. These are the first records of this species for Liberia.

Tringa hypoleucos — Common Sandpiper

SPECIMENS. 2 ♂♂, Mar. 1968, Nov. 1967. 2 ♀♀, Aug. 1967, Sept. 1969.

IMPERMANENT COLOURS. Legs yellowish-green. Iris brown. Bill grey.

STOMACH CONTENTS. Insects, including small beetles.

HABITAT AND STATUS. This Palaearctic migrant was regularly observed at Nimba between 1963 and 1966, but in the following years it became a less regular visitor, probably due to the destruction of the river shores, its main habitat.

Family Recurvirostridae

Himantopus himantopus — Black-winged Stilt

This species was observed at Yekepa in February 1971 (AF-W, JK & SK). This is the second record for Liberia; see Rand (1951). In West Africa wintering birds from Eurasia are more numerous than the resident African birds. The species has not been found breeding in Liberia but does so in the interior of Ivory Coast.

Family Columbidae

Columba unicincta — African Wood Pigeon

SPECIMENS. 2 ♂, Apr. 1970, Jun. 1967. 1 ♀, Apr. 1970.

IMPERMANENT COLOURS. Legs pale grey. Iris bright red. Bare skin round eye purple-red. Bill grey; cere tinged greenish.

STOMACH CONTENTS. Large white pointed ribbed seeds and grit.

ANNUAL CYCLE. The two April birds (not examined for breeding condition) were both in wing-moult, the male renewing the 9th and the female the 6th primary. The June male was in fresh plumage, with testes 11 mm.

DISTRIBUTION AND HABITAT. Liberia represents the western limit of occurrence of this species. It inhabits primary forest, and most of the observations (mainly by hearing) were from below the 900 m contour, but occasionally at higher levels, even on the top of Mount Nimba (KC-L).

Columba iriditorques — Bronze-naped Pigeon

SPECIMENS. 15 ♂♂, Jan. 1966, 1969 (3), Jun. 1971, Jul. 1967 (2), 68 (2), Sept. 1967, Nov. 1968 (5). 18 ♀♀, Jan. 1969 (3), Apr., May 1968, Jun. 1970, Jul. 1968 (2), Sept. 1967 (2), Nov. 1968 (7), Dec. 1964. 1 juv. ♀, Mar. 1969.

IMPERMANENT COLOURS. Legs pink. Iris pinky-red. Bare skin around eye reddish. Bill grey.

STOMACH CONTENTS. Seeds, small fruits, vegetable matter, fibres and grit.

ANNUAL CYCLE. The juvenile was taken from a nest on 29 March. Three females gave evidence of breeding activity: one with ovary 13 mm, ova to 1.5 mm, in April; one noted as having laid, July; and one with ovary 15 mm, September (gonad state was not noted for the January and December birds). These three females, and another female, January, all had interrupted a wing-moult, and show a clear contrast between fresh inner and worn outer primaries. Of the seven females collected in November, four had ovaries of 5 mm or less and the maximum was 10.5 mm, suggesting a low level of breeding in this month. Birds in active wing-moult were collected in January, May, June, July, September and November. None of the males showed evidence of interrupted moult.

HABITAT. Found in both primary and secondary forest at Nimba up to about 900 m.

Streptopelia semitorquata — Red-eyed Dove

SPECIMEN. 1 ♀, Sept. 1968; in breeding condition (ova to 5.5 mm).

IMPERMANENT COLOURS. Legs maroon-pink. Iris dark brown. Bare skin round eye maroon-purple. Bill black, purple basally.

STOMACH CONTENTS. Round green fruits and pale green vegetable matter.

HABITAT. A common dove at Nimba in all kinds of habitats from forests to gardens and inhabited areas. The opening up of the Nimba region may have favoured this species, as it is now more common than in the 1960s.

Turtur tympanistria — Tambourine Dove

SPECIMENS. 9 ♂♂, Jun. (6), Jul., Aug. 1967, Sept. 1970. 6 ♀♀, Jun. 1967, 1968, Jul. (2), Sept. 1967, Nov. 1970. 2 juv. ♀♀, Jun. 1967, Oct. 1970.

IMPERMANENT COLOURS. Legs pinkish-purple. Iris dark brown. Bill black. Cere purple-black.

STOMACH CONTENTS. Vegetable matter, including hard seeds and fibres.

ANNUAL CYCLE. The only indication of the breeding season comes from the juvenile collected on 30 October, which was apparently not long out of the nest. Two, and possibly three, of the seven adults collected in June were in wing-moult, but none of those collected July to November.

HABITAT. Occurs in both primary and secondary forest up to about 1000–1100 m, but seems to prefer secondary growth. As it feeds entirely on the ground its foraging may have been facilitated by the opening up of the Nimba area.

Turtur afer — Blue-spotted Wood-dove

SPECIMENS. 2 ♂♂, Feb. 1968, Aug. 1967. 2 ♀♀, Feb., Oct. 1968.

IMPERMANENT COLOURS. Legs purple. Iris dark brown. Bill pale orange-pink with the base dark purple. Cere purple.

STOMACH CONTENTS. Hard seeds and yellow vegetable matter.

ANNUAL CYCLE. No indication of breeding from gonads. The October and February females were in worn plumage, the February male in an early stage of wing-moult, and the August male in fresh plumage.

HABITATS AND HABITS. A common dove at Nimba colonizing all kinds of tree vegetation along roads and paths which have been opened up at higher elevations, and even on the ridges at about 1200 m. Frequently seen in pairs searching for food on the ground, often beside roads, and in clearings with short grass and scrub.

Turtur brehmeri — Blue-headed Dove

SPECIMENS. 7 ♂♂, Jan., Feb. 1970, Jun. 1967, 1968, 1971, Aug. 1968, Oct. 1967. 4 ♀♀, Jan. (2) 1969, Oct. 1974, Dec. 1968. — *T. b. infelix* (Sierra Leone to Cameroon).

IMPERMANENT COLOURS. Legs pinkish-purple. Iris brown tinged chestnut. Bill grey.

STOMACH CONTENTS. Various hard seeds, vegetable matter and insects.

ANNUAL CYCLE. Gonad data incomplete, but August and October males with testes 9 mm (*cf.* 6 mm for two June males) suggest breeding in latter half of year. Two males in late stages of wing-moult in June and August, and a female finishing wing-moult (outer primaries growing) in October.

HABITATS AND HABITS. A lowland forest dove with habits similar to the preceding species, but usually more retiring and rarely found above 700–750 m. During recent years it has gradually ventured out of the forests and is found feeding in gardens and on lawns, e.g. at Grassfield and Yekepa, though there are always patches of forest nearby.

Aplopelia larvata — Lemon Dove

SPECIMENS. 2 ♂♂, Feb. 1966, Apr. 1970. 1 ♀, Sept. 1966. — *A. l. simplex* (Liberia, Cameroon, Gulf of Guinea islands, and locally in Gabon and Zaire).

IMPERMANENT COLOURS. Legs red. Iris dark yellow. Bill black.

DISTRIBUTION. The only other Liberian record of this ground-feeding forest dove is from Paiata, 140 km SW. of Nimba (Allen, 1930). There appear to be no records of the species between Liberia and Cameroon.

Treron calva — Green Pigeon

SPECIMENS. 4 ♂♂, Feb. (2) 1968, 1974, Apr. 1969, Aug. 1968. 4 ♀♀, Jul. 1970, 1974, Sept. 1975, Oct. 1968. — *T. c. sharpei* (Sierra Leone to Nigeria).

IMPERMANENT COLOURS. Legs yellow. Iris bright pale blue. Bill whitish. Cere and soft skin at base of lower mandible, deep orange-red.

STOMACH CONTENTS. Fruit pulp and seeds.

ANNUAL CYCLE. The October female was apparently approaching breeding condition, with ova to 1.5 mm (other females without gonad data). A February male was just beginning a wing-moult, the April male was at a late stage, and a female collected 1 July was just finishing its wing-moult (outermost primary not full grown). Four birds collected 18 July to 20 October all had fresh plumage.

HABITAT AND HABITS. This is a common species at Nimba, occurring in all kinds of woods and forests from the lowland up to about 1100 m. It is social and appears usually in small groups of 3–4 birds, or in pairs. It feeds in the trees. There are local movements of birds but the pattern is irregular, probably depending on the ripening of fruits.

Family Psittacidae

Psittacus erithacus — Grey Parrot

This parrot was observed at Nimba in 1971 (KC-L), and in 1976 (AF-W, JK & SK). It inhabits tropical forest and adjacent cleared land. It is remarkable that this species is so rare in the lowland rain forests around Nimba compared with its frequency in equatorial forests, even montane rain forests, elsewhere in Africa, as in Zaire (Curry-Lindahl, 1961).

Family Musophagidae

Tauraco persa — Green-crested Turaco

SPECIMENS. 1 ♂, Nov. 1968. 3 ♀♀, Jan. 1968, Jul. 1970, Oct. 1964. — *T. p. buffoni* (Gambia to Liberia).

IMPERMANENT COLOURS. Legs black. Iris brown. Eye-wattle bright red. Bill dull red, tip blackish.

STOMACH CONTENTS. Fruit pulp and seeds.

ANNUAL CYCLE. The January female was in full breeding condition, with ovary 19 mm and ova to 4.5 mm (gonad state of other females not recorded).

HABITAT AND HABITS. This is a common arboreal species at Nimba, often seen in pairs. Throughout the year, but particularly December to April, it calls energetically, widely announcing its presence both in primary (including *Parinari*-dominated), and in secondary forest at all levels from the lowland up to about 1100 m.

Tauraco macrorhynchus — Black-tip Crested Turaco

SPECIMENS. 3 ♂♂, Feb. 1970, Apr. 1969, Nov. 1968. 8 ♀♀, Jan. 1969, May 1966, Jun. 1967 (2), 1970, Jul. 1970 (2), Sept. 1967. — *T. m. macrorhynchus* (Sierra Leone to Ghana).

IMPERMANENT COLOURS. Legs black. Iris brown. Eye-wattle bright red. Bill bright yellow, base dark red.

STOMACH CONTENTS. Fruit pulp, vegetable matter, including shoots and seeds.

ANNUAL CYCLE. Two June females had ovaries of 15 and 16 mm, and the September female an ovary of 12 mm (gonad size of others not recorded). Four of the seven birds collected January to June were in wing-moult, and none of the four collected July to November.

HABITAT AND HABITS. This species shares habitats with the preceding one but appears to keep more to the higher forest strata than its relative. It does not normally enter the *Parinari*-dominated associations, is sometimes seen visiting *Musanga* growths. To judge by the amount of calling (mainly November–April) the Black-tip Crested Turaco is more common at Nimba than the Green-crested Turaco.

Corythaeola cristata — Great Blue Turaco

SPECIMEN. 1 ♀, Aug. 1968, ovary 4 mm.

IMPERMANENT COLOURS. Legs black. Iris deep chestnut-brown. Bare face blackish. Bill bright yellow with a red tip.

STOMACH CONTENTS. Fruit pulp, probably from the umbrella tree, *Musanga*.

HABITAT AND HABITS. A common bird at Nimba though heard less often than the two preceding species, probably due to its habit of calling mainly in the early mornings and late afternoons, not during the whole day like the others. It is especially vocal from November to March. It is a canopy-dweller, found in both primary and secondary high forest, usually in groups of 3–6 birds, and does not normally ascend above 900 m.

Family Cuculidae

Clamator glandarius — Great Spotted Cuckoo

This cuckoo was observed at Nimba in 1967 or 1968 (AF-W). There are at least seven isolated areas, scattered in all climatic regions of Africa, where this cuckoo breeds, one of them in nearby Sierra Leone. In addition, it is likely that a considerable proportion of Palaearctic migrants winter in West Africa.

Clamator levaillantii — Striped Cuckoo

SPECIMENS. 5 ♂♂, Mar. 1968, Aug., Nov. (2), Dec. 1967. 1 ♀, Nov. 1967.

IMPERMANENT COLOURS. Legs grey. Iris brown. Bill black.

STOMACH CONTENTS. Insects, including grasshoppers and hairy caterpillars.

ANNUAL CYCLE. The birds were in non-breeding condition. The August male was in fresh plumage and the remaining birds were in varying stages of moult.

HABITAT AND STATUS. This is a pronounced intra-African migrant, although its movements so far are little understood. In addition to the birds collected at Nimba there are observations for January (KC-L) and July (AF-W & DT). Thus, this species seems to spend a large part of the year at Nimba. It has been observed mainly in secondary growth and woodland around Grassfield and Yekepa (KC-L).

Cuculus solitarius — Red-chested Cuckoo

SPECIMENS. 1 ♀, Nov. 1968. 1 o, Nov. 1970. — *C. s. solitarius* (Gambia to Eritrea, south to Cape Province).

IMPERMANENT COLOURS. Legs yellow. Iris dark brown. Eye-rim chrome yellow. Bill black, yellow at the base of the lower mandible. Gape orange.

STOMACH CONTENTS. Hairy caterpillars.

HABITAT AND STATUS. The Red-chested Cuckoo was observed at Nimba in 1964, 1966 and several subsequent years (KC-L), and also recorded in 1966 by Verschuren (1979). These are the first records of this cuckoo for Liberia. It frequents all kinds of forest, both primary and secondary, as well as woodlands and gardens. It calls intensely at Nimba during December to April, but it may also be heard occasionally in other months.

Cuculus clamosus — Black Cuckoo

This cuckoo was observed at Nimba in February or March 1971 by AF-W and SK. In February 1976 an individual of the rufous-chested forest race (*gabonensis*) was seen in forest along a mine road at about 950 m (KC-L). This species has a characteristic voice and may often be heard calling at night. As it has been recorded calling in all months of the year, at least the forest population is sedentary at Nimba. Elsewhere the species is known to be migratory, but its movements are not well understood. It is possible that the non-forest race (*clamosus*) is migratory and that the forest race may be locally or entirely resident.

Cuculus canorus — Cuckoo

SPECIMENS. 3 ♂♂, Nov. 1964, 1967 (2), Dec. 1967. 3 ♀♀, Nov (2), Dec. 1967. — *C. c. canorus* (Palaearctic, winter visitor to Africa).

IMPERMANENT COLOURS. Legs yellow-orange. Iris brown. Bill black, green at base.

STOMACH CONTENTS. Insects.

HABITAT AND STATUS. As the nominate race is usually silent in Africa it usually escapes notice in forested country. However, a female was found dead in February on a Nimba mine road, surrounded by montane forest, at about 1000 m. The bird was intact and had probably been on migration. On other occasions KC-L has found dead migrants of other species along the same road during migration periods. They have all been intact, apart from being invaded by ants, and the reason for this mortality remains a mystery.

Pachycoccyx audeberti — Thick-billed Cuckoo

This cuckoo was observed at Nimba in 1967 or 1968 by AF-W. It is a solitary species and everywhere uncommon. Its breeding distribution follows that of its breeding hosts – species of *Prionops* (PRC). This is the first record of the species for Liberia.

Cercococcyx mechowi — Dusky Long-tailed Cuckoo

SPECIMENS. 1 ♂, Aug. 1967. 1 imm. ♀, Nov. 1970.

IMPERMANENT COLOURS. Legs lemon-yellow. Iris dark brown. Eye-rim lemon-yellow. Bill black above, yellow below tipped black. Gape greenish.

STOMACH CONTENTS. Hairy caterpillars.

HABITAT. Observed in October 1963 in dense lowland primary forest (KC-L). It is a very unobtrusive, skulking species of primary forest tree-tops, and if it were not for its distinctive call it would be considered rare, but it is actually fairly common (AF-W).

Cercococcyx olivinus — Olive Long-tailed Cuckoo

SPECIMENS. 2 ♂♂, Sept., Oct. 1967.

IMPERMANENT COLOURS. Legs yellow. Iris brown. Eye-rim yellow-green. Bill black, yellowish-green below. Gape yellow.

STOMACH CONTENTS. Insects, including caterpillars.

HABITAT AND STATUS. These are the first records for Liberia of this little known forest cuckoo. It represents an important extension of range some 750 km west. It was also observed in February 1971 (JK) and was heard calling in July 1976 (AF-W & DT). Like the previous species, it is unobtrusive and skulking, but is probably not uncommon.

Chrysococcyx klaas — Klaas's Cuckoo

SPECIMENS. 3 imm. ♂♂, Feb. Apr. 1968, Nov. 1964. 1 ♀, Oct. 1968. 3 imm. ♀♀, Jun. 1968, 1971, Nov. 1972.

IMPERMANENT COLOURS. Legs olive-green. Iris clear pale creamy-brown; brown in immature. Bill blackish, tinged bluish at base of lower mandible.

STOMACH CONTENTS. Insects, mostly caterpillars and also a few beetles.

ANNUAL CYCLE. The October female was in breeding condition (ovary with yolks to 8 mm).

HABITAT AND STATUS. Seen and heard in most months of the year in a wide range of habitats, from gardens and cultivation to primary lowland forest, particularly in valley bottoms.

Chrysococcyx caprius — Didric Cuckoo

SPECIMENS. 3 ♂♂, Apr. 1974, Aug., Oct. 1967. 4 imm. ♂♂, Jan. 1968, Dec. (3) 1967. 2 ♀♀, Jan., Apr. 1968. 1 imm. ♀, Jan. 1968. 1 imm. o, Dec. 1971.

IMPERMANENT COLOURS. Legs dark grey or black. Iris: male — red or orange, yellow internally; female — pale creamy, browner near pupil; immature — brown. Eye-rim orange or pinkish. Bill blackish, paler horn below.

STOMACH CONTENTS. Insects, including caterpillars; also 2 hard seeds.

ANNUAL CYCLE. The specimens gave no evidence of breeding. Of the adults, the April female was in wing-moult and the August and October males in fresh plumage.

HABITAT AND STATUS. The species was seen and heard in many years and in all months, chiefly in the gallery forests in valley bottoms and in most other habitats except those at higher levels, where *Parinari* predominates.

Chrysococcyx cupreus — Emerald Cuckoo

SPECIMENS. 7 ♂♂ Jan. 1972, Aug. 1968 (2), Sept. 1968, 1969, Oct. 1967, 1968. 1 imm. ♂, Jun. 1975. 7 ♀♀, Mar. 1968, Jun. 1970, Aug. (2), Sept. 1968, Nov. 1964, Dec. 1967. — *C. c. cupreus* (mainland Africa to the Zambesi).

IMPERMANENT COLOURS. Legs blue. Iris brown. Eye-rim green in the male, bright blue in the female. Bill green tinged yellow-horn apically in the male, bluish-black with a green base in the female. Gape blue.

STOMACH CONTENTS. Many hairy caterpillars.

ANNUAL CYCLE. The August–September females were all in breeding condition (oviduct egg broken, 27 Aug.; had laid, 30 Aug.; yolks to 8.5 mm, 11 Sept.). Two were also in wing-moult, the 27 August female with a primary growing in each wing (not symmetrical) and the 30 August female with a primary growing in one wing only. No other birds were in active wing-moult.

HABITAT AND STATUS. Since 1965 this species has been observed in the remaining high forested areas of the Seka Valley, as well as in other remnants of lowland rain forest, both primary and secondary. It calls throughout the year.

Ceuthmochares aereus — Yellowbill

SPECIMENS. 6 ♂♂, Jun. 1966, Jul., Sept. 1967, Dec. 1964, 1967, 1971. 1 juv. ♂, Jan. 1968. 2 ♀♀, Jan. 1968, Oct. 1967. – *C. a. flavirostris* (Senegal to western Nigeria).

IMPERMANENT COLOURS. Legs black. Iris red or red-brown, brown in juvenile. Bill bright yellow with a small triangle of black at the base of the culmen; blackish in juvenile. Bare skin of face yellow, tinged green at eye; dark grey, bluish in front of eye, in juvenile.

STOMACH CONTENTS. Insects, including caterpillars, beetles and grasshoppers.

ANNUAL CYCLE. The January female was collected with the juvenile, which had recently left the nest, and was in worn condition. The July–October birds were in fresh plumage, and the December males in more or less worn condition.

HABITAT. Birds observed have been in *Musanga*-dominated second-growth thickets along an abandoned road between 700 and 900 m.

Centropus leucogaster — Black-throated Coucal

SPECIMENS. 1 ♂, Aug. 1967. 1 juv. ♂, Dec. 1967. 2 ♀♀, Jan. 1968, Dec. 1967. — *C. l. leucogaster* (Guinea to southern Nigeria).

IMPERMANENT COLOURS. Legs blue-grey. Iris dark red, grey in juvenile. Bill black.

STOMACH CONTENTS. Insects, including grasshoppers, caterpillars, beetles and a cockroach.

ANNUAL CYCLE. The juvenile had a very short tail and had only recently left the nest (2 Dec.).

HABITAT. This bird has usually been seen flying low across a road or path between thick vegetation belts. The surrounding high forest has been both primary and secondary, and the altitude has varied from 500 to about 800 m.

Centropus senegalensis — Senegal Coucal

SPECIMENS. 2 ♂♂, Apr. 1969, Jul. 1967. — *C. s. senegalensis* (Senegal to Somalia, south to Zaire and northern Angola).

IMPERMANENT COLOURS. Legs grey. Iris bright red. Bill black.

STOMACH CONTENTS. Insects, including caterpillars and grasshoppers, small centipedes; also amphibian bones in one bird.

HABITAT. A common bird at lower levels in the Nimba area. It has a wide ecological range from savannas and bush country with thickets to plantations, reed-beds in dry ground, secondary growth and also shrubby clearings within primary forest.

Family Strigidae

Tyto alba — Barn Owl

SPECIMEN. 1 ♀, Nov. 1968; ovary small, fresh plumage. — *T. a. affinis* (sub-Saharan Africa).

IMPERMANENT COLOURS. Legs dusky-grey. Iris dark brown. Bill pale whitish-horn. Cere pinkish.

HABITAT AND STATUS. This owl is rather common at Nimba, and has certainly been favoured by the human encroachment which has led to an increase in certain rodents. It has a wide range of habitats in the lowland to about 600 m, but is absent in the highlands, probably because of the lack of human habitations.

The 'Christmas Tree' Club Moss (*Lycopodium cernuum*) is a rapid coloniser of lateritic soil accumulations along all tracks at Nimba, providing cover for many small vertebrates, including ground birds. Photograph Malcolm Coe.

Otus icterorhynchus   Cinnamon Scops Owl

SPECIMENS. 2 ♂♂, Jun. 1967, Jul. 1968. 2 ♀♀, Jan., Sept. 1967.

IMPERMANENT COLOURS. Legs pale whitish-pink. Iris bright yellow. Bill whitish. Cere tinged orange.

STOMACH CONTENTS. Insects, including grasshoppers and beetles.

ANNUAL CYCLE. The males' gonads were small (2, 3 mm). The September female had an enlarged ovary (11.5 mm, ova to 3.5 mm). The January female was in moult, and the other birds in fresh plumage.

DISTRIBUTION. Nimba birds do not differ from the type of *O. i. icterorhynchus* from Fantee, Ghana. These are the first records for Liberia and represent an extension of range 750 km west. Prior to this the nominate form was only known from two specimens from Ghana. It is a lowland forest species so far known from Liberia, Ghana, Cameroon and Zaire.

HABITAT. Forests up to about 1000 m and in the forest-shrub-grassland mosaic at Grassfield.

Otus scops   Scops Owl

SPECIMENS. 1 ♂, Dec. 1967. 4 ♀♀, Jan. (2), Feb. 1968, Dec. 1967. — *O. s. scops* (breeds Eurasia and north Africa).

IMPERMANENT COLOURS. Legs grey. Iris yellow. Bill dark grey. Cere yellowish.

STOMACH CONTENTS. Insects.

ANNUAL CYCLE. Both December birds were in late stages of wing-moult (7 Dec., 8th–10th primaries growing; 27 Dec., 8th primary growing, 9th and 10th old), and the January–February birds in fresh plumage.

DISTRIBUTION. Wintering Palaearctic Scops Owls have been recorded in several West African countries, and in central and eastern Africa. These are the first records for Liberia.

HABITAT. The forest-shrub-grassland mosaic.

Otus leucotis   White-faced Scops Owl

SPECIMEN. 1 ♀, Aug. 1967; fresh plumage. — *O. l. leucotis* (Senegal to Somalia).

IMPERMANENT COLOURS. Legs yellow. Iris yellow. Bill grey.

HABITAT AND STATUS. This owl has been heard and seen in gardens at both Grassfield and Yekepa as well as in other types of opened up country. Curry-Lindahl did not hear its characteristic call until the late 1960s, and it is possible that the species colonised the Nimba area after the creation of the mosaic landscape.

Jubula lettii   Maned Owl

SPECIMEN. 1 ♀, Aug. 1971.

IMPERMANENT COLOURS. Legs yellow. Iris orange. Bill yellow.

ANNUAL CYCLE. A pair with a full-grown young were seen in forest on 19 February 1971 (JK & SK). The August female was in worn plumage.

HABITAT. In 1969 Curry-Lindahl came upon a hunter in the forest at Nimba who had killed a specimen of this little known owl. It had been shot about an hour earlier. He asked the man to show him the exact locality which was in dense lowland primary forest. The hunter later told him that he had not previously seen this species.

Bubo africanus   Spotted Eagle-Owl

SPECIMEN. 1 ♀, Apr. 1971; fresh plumage. — *B. a. cinerascens* (Senegal to Somalia, south to about the equator).

IMPERMANENT COLOURS. Legs yellow. Iris brown. Bill black.

FIELD NOTES. Curry-Lindahl encountered this owl at night, in all months of the year, along an abandoned mountain road from about 500 to 1200 m. During the dry months it was recorded hooting from the forest slopes and perching on rocky outcrops, behaviour that may indicate breeding activity.

Bubo poensis   Fraser's Eagle Owl

SPECIMENS. 3 ♀♀, Jan. 1968, Sept. 1967, Nov. 1968. 2 juv. ♀♀, Jun. 1968, Aug. 1967. — *B. p. poensis* (Liberia to western Zaire).

IMPERMANENT COLOURS. Legs whitish. Iris dark brown. Bill whitish or pale bluish. Cere grey.

STOMACH CONTENTS. Small rodents, birds, beetles and grasshoppers.

ANNUAL CYCLE. All three females had enlarged ovaries (Jan., 17 mm, ova to 3 mm; Sept., 27 mm; Nov., ova to 3 mm). The juveniles, taken on 6 June and 4 August, were nearly full-grown and well-feathered.

HABITAT. A forest owl, occurring mainly in primary forest but also in secondary forest areas. Despite the fact that this is a new record for Liberia it may be widely distributed in suitable forest, as it is not uncommon at Grassfield (AF-W).

Bubo shelleyi   Shelley's Eagle-Owl

SPECIMEN. 1 ♀, Nov. 1968; in non-breeding condition.

IMPERMANENT COLOURS. Legs dull whitish, claws black. Iris dark brown. Bill pale creamy-horn, tinged bluish at base. Cere pale dull blue-grey.

HABITAT AND STATUS. This very large forest owl was also recorded in March 1979, when its persistent calls were heard (KC-L) in the lowland rain forest of the Seka Valley. The species is otherwise known from a few specimens obtained in the lowland forests of Liberia, Ghana, south Cameroon and Zaire.

Bubo lacteus   Milky Eagle-Owl

This large owl was seen at Nimba (AF-W) in 1967 or 1968. In the following years it was heard calling at two sites several times during the dry season by Curry-Lindahl who knew this species well from other areas of Africa. These are the first records for Liberia. The species also occurs in Guinean Nimba. In western Africa it is widely but rather thinly distributed in the dry open belt north of the forest, from southern Mauretania and Senegal east to the Central African Republic. Both sites where this owl was heard calling were isolated patches of secondary forest surrounding a few very tall trees, probably relics of the ancient forest. These patches of forest were located in bush country with grass and scrub.

Bubo leucostictus   Akun Eagle-Owl

SPECIMENS. 2 ♂♂, Jul. 1967 (2). 2 ♀♀, Jul. 1967, Aug. 1970. 1 juv. ♀, Jul. 1967. 1 o, no date.

IMPERMANENT COLOURS. Legs pale yellow with black claws. Iris pale yellow. Bill and cere pale greenish-yellow.

STOMACH CONTENTS. Insects, including cockroaches, katydids, click-beetles, and other large beetles.

ANNUAL CYCLE. The young bird, presumably taken from the nest, was almost fully grown but still retained a lot of body down. All adults were in fresh plumage except for the July female, which was worn.

FIELD NOTES. One July male was followed by call at Grassfield (1840–1915 hrs). Forbes-Watson says in his notes: 'It started (to call) in the forest, but later came out into the open, where I saw it on top of an aerial mast. It flew back into the forest, where I saw it by torchlight sitting in the top of a tree — its eyes shone red like a nightjar's, and this is the first time I've seen an owl's shine. The call is a deep, measured soft grunting *hu* (2 sec interval) *hu* . . . and does not carry very far.' The same call was heard (KC-L) in subsequent years, but usually during the dry months.

Scotopelia ussheri   Rufous Fishing Owl

SPECIMEN. 1 juv. ♂, Jul. 1967; moulting into ad plumage.

IMPERMANENT COLOURS. Legs pale creamy-yellow. Iris deep brown. Bill black with a creamy base to the lower mandible. Cere and gape pale creamy-yellow. Eye-rim dull creamy-yellow with irregular liverish swellings.

STOMACH CONTENTS. Bones of a catfish, including the bony head-plates.

HABITAT AND STATUS. The specimen was collected near Grassfield in a forest-shrub-river mosaic. This appears to be the fifth known locality for the species, which is found along forested rivers from Sierra Leone to Ghana.

Glaucidium tephronotum   Red-chested Owlet

SPECIMENS. 3 ♂♂, Mar. 1968, Jun. 1967, Sept. 1968. 1 ♀, Aug. 1967.

IMPERMANENT COLOURS. Legs yellow. Iris bright yellow. Eye-rim orange. Bill greenish-yellow. Cere waxy-yellow.

STOMACH CONTENTS. Insects, including cockroaches, cockchafers, earwigs and crickets.

ANNUAL CYCLE. The specimens gave no evidence of breeding. The June male was in wing-moult, the August–September birds in worn plumage, and the March male in fresh plumage.

DISTRIBUTION. Nimba birds do not differ from the only BM(NH) specimen of the nominate form, collected in lowland forest in Ghana. Only two previous specimens of *G. t. tephronotum* are known, both from dense forest in Ghana. This is a new species for Liberia and it represents a range extension of some 650 km west.

HABITAT. Forests and forest-shrub mosaic (KC-L). Forbes-Watson records it as generally confined to primary forest, but in the evening appearing at edges.

Glaucidium capense — Barred Owlet

SPECIMENS. 1 ♂, Aug. 1967. 2 ♀♀, Aug., Dec. 1967.

IMPERMANENT COLOURS. Legs dull yellow. Iris bright yellow. Bill yellowish-green. Cere dusky yellowish-green.

STOMACH CONTENTS. Insects, including large grasshoppers.

ANNUAL CYCLE. The December female, with ovary 12.5 mm, was possibly in breeding condition. The August female, with ovary 9 mm and ova to 1.5 mm, was in wing-moult. The August male was in fresh plumage, with small gonads (2.5 mm).

DISTRIBUTION. The occurrence in West Africa of this forest owlet is based on only four specimens: one from Lamto, Ivory Coast, and the three recorded from Nimba near the Ivory Coast border. The Lamto specimen has been described by Roux (1983) as a race *etchecopari* of *G. capense*, and the Nimba birds are thought to be similar. This is a new species for Liberia.

Strix woodfordi — African Wood-Owl

SPECIMENS. 4 ♂♂, Apr. 1968, May 1970, Nov. 1968 (2). 1 juv. ♂, Jul. 1967. 1 ♀, Mar. 1972. — *S. w. nuchalis* (Sierra Leone to southern Sudan, south to Angola).

IMPERMANENT COLOURS. Legs yellow. Iris dark brown, eye-rim pale orange. Bill yellow with grey-green cutting edges.

STOMACH CONTENTS. Insects, including katydids, grasshoppers, cockroaches and beetles.

ANNUAL CYCLE. The specimens gave no evidence of breeding. The juvenile, which still retained some down on the head and chest, was taken on 17 July. Unfledged begging young have been found out of the nest in February and March (KC-L). The three March–May adults were all in wing-moult.

HABITAT AND HABITS. This is a common owl at Nimba, occurring at the edges of primary and secondary forest up to about 1100 m; also in woodlands, patches of partly opened up forest, clearings and even gardens. Its habits and activities are very similar to those of the Palaearctic *S. aluco*. It has a highly variable vocabulary and will sometimes call loudly during December–February (i.e. in the dry months).

Family Caprimulgidae

Caprimulgus binotatus — Brown Nightjar

SPECIMENS. 1 ♂, Jan. 1971; fresh plumage. 1 o, Jan. 1971; in moult.

IMPERMANENT COLOURS. Legs black. Iris brown. Bill black.

DISTRIBUTION. The type was collected in Ghana, probably inland from Takoradi, in 1850. The species has not been found in the western part of the West African rain forest since, so that its discovery in the Nimba forests at Grassfield is extremely interesting. It is evidently a very hard bird to find. It occurs in southern Cameroon and there are also a few records from Zaire. This is a new species for Liberia and it represents an extension of range some 700 km west.

HABITAT AND HABITS. Lowland forest. The two specimens were first seen hawking from the forest canopy near Grassfield.

Caprimulgus inornatus — Plain Nightjar

SPECIMENS. 2 ♂♂, Nov. 1964, 1971. 1 nestling ♂, Jun. 1968. 5 ♀♀, Nov. 1964 (4), Dec. 1967. The 2 ♂♂ grey-phase, the remainder all rufous-phase birds.

IMPERMANENT COLOURS. Legs brown. Iris brown. Bill black.

STOMACH CONTENTS. Beetles and other insect fragments.

ANNUAL CYCLE. The only adult whose gonads were examined (1 Nov. ♀) was not in breeding condition (ovary 3.5 mm), and was in wing-moult. No other specimens were in moult. The nestling, which was picked up near the nest on 26 June, was about half grown.

FIELD NOTES. In addition to the specimens listed above, a dead male of the rufous phase, was found intact at 09 15 on 12 January 1982 on a road surrounded by forest at about 960 m. It was completely fresh with the colour of the eyes slowly fading, and had not so far been touched by ants. Curry-Lindahl had passed the same spot an hour earlier without observing the bird. His car was the only one on this closed mountain mine road, so that the bird could not have been killed by a vehicle. Strong *Harmattan* winds had been blowing for several days previously.

Caprimulgus tristigma — Freckled Nightjar

On 28 February 1976 a Freckled Nightjar was found dead (KC-L) on a road in the mining area of Mount Nimba at about 1200 m. In March 1979 he was shown another specimen from the same area. Both birds had apparently been killed by cars. There is heavy motor traffic in the mine area throughout the night. This is a new species for Liberia.

From 1976 onwards Curry-Lindahl found that nightjars had taken up the habit of hunting insects which were attracted by the strong road lights in the mine area. Many birds were noted resting on the roads at night and were examined closely in the headlights of the car; most of them appeared to be *C. tristigma*. Moreover, in February–March some nightjars were heard calling with a characteristic musical *pew-hew* (in falling scale), similar to the call of *C. tristigma* heard (KC-L) in Zaire. The rocky habitat in the mine area seems to correspond well with the ecological requirements of this species, which evidently colonized the area after the forest had been cleared and the rocks exposed.

Caprimulgus climacurus   Long-tailed Nightjar

SPECIMENS. 1 ♂, Jan. 1968. 2 ♀♀, Apr. 1968, Dec. 1967. — *C. c. sclateri* (Sierra Leone to Zaire).

IMPERMANENT COLOURS. Legs brown. Iris brown. Bill brown.

STOMACH CONTENTS. Insects, including beetles.

ANNUAL CYCLE. The April female had an enlarged ovary (10.5 mm); the other two were in non-breeding condition. The December bird was in slightly worn condition and the other two in fresh plumage.

HABITAT. Forest clearings and along roads in both the lowland and the highlands up to about 1000 m.

Macrodipteryx longipennis
Standard-wing Nightjar

SPECIMENS. 5 ♂♂, Jan. 1968 (2), Feb. 1966, Mar. 1968, Dec. 1967. 7 ♀♀, Jan. 1968, Feb. 1966, 1968, Mar., Nov. 1968, Dec. 1967 (2).

IMPERMANENT COLOURS. Legs brown. Iris brown. Bill black.

STOMACH CONTENTS. Insects.

ANNUAL CYCLE. The only evidence of breeding is from a February female with ovary 12 mm and ova 3.5 mm. Two males (10 Jan., 1 Feb.) had elongated wing-pennants. No birds were in wing-moult; the November–December birds were in freshish plumage.

HABITAT. Short grassy lawns and paved parking areas.

DISPLAYS. Males have elongated wing pennants during December–March. Earliest dates of such birds observed (KC-L) are 26 November and 20 December. From the latter half of February the display is in full swing. At Nimba there are two 'display arenas', located on the only two extensively paved parking lots at Yekepa. Here 1–3 males may congregate, the females usually being

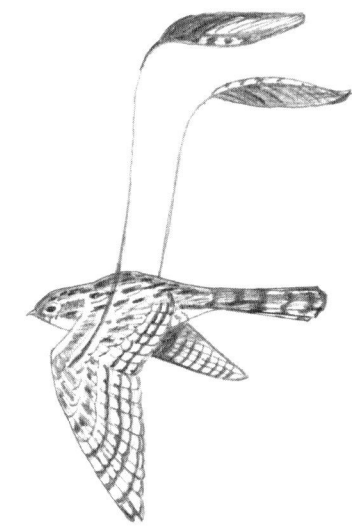

more numerous. Once there were as many as 6 males, but at that time only 4 females were spectators. Males with elongated feathers court females by 'dancing' around them in a bouncing, 'slow motion' flight about 0.3–0.5 m above the ground, holding the elongated wing pennants vertically upwards with webs flashing. The latter are kept in a horizontal position probably due to the effect of air resistance. The most intense dancing displays have been between 21.00 and 23.30 hours. The males do not perform every night; for example 25 February 1980 there was intense dancing activity, but the following night there was none although males and females were present.

During the 1980 display season 3 males in each of the two arenas tended to occupy special sites, where Curry-Lindahl could find them resting or watching night after night, while in this respect the females were more irregular. From these sites the males flew to join the females in order to perform their dance in front of them.

The males were silent while displaying, but when perched on the ground they frequently uttered a barely audible, thinly whistled song, somewhat resembling the call of a shrew (*Sorex*).

MIGRATION. The Standard-wing Nightjar used to arrive at Nimba in November–December to breed in February–March, departing in May. It migrates north and eastwards to more northerly savannas probably in Mali, Upper Volta and Nigeria.

Family Apodidae

Apus apus   Common Swift

SPECIMENS. 2 ♂♂, Feb. 1968. 4 ♀♀, Feb (3), Mar. 1968. — *A. a. apus* (Palaearctic breeder, wintering in Africa).

IMPERMANENT COLOURS. Legs black. Iris brown. Bill black.

STOMACH CONTENTS. Insects, including black flying ants.

HABITAT. The airspace above all types of habitat including the mine landscape.

Apus melba — Alpine Swift

A flock giving their characteristic calls was observed at Nimba in 1966 (KC-L). In 1967 or 1968 this species was also seen (AF-W). These are the first records for Liberia. The three African races are found mainly in East Africa, south from Somalia to Cape Province. *Apus m. melba* of the Palaearctic region has been found on passage or wintering in Mali, Togo, Ghana, Nigeria, the Sudan and Uganda. It seems most likely that the Liberian birds were of Palaearctic origin.

Apus batesi — Bates's Black Swift

This little known evergreen-forest swift was observed at Grassfield and near the ridge of Mount Nimba (AF-W) in 1967 and, or, 1968. This is the first record for Liberia and represents a considerable extension of the species' range. Its occurrence west of Cameroon is so far based only on sight records: in addition to the Nimba record, Ghana (Macdonald & Taylor, 1977) and Nigeria (Elgood, 1982).

Apus affinis — Little Swift

This gregarious town-dwelling swift was observed at Nimba in 1967 and 1968 (AF-W) and in the 1970s and 1980s (KC-L). It began to breed on buildings in Yekepa in 1971 and has since then increased in number.

Cypsiurus parvus — Palm Swift

SPECIMEN. 1 o, Oct. 1968; fresh plumage. — *C. p. brachypterus* (Sierra Leone to Zaire).

IMPERMANENT COLOURS. Legs dark grey. Iris brown. Bill black.

STOMACH CONTENTS. Masses of small black flying ants.

HABITAT. Probably due to the presence of oil palms, this swift is fairly widespread in the Nimba area, chiefly at lower levels outside the forest. The species has bred regularly at Yekepa, at least from 1967, and may be a newcomer there. It nests in buildings and on palm-leaves.

Raphidura sabini — Sabine's Spinetail

SPECIMENS. 5 ♂♂, Mar. (3), Apr. (2) 1968. 4 ♀♀, Mar. 1968 (4). 1 juv. ♀, Jul. 1967. 1 o, Mar. 1968.

IMPERMANENT COLOURS. Legs purplish. Irish brown. Bill black.

STOMACH CONTENTS. Black flying ants.

ANNUAL CYCLE. Two of the three March males (6, 12 mm) and both the April females (6, 8 mm) had enlarged gonads. March females ovaries were enlarged (7–10 mm, ova to *c*.1 mm). None was in moult. The July female was examined by Brooke (1971); he considered it an adult with unusually dull plumage, lacking gloss, but we have re-examined the specimen and think that it is in juvenile plumage.

DISTRIBUTION. This lowland-forest swift is widespread in the Lower Guinea forest, and probably in Upper Guinea also, since in addition to the present records there are specimens from Sierra Leone and acceptable sight records from Ghana and Nigeria. These are the first records of this species for Liberia.

Neafrapus cassini — Cassin's Spinetail

SPECIMENS. 1 ♂, Jan. 1968. 1 ♀, Jan. 1968.

IMPERMANENT COLOURS. Legs dull purplish-black. Iris dark brown. Bill black.

STOMACH CONTENTS. Black flying ants.

ANNUAL CYCLE. Both birds were in non-breeding condition. The male had almost completed a moult, outermost primary half-grown; the female was in fresh plumage.

DISTRIBUTION. This is a new record for Liberia. Like Sabine's Spinetail, it is widespread in the Lower Guinea forest, but so far known only from a few localities in Upper Guinea, Nigeria, Ghana and Liberia.

Telacanthura ussheri   Ussher's Spinetail

This species was observed in 1967 and, or, 1968 (AF-W), in subsequent years (KC-L) and in July–September 1978 (RW). Birds observed by Curry-Lindahl were above the forest-grassland mosaic at Grassfield. These are the first records for Liberia. In West Africa it is locally distributed in both forest and savanna from Senegal and Gambia to Cameroon.

Telacanthura melanopygia   Mottled-throated Spinetail

This swift was observed at Nimba in 1967 and, or, 1968 (AF-W); the first record for Liberia. As recently as 1966 the species was considered endemic to the Congo rainforest (Moreau, 1966). In addition to Liberia, it has subsequently been found in Cameroon (Mackworth-Praed & Grant, 1970), Nigeria (Elgood, 1982), Ghana, where it is 'in places common in forest reserves, cocoa farms and mosaic forest' (Macdonald & Taylor, 1977). Whether this species has been overlooked in the past, or has recently colonised the Upper Guinea forest, remains unknown.

Family Trogonidae

Apaloderma narina   Narina's Trogon

SPECIMENS. 5 ♂♂, Mar. 1968, 1974, Aug. 1968 (2), Sept. 1967. 1 ♀, Aug. 1968. — *A. n. constantia* (Sierra Leone to Nigeria).

IMPERMANENT COLOURS. Legs pink or pale purplish. Iris chestnut-brown. Bare skin around eye bright yellow in male, lead-blue in female. Bill pearly greenish-yellow.

STOMACH CONTENTS. Insects, including grasshoppers and caterpillars; also spiders.

ANNUAL CYCLE. Both March males were in wing-moult, one in an early stage and the other in a late stage, and the September male was just finishing. The female's ovary was slightly enlarged (8 mm).

HABITAT. All the trogons observed have been in high forest, up to an altitude of about 1000 m. The species has been heard more frequently in the Iti valley than elsewhere at Nimba.

Family Alcedinidae

Ceryle maxima   Giant Kingfisher

SPECIMENS. 1 ♂, Dec. 1970. 2 ♀♀, May 1970, Jun. 1967.

IMPERMANENT COLOURS. Legs grey. Iris dark brown. Bill black.

STOMACH CONTENTS. Crabs.

HABITAT AND HABITS. Wooded streams with clear water and sufficient depth to let the Giant Kingfisher dive safely are usually a requirement. As such waters hardly exist any longer in the Nimba area this species is becoming rare. However, on three occasions Curry-Lindahl has observed it hovering above the muddy waters of the Yah River and catching prey on or just below the surface. He has also seen this species hovering in Zaire and Tanzania. It is not a common habit in this species.

Ceryle rudis   Pied Kingfisher

SPECIMEN. 1 ♀, Apr. 1973; fresh plumage. — *C. r. rudis* (widely distributed south of 17°N).

IMPERMANENT COLOURS. Legs black. Iris blue. Bill black.

HABITAT. The bird is rare at Nimba but was still seen in the early 1980s hovering over the muddy Yah River. Previous records have been from coastal regions.

Alcedo quadribrachys   Shining-blue Kingfisher

SPECIMENS. 5 ♂♂, Apr. 1970, Jun. 1967 (2), Jul. 1968 (2). 1 imm. ♂, Feb. 1968. 4 ♀♀, Jan. 1971, Mar. 1968, Apr. 1970, Jun. 1967. — *A. q. quadribrachys* (Gambia to northern Nigeria).

IMPERMANENT COLOURS. Legs waxy orange-red. Iris brown. Bill black with a pinkish base.

STOMACH CONTENTS. Small fish and a 20 mm crab.

ANNUAL CYCLE. The birds were in non-breeding condition. The January female and the April male were in worn condition, and the June female in wing-moult. The remaining adults were in fresh plumage.

HABITAT. Curry-Lindahl has seen this species at Nimba, only in dense riverine forest along the Iti river and in the forest-shrub-river mosaic near Grassfield.

Alcedo cristata   Malachite Kingfisher

SPECIMENS. 2 ♂♂, Feb., Apr. 1968; testes 1 mm, 6 mm, no moult.

IMPERMANENT COLOURS. Legs waxy orange-red. Iris brown. Bill orange-red.

STOMACH CONTENTS. Insects and a small fish.

HABITAT. A common bird at Nimba occupying the vegetation along small streams or pools, but sometimes far from water.

Alcedo leucogaster   White-bellied Kingfisher

SPECIMENS. 12 ♂♂, Feb. 1968 (2), Apr. 1965, May 1968, Jun. 1967, 1968, Jul. 1967 (3), Aug. 1967, 1968, Nov. 1968. 14 ♀♀, Jan. 1966, 1969 (2), Feb. 1966 (2), 1968, Apr. 1965, 1966, Jun. (2), Aug. 1967, Sept. 1967, 1968, Oct. 1968. 1 o, Mar. 1968. — *A. l. bowdleri* (Guinea Bissau to southwest Nigeria).

IMPERMANENT COLOURS. Legs waxy-pink or orange. Iris brown. Bill orange or orange-red but dusky pink in 3 males for May, June and November and 1 female for June.

STOMACH CONTENTS. Insects and small frogs.

ANNUAL CYCLE. The specimens gave no definite evidence of breeding. The males' gonads were small (max 3 mm); three females had enlarged ovaries in June (6.5 mm), August (9 mm) and September (8 mm). One February and two June birds were in late stages of wing-moult.

Ispidina lecontei
Red-headed Dwarf Kingfisher

SPECIMENS. 1 ♂, Jun. 1968. 1 imm. ♂, Oct. 1967.

IMPERMANENT COLOURS. Legs red. Iris brown. Bill bright orange.

STOMACH CONTENTS. Insects.

ANNUAL CYCLE. The June male was in non-breeding condition and in fresh plumage. The immature male was moulting into adult plumage. The bill tip was blunt like the adult's and not pointed as in the young bird.

DISTRIBUTION. This is a new record for Liberia. It is a lowland forest kingfisher, found from Guinea to Uganda, south to northwest Angola.

Ispidina picta   Pigmy Kingfisher

SPECIMENS. 8 ♂♂, Feb., Mar., Oct. 1968, Nov. 1967 (2), 1968 (2), 1970. 6 ♀♀, Feb., Apr. 1968, Nov. 1964, 1967, 1968 (2). 1 o, Nov. 1964. — *I. p. picta* (Sierra Leone to southern Sudan, south to northern Angola). Two specimens are darker rufous below and agree with equatorial forest birds *I. p. ferrugina*, while paler nominate *picta* are presumably migrants from the north.

IMPERMANENT COLOURS. Legs waxy-red. Iris brown. Bill orange-red.

STOMACH CONTENTS. Insects.

ANNUAL CYCLE. The gonads of a November male were enlarged (5 mm); those of the other males small (max 2.5 mm), and those of the females small (max 4 mm). The February–April birds were in wing-moult, the April female at a late stage, outermost primary growing.

HABITAT. Dry country hills, grassy or bush vegetation, edges of forest and river banks.

Halcyon senegalensis   Woodland Kingfisher

SPECIMENS. 2 ♂♂, Aug., Nov. 1968. 1 imm. ♂, May 1974. 3 ♀♀, Jan. 1968, Jul. 1966, Oct. 1968.

IMPERMANENT COLOURS. Legs black. Iris dark brown. Bill dusky-red above, black below, completely black in the young male.

STOMACH CONTENTS. Insects, including grasshoppers and beetles.

ANNUAL CYCLE. The specimens give no definite evidence of breeding, but the January female had an enlarged ovary (9 mm) and may have been approaching breeding condition. The July–August birds were in worn plumage, the October bird in wing-moult, and the November–January in fresh plumage.

HABITAT. A common bird at Nimba in the Yah valley and other grassy or cultivated habitats, and in towns and villages such as Yekepa and Grassfield; rarely found above 600 m.

Halcyon malimbica   Blue-breasted Kingfisher

SPECIMENS. 12 ♂♂, Mar. 1968, Apr. 1965, May, Jun. 1968, Jul., Oct. 1967, Nov. 1968 (2), 1970 (3), Dec. 1967. 6 ♀♀, Jan. 1969, Feb. 1968, Apr. 1969, Jun. 1967, 1968, Oct. 1968. 1 imm. ♀, Jun. 1967. — *H. m. forbesi* (Sierra Leone to Nigeria).

IMPERMANENT COLOURS. Legs pale orange-red to bright red. Iris brown. Bill orange-red to dark red with the lower mandible black.

STOMACH CONTENTS. Insects, beetles and grasshoppers. Also frogs.

ANNUAL CYCLE. The specimens gave no evidence of breeding, except for a June female with an enlarged ovary (12 mm) which may have been approaching breeding condition. This bird and all others collected in June–July were in middle stages of wing-moult, and an October female was in a late stage of moult, two outermost primaries old, 8th growing.

HABITAT. Common at Nimba along forest edges and clearings in both lowlands and highlands up to 800 m.

Halcyon badia   Chocolate-backed Kingfisher

SPECIMENS. 2 ♂♂, Jan. 1966, Apr. 1968. 1 juv. ♂, Apr. 1968. 1 ♀, Dec. 1969. 1 imm. ♀, Jun. 1968. 1 o, Mar. 1968.

IMPERMANENT COLOURS. Legs dark red to dark purple. Iris dark brown. Bill orange-red, dark purple at the tip; black with a yellow tip in juv.

STOMACH CONTENTS. Insects, including beetles, grasshoppers, a mantis and naked caterpillars.

ANNUAL CYCLE. Gonad data incomplete; no evidence of breeding. The juvenile, collected 26 April, had barely left the nest and its bill was half size. The March bird was in wing-moult, renewing inner primaries: the January bird, probably in wing-moult, one wing only; asymmetric, or replacement of accidentally lost feathers.

Halcyon leucocephala   Grey-headed Kingfisher

SPECIMENS. 4 ♂♂, Feb. 1970, Nov., Dec. (2) 1967. 2 ♀♀, Jan. 1968, Dec. 1967. — *H. l. leucocephala* (widespread in West Africa).

IMPERMANENT COLOURS. Legs red. Iris brown. Bill red.

STOMACH CONTENTS. Insects, including grasshoppers and one caterpillar.

ANNUAL CYCLE. The specimens provided no definite evidence of breeding, but the December female (ovary 8.5 mm) and January female (ovary 7.0 mm) may have been approaching breeding condition. The November and February males were both in late stages of wing-moult, and the December-January birds all in fresh plumage. Elsewhere in West Africa this species is known to be a pronounced migrant, breeding in the Guinean savanna belt January to June and then migrating north to spend the months May to October in the Sudan and Sahel belts.

HABITAT. A common bird at Nimba, where it is chiefly a forest and woodland species. In forests it frequents edges, clearings, burnt forest, and areas where the forest has been thinned by selective felling. It occurs in both lowland and highland habitats up to about 1000 m.

Family Meropidae

Merops apiaster   European Bee-eater

SPECIMENS. 3 ♂♂, Jan. 1972, Feb. 1968, Dec. 1971. 2 ♀♀, Jan. 1968, 1972.

IMPERMANENT COLOURS. Legs black. Iris red. Bill black.

STOMACH CONTENTS. Insects, including green beetles and black flying ants.

ANNUAL CYCLE. The February male was in fresh plumage and had small gonads. The January and December birds were all in late stages of wing-moult.

HABITAT AND HABITS. The entire airspace of the Nimba area is utilized by flocks of European Bee-eaters. They were first observed in 1966 (which was the first record of this species for Liberia). They are particularly common at Nimba during February–March, and in 1976 there was a spectacular invasion of several flocks, each of them consisting of about 500–600 birds, and the whole sky was filled with their musical calls. In 1982 the first bee-eaters arrived at Nimba on 10–11 January.

Merops albicollis   White-throated Bee-eater

SPECIMENS. 7 ♂♂, Apr. 1965, 1968, Oct. 1967 (3), 1968, Dec. 1967. 1 ♀, Nov. 1964.

IMPERMANENT COLOURS. Legs pale greenish. Iris red. Bill black.

STOMACH CONTENTS. Insects, including large black flying ants and small metallic beetles.

ANNUAL CYCLE. None of the birds was in breeding condition (see below, under Migration). Two of the October birds were in wing-moult, the other two in worn plumage. The November–December birds were in wing-moult. One of the April birds was just finishing its wing-moult, outermost primary growing, and the other was in fresh plumage.

HABITS. This bee-eater was often seen perched on open ground near river banks or roads without traffic, and would fly up to catch insects 2–10 m in the air, afterwards settling on the ground again.

MIGRATION. Since 1966 flocks of this species have been observed at Nimba between October–May. It is a trans-equatorial migrant, moving southwards to southern savannas, but has often been seen above rain forest both in West Africa and in Zaire. It is probable that the White-throated Bee-eaters visiting Nimba annually are not passage migrants, but spend the non-breeding season in this part of Liberia, and the neighbouring areas of Guinea and the Ivory Coast.

Merops pusillus — Little Bee-eater

SPECIMENS. 3 ♂♂, Jan. 1966, Feb. 1968, Sept. 1968. 1 imm. ♂, Aug. 1968. 2 ♀♀, Jan. 1966, Sept. 1968. — *M. p. pusillus* (widespread in West Africa).

IMPERMANENT COLOURS. Legs dark grey. Iris red. Bill black.

STOMACH CONTENTS. Insects, including black flying ants and small metallic beetles.

ANNUAL CYCLE. No indication of breeding. The two January birds were in worn plumage, and of the two September birds, one was at a late stage of wing-moult and the other in fresh plumage.

HABITAT AND HABITS. The Little Bee-eater is rather common at Nimba. It has a wide range of habitats, from grasslands, scrub and bush to secondary growth and clearings, in both lowland and montane forest up to about 1000 m. Often found in small groups of 3–6 birds hawking for insects from low perches.

MIGRATION. In West Africa it has migratory tendencies, particularly in Ghana and Nigeria. Migration has been suggested for Liberian birds (Allen, 1930) but at Nimba birds have been observed in every month of the year.

Merops gularis — Black Bee-eater

SPECIMENS. 9 ♂♂, Jan. 1968, 1976, Feb. 1968, 1975, Aug. 1970, Sept. 1967 (2), Dec. 1968 (2). 1 juv. ♂, Jun. 1967. 5 ♀♀, Jan. 1966, 1976, Feb. 1968, Sept. 1967, Dec. 1971. — *M. g. gularis* (Sierra Leone to Nigeria).

IMPERMANENT COLOURS. Legs black. Iris dark red, brown in imm. Bill black.

STOMACH CONTENTS. Insects, including black flying ants.

ANNUAL CYCLE. The adults gave no evidence of breeding, but gonad measurements are available for only 6 of the 14 specimens. Nest-holes are occupied in March (see next section). The juvenile, collected 18 June, had recently left the nest; its bill was two-thirds grown and its tail was not full length. The August and two September specimens were in late stages of wing-moult, 9th or 10th primaries growing, the other September bird being in fresh plumage. In addition one January male was in wing-moult.

HABITAT AND HABITS. The Black Bee-eater frequents the outskirts of primary and secondary forests, as well as clearings both in the lowland and up to about 1300 m. There is an area of beautiful high forest situated at about 1200 m on Nimba, both above and below a little plateau which had been cleared in the mid-1960s. Since 1974 Curry-Lindahl has always found some 6–12 Black Bee-eaters perched in the trees or bushes there, and regularly flying out to catch insects. The birds appear very social at all times of the year. In March 1979 they bred in a nearby road bank, closed to traffic for years, where at least two nests were occupied, although there were up to 12 birds present. In the same period of 1980 there were 7 nest-holes and in 1981 eight.

In another locality at Nimba, at the edge of lowland rain forest, another group of Black Bee-eaters was also resident and had been present at the same spot for many years. Thus it appears that the Black Bee-eater is much less nomadic within its home-range than many of its relatives.

MIGRATION. Observations of *M. gularis* have been made at Nimba in all months of the year. Yet there is apparently, at least in some years, an influx of birds with the onset of the rains in February or March. In some years a reduction in the numbers at the more favourite sites seems to take place during November–December, which is usually when the short dry period begins. For about two hours on 2–4 February 1979 Curry-Lindahl witnessed flock after flock of 10–30 migrating Black Bee-eaters flying westwards across Mount Nimba and over the Liberian lowland rain forest on both sides of southern Mount Nimba. Four of these flocks, after having passed over the Nimba ridge, headed downwards on the western side of the mountain gliding with spread wings until they disappeared into the canopy. A few flocks were again seen on 1 March 1981, migrating westwards above the lowland forest southwest of Mount Nimba.

From these scattered observations made during the period 1963–1982 one may perhaps conclude that the Black Bee-eater is a partial migrant in the Nimba region and that the majority of birds are present during the rainy season, i.e. from February–March to November–December, although some small parties of the species also remain during the dry month of January. Furthermore, the parties arriving at, or passing, Nimba come from the east which could be from any of the lowland rain forests of Africa.

Merops muelleri Blue-headed Bee-eater

SPECIMENS. 5 ♂♂, Jul. 1965, 1967, Aug., Sept. 1967, Nov. 1968. 2 imm. ♂♂, Jul. 1967, 1968. 3 ♀♀, Jul. 1965, Aug., Sept. 1967. — *M. m. mentalis* (Sierra Leone to Cameroon).

IMPERMANENT COLOURS. Legs black. Iris red. Bill black.

STOMACH CONTENTS. Insects, including bees and black flying ants.

ANNUAL CYCLE. The specimens gave no definite evidence of breeding, but the August and September females, with ovaries measuring 7 mm, may have been approaching breeding condition. All three July birds were in middle to late stages of wing-moult, one August and one September bird were near the end of their wing-moult, and the remainder were in fresh plumage.

HABITAT AND HABITS. This bee-eater is found along forest edges, in clearings and along roads in the lowland and up to about 800 m. Small groups of 2–4 birds perch on low branches, flying out to hawk for insects in the clearings or just above the canopy. A new species for Liberia.

Family Coraciidae

Coracias abyssinica Abyssinian Roller

SPECIMENS. 2 ♂♂, Feb.1979, May 1968. 1 ♀, Feb. 1976.

IMPERMANENT COLOURS. Legs dull brownish-yellow. Iris brown. Bill black.

STOMACH CONTENTS. Mainly grasshoppers.

ANNUAL CYCLE. All three specimens were in more or less worn plumage. No evidence of breeding, but gonad data only for the May male (testes 3 mm).

DISTRIBUTION, HABITAT AND HABITS. Although ranging from Senegal and Sierra Leone to the Red Sea this species had not previously been found in Liberia, where it was first recorded (1965) in the savanna close to the Guinean border. It has since been observed in the same area during October to May. When there are grass fires in Guinea, just on the other side of the Liberian border, up to half a dozen Abyssinian Rollers may congregate to catch insects in front of the flames. This species is migratory in West Africa, breeding in the Sudanese savanna belt and moving south to the Guinean savanna belt in the dry season.

Eurystomus glaucurus Broad-billed Roller

SPECIMENS. 1 ♂, Nov. 1969. 2 ♀♀, Jan. 1976, Dec. 1968. — *E. g. afer* (Senegal to Eritrea).

IMPERMANENT COLOURS. Legs olive-green. Iris brown. Bill yellowish-brown.

STOMACH CONTENTS. Large beetles.

ANNUAL CYCLE. The November male was in the final stage of wing-moult (10th primary growing), and the other two birds in fresh plumage. No evidence of breeding, but gonads of only the December female recorded (ovary 6 mm).

HABITAT AND HABITS. The Broad-billed Roller has been observed at Nimba since 1963, in the months of October to April. It frequents forest edges and clearings, or any group of tall trees on open land. At Nimba it has not been seen above 900 m. It is a migratory species in West Africa, moving south after breeding in the Sudanese savanna belt to the Guinean woodland savanna belt and parts of the rain forest area.

Eurystomus gularis Blue-throated Roller

SPECIMENS. 4 ♂♂, Feb. 1972, Mar. 1968, Nov. 1964, Dec. 1967. 2 imm. ♂♂, Jun. 1967 (2). 4 ♀♀, Feb. 1968, Apr. 1969, Nov. 1964, Dec. 1973. — *E. g. gularis* (Sierra Leone to Cameroon).

IMPERMANENT COLOURS. Legs dark brown. Iris dark brown. Bill yellow, yellowish-brown in the immature.

STOMACH CONTENTS. Insects, including many flying termites and beetles. Also one large pebble.

ANNUAL CYCLE. The February female, with ovary 13.5 mm and ova 3 mm, was apparently in breeding condition, gonads of the other females not recorded. The February–March birds were in fresh plumage and the November–December birds in worn plumage, except for the November male which was in a late stage of wing-moult (9th and 10th primaries growing).

HABITAT AND HABITS. This is a resident forest counterpart of the migratory savanna species. It is rather common at Nimba inside forest, at their edges or beside clearings. Apparently there is competition between the two *Eurystomus* when both species are present at Nimba, because the habitats occupied by the larger *E. glaucurus* during its stay at Nimba are apparently evacuated by *E. gularis*. When the former species leaves the area in April, the latter returns to these probably optimal habitats.

Family Phoeniculidae

Phoeniculus bollei Buff-headed Wood-hoopoe

SPECIMENS. 2 ♂♂, Feb. 1968, Dec. 1972. 1 ♀, Feb. 1968. — *P. b. bollei* (Liberia to southern Cameroon and Ubangi).

Family Bucerotidae

IMPERMANENT COLOURS. Legs dusky-red. Iris brown. Eye-ring red. Bill red or purplish-red.

STOMACH CONTENTS. Insects and beetle larvae.

ANNUAL CYCLE. The December male was in the middle of a wing-moult (4th primary being replaced, 5–10th old), the February female near the end of its moult (8th primary growing, 9–10th old), and the February male in fresh plumage. No indication of breeding.

HABITAT AND STATUS. Usually found in tall trees of dense forest up to an altitude of about 800 m, but four birds were once observed in a *Gmelina* plantation, which is a more open deciduous wood. A new species for Liberia.

Phoeniculus castaneiceps Forest Wood-hoopoe

SPECIMENS. 5 ♂♂, Mar. 1972, Apr. 1969, May 1970, Jun. 1971, Jul. 1968. 1 ♀, Apr. 1968. 1 o, Jul. 1966. — *P. c. castaneiceps* (Liberia to Cameroon).

IMPERMANENT COLOURS. Legs black. Iris dark brown. Bill dark horn with a pale yellow cutting edge.

STOMACH CONTENTS. Insects, including beetles and caterpillars.

ANNUAL CYCLE. Three of the four March–May birds were in wing-moult. No evidence of breeding, but gonads of only two birds were measured, April and July, both small.

HABITAT AND HABITS. This is a primary and secondary forest species at Nimba, keeping to leafy tree-tops where it is seldom seen but its calls reveal its presence. It has been observed in small flocks feeding on fruits or excavating insects from them. A new record for Liberia.

Family Bucerotidae

Tockus camurus Dwarf Red-billed Hornbill

SPECIMENS. 5 ♂♂, Mar., May 1968, Jun., Jul. 1967, Dec. 1971. 2 ♀♀, Jun. 1967, Jul. 1970. 1 o, Mar. 1972. — *T. c. pulchrirostris* (Liberia to southern Nigeria).

IMPERMANENT COLOURS. Legs dark blackish-brown. Iris pale clear yellow. Bare skin around eye greenish-grey. Bill orange.

STOMACH CONTENTS. Insect fragments including large beetles and grasshoppers.

ANNUAL CYCLE. The specimens provided no evidence of breeding, except perhaps the June female which had an ovary measuring 11 mm. The two March birds were in worn plumage, and a May and a July bird were in wing-moult.

HABITAT AND HABITS. Rather common at Nimba in secondary lowland forests, gallery forests and what remains of ancient swamp forests. Usually seen in small groups of 3–4 birds.

Tockus hartlaubi Black Dwarf Hornbill

SPECIMENS. 4 ♂♂, Jul. 1965, 1967, 1968, 1970. 3 ♀♀, Jun., Aug. 1970, Sept. 1964. — *T. h. hartlaubi* (Sierra Leone to Cameroon).

IMPERMANENT COLOURS. Legs dark grey. Iris brown. Bare skin of face grey; sides of throat below bill pink. Bill black with a red tip; all black in the female.

STOMACH CONTENTS. Insects including grasshoppers, beetles and a very bright green bug.

ANNUAL CYCLE. No evidence of breeding. A July male was in a stage of slow, possibly interrupted, wing-moult.

HABITAT AND HABITS. Lowland high forest. Usually 2–4 birds seen together.

Tockus fasciatus Pied Hornbill

SPECIMENS. 1 ♂, Jun. 1967. 3 ♀♀, May, Jul., Aug. 1968. 2 o, Aug. 1968, Sept. 1964. — *T. f. semifasciatus* (Senegal to Nigeria).

IMPERMANENT COLOURS. Legs blackish. Iris dark brown. Bill whitish-cream and black, dark red-brown near nostrils.

STOMACH CONTENTS. Insects, including beetles and caterpillars. Also vegetable matter, fibres and yellow fruits.

ANNUAL CYCLE. The specimens give no evidence of breeding. The June and September birds were in wing-moult. In different years three nest-holes have been occupied between December and February (KC-L).

HABITAT AND HABITS. Almost ubiquitous at Nimba where there are trees, frequenting primary and secondary lowland and montane forest, isolated stands of trees, cultivated areas and plantations etc. Usually does not exceed 900 m. At Nimba its presence is probably favoured by the oil palm (*Elaeis guineensis*), of which the fruits are eaten. This species may form large flocks. The largest seen at Nimba contained 9 birds, but elsewhere in Liberia up to 70 have been observed (Rand, 1951).

Ceratogymna atrata   Black-casqued Hornbill

SPECIMENS. 2 ♂♂, Jul., Aug. 1968. 2 ♀♀, Mar. 1970, Jul. 1968.

IMPERMANENT COLOURS. Legs black. Iris red-brown. Bare facial skin around eye and wattle, dark blue, black at the angle of the jaw. Wattle below eye in ♀ pale pink. Bill black, brownish on rough patches.

STOMACH CONTENTS. Orange fruits with hard stones, and palm nuts.

ANNUAL CYCLE. The July female was probably approaching breeding condition (ovary 20 mm, ova to 1 mm), and was noted as being exceedingly fat. The three other birds were all in wing-moult, the two males with small gonads.

HABITAT AND HABITS. In view of its size, which makes it an easy target for hunters, this species is surprisingly common at Nimba in primary forest and secondary forests with tall trees remaining. In dense forest the tremendous noise produced by its wing beats confirms how common this impressive bird is.

Ceratogymna elata   Yellow-casqued Hornbill

This large forest-inhabiting, mainly frugivorous hornbill was observed in 1963–1965 and on almost every subsequent visit made to Nimba (KC-L), and was also seen in 1967–1968 (AF-W). It is rather common at Nimba in lowland and montane forest where there are tall trees but it also visits secondary forest. It can be found up to about 1000 m. Often seen in groups of 2–4 birds. When crossing a clearing or a road they fly across separately one by one, at intervals of up to a minute. The species likes the fruits of the oil palm.

Tropicranus albocristatus   White-crested Hornbill

SPECIMENS. 7 ♂♂, Apr. 1968, 1969, Aug. 1967, 1971, Sept. 1967, Oct. 1968 (2). — *T. a. albocristatus* (Sierra Leone, Liberia and Guinea).

IMPERMANENT COLOURS. Legs grey. Iris white or creamy. Bare skin black. Bill black with a creamy patch at the base of the upper mandible.

STOMACH CONTENTS. Insects, including grasshoppers, metallic beetles, and caterpillars. Also fruit and palm nut remains.

ANNUAL CYCLE. The September–October males had enlarged gonads (13, 13, 8 mm). None of the birds was in active wing-moult, but an August male had apparently arrested a moult (7 inner primaries fresh, 3 outer primaries old and worn).

HABITAT AND HABITS. Primary and secondary lowland and montane forests up to about 900 m. Flies around a good deal in the forest usually keeping below the canopy.

Bycanistes fistulator   Piping Hornbill

This species was seen (KC-L) at Nimba in 1964–65, and in subsequent years, in flocks of up to 10–15 birds flying around and giving very noisy calls between primary and secondary lowland forests. It seldom exceeds the 600 m contour. In 1971 it was also observed (AF-W & DT). One individual was collected in 1980 and kept in the collection of the Nimba Research Laboratory at Grassfield.

Bycanistes cylindricus   Brown-cheeked Hornbill

SPECIMEN. 1 ♀, Jan. 1968; ovary 18 mm, in wing- and tail-moult. — *B. c. cylindricus* (Sierra Leone to Ghana).

IMPERMANENT COLOURS. Legs dull blackish and blue-grey. Iris brown. Bare skin around eye whitish-pink. Bill creamy-white and brownish-black.

HABITAT. Those birds which have been identified with certainty in the field at Nimba have all been in the more or less intact parts of the lowland rain forest.

Family Capitonidae

Lybius bidentatus — Tooth-billed Barbet

This large barbet, already known from Liberia and from many other localities in the Upper Guinea forest, was observed at Yekepa in 1967 or 1968 (AF-W).

Lybius vieilloti — Vieillot's Barbet

This species was observed at Yekepa in February 1971 (AF-W, JK & SK). This is the first record for Liberia. It is known to occur on the French-Guinean side of Nimba. In February 1978 Curry-Lindahl heard a pair of this species duetting on several occasions at the same site near Yekepa. When the birds meet each other after having been separated for a while they frequently greet each other by duetting. The species was also observed at Nimba in 1979–1981.

Lybius hirsutus — Hairy-breasted Barbet

SPECIMENS. 4 ♂♂, Apr. 1968, 1969, Jul., Aug. 1967. 6 ♀♀, Mar. 1970, Apr., May, Aug. 1968, Aug., Sept. 1970. — *L. h. hirsutus* (Sierra Leone to Togo).

IMPERMANENT COLOURS. Legs dark grey. Iris dark red. Bill black or blackish-horn.

STOMACH CONTENTS. Fruit pulp and large flat seeds.

ANNUAL CYCLE. No evidence of breeding, but one August female, with ovary 10 mm and ova to 1 mm, may have been approaching breeding condition. All three April birds and the July bird were in wing-moult, and August birds in fresh plumage.

HABITAT. Permanently present in the forest-grassland mosaic at Grassfield, where it kept to the inside of, or on the outskirts of, both primary and secondary forest patches and larger complexes.

Gymnobucco calvus — Naked-faced Barbet

SPECIMENS. 9 ♂♂, Jun. 1968 (2), Jul. 1967 (2), Aug., Sept. 1967 (3), 1970. 6 ♀♀, Jun. 1967, Jul. 1967, 1970 (2), Sept. 1967, Nov. 1968. — *G. c. calvus* (Sierra Leone to Cameroon and Gabon).

IMPERMANENT COLOURS. Legs dark brown. Iris brown. Bill pale brown with dark patches. Ear holes yellow. Bare skin on head black.

STOMACH CONTENTS. Fruit pulp and seeds. Insects including beetles and ants.

ANNUAL CYCLE. No definite evidence of breeding, but a July male with testes 9 mm may have been in breeding condition. One June, one July and two September birds were in wing-moult.

HABITAT AND HABITS. This species utilizes a number of habitats where there are ripe or over-ripe fresh fruits available. It wanders around in flocks in various kinds of forest up to 1200 m as well as in cultivation, gardens and villages. It is particularly fond of mangos and papayas, and may return day after day to the same tree when the fruits are ripe. The birds cluster to the fruit, clinging in all kinds of positions, and may feed for hours. Birds have occasionally been seen with black bills; on 1 March 1980, a flock of 8 birds had completely black bills. Possibly the colour-change is seasonal.

Pogoniulus duchaillui — Yellow-spotted Barbet

SPECIMENS. 15 ♂♂, Apr. 1969, Jun., Jul., Aug. 1967 (3), Sept. 1967 (5), 1970 (3), Nov. 1964. 1 imm. ♂, Feb. 1968. 6 ♀♀, Aug. (2), Sept. 1967 (4). 1 juv. ♀, Nov. 1968. — *P. d. duchaillui* (Sierra Leone to Zaire).

IMPERMANENT COLOURS. Legs dark grey, pinkish-grey in juvenile. Iris brown, grey in juvenile. Bill black, but mostly yellow in juvenile with a black tip. Bare skin around eye black, dull pale pink in juvenile.

STOMACH CONTENTS. Hard yellow fruits, purple or pink fruit pulp.

ANNUAL CYCLE. A September male with testes 12.5 mm, and August and September females with ovaries 10.0 and 11.5 mm respectively, were probably in breeding condition. The juvenile had not long left the nest (7 Nov.), its bill being only half-grown. No birds were in wing-moult; the November male and some September birds were in worn plumage.

HABITAT. Primary and secondary forest.

Pogoniulus scolopaceus — Speckled Tinker-bird

SPECIMENS. 11 ♂♂, Jan. 1971, Feb. 1968, Jun. 1967 (3), Jul. 1967 (4), Sept. 1965, 1967. 7 ♀♀, Feb. 1968, Jun. (4), Jul., Aug. 1967. 1 juv. ♀, Jan. 1968. — *P. s. scolopaceus* (Sierra Leone to Nigeria).

IMPERMANENT COLOURS. Legs olive-grey, brownish in juvenile. Iris clear yellow or creamy yellow, brown in juvenile. Bill black with the lower mandible grey-horn. Gape yellow in juvenile.

STOMACH CONTENTS. Insects, hard seeds, round red fruits and other vegetable matter.

ANNUAL CYCLE. The juvenile, taken from the nest on 30 January, was well-feathered, with short wings and tail, and the bill about half-grown. No other definite evidence of breeding, but a September male, with testis 5 mm, may have been approaching breeding condition (maximum of 3 mm for ♂♂ in other months). The February and two June females were in early stages of wing-moult.

HABITAT. Primary and secondary lowland forests, clearing, cultivated land with trees and gardens.

Pogoniulus leucolaima Lemon-rumped Tinker-bird

This species was heard and seen at Nimba in 1978–1982 (KC-L). A bird was collected in 1979 and kept in the Nimba Research Laboratory at Grassfield. In 1980 another bird was collected at Grassfield (Louette, 1981).

Pogoniulus subsulphureus Yellow-throated Tinker-bird

SPECIMENS. 15 ♂♂, Jan. (3), Feb., Apr. 1968 (2), Jun. 1967, Aug. 1968 (2), Sept. 1967 (3), Oct. 1968 (3). 2 imm. ♂♂, Apr. 1968 (2). 9 ♀♀, Feb. 1966, 1968, Mar. 1968, Jun. 1967, Jul. 1968 (3), Aug. 1968, Sept. 1967. — *P. s. chrysopygus* (Guinea and Sierra Leone to Ghana).

IMPERMANENT COLOURS. Legs dark grey. Iris brown. Bill black.

STOMACH CONTENTS. Insects and fruit pulp.

ANNUAL CYCLE. The specimens gave no definite evidence of breeding, and none was in wing-moult. Females with ovaries 7.0–7.5 mm in February, July and September may have been in breeding condition. Males had enlarged gonads (5 mm) in January–February, and one in June (5.5 mm), the maximum in other months being 4 mm.

HABITAT. Familiarity with the call of this species in eastern Zaire facilitated Curry-Lindahl in noting how common this bird was at Nimba. It frequents primary and secondary lowland and montane forest up to about 1000 m as well as the forest-grassland mosaic at Grassfield.

Pogoniulus atroflavus Red-rumped Tinker-bird

SPECIMENS. 6 ♂♂, Feb. 1966, 1968, Apr., May 1968, Jun, Jul. 1967. 2 juv. ♂♂, Apr., Aug. 1968. 3 ♀♀, Apr., May, Jul. 1968.

IMPERMANENT COLOURS. Legs dark grey. Iris brown. Bare skin around eye black. Bill black, pinkish at base of lower mandible in juvenile.

STOMACH CONTENTS. Insects, purple fruit pulp and seeds.

ANNUAL CYCLE. No definite evidence of breeding, but the April male with testes 6 mm may have been in breeding condition. One February male and the May male were in the middle of a wing-moult, both with 5th primary growing.

HABITAT. Clearings, cultivated ground, gardens, woodlands and forest edges.

Trachyphonus purpuratus Yellow-billed Barbet

SPECIMENS. 1 ♂, Apr. 1969. 1 ♀, Oct. 1968. — *T. p. goffinii* (Sierra Leone to Ghana).

IMPERMANENT COLOURS. Legs grey. Iris deep red. Bare skin around eye black. Bill deep yellow.

STOMACH CONTENTS. Insects and gastropods.

ANNUAL CYCLE. The April male was beginning a wing-moult (innermost primary growing), and the October female was in fresh plumage, with ovary 2.5 mm.

HABITAT. Primary and secondary lowland and montane forests up to about 1000 m.

Family Indicatoridae

Indicator maculatus Spotted Honeyguide

SPECIMENS. 11 ♂♂, Apr. 1968, Jul. 1967 (3), Aug. 1967, 1968, Oct., Nov. 1968 (4). 12 ♀♀, Jan. 1972, Mar. 1968 (2), Jun. (2), Aug., Oct. 1967, Nov. 1968 (5). 2 o, Jul., Aug. 1967. — *I. m. maculatus* (Gambia to western Nigeria).

IMPERMANENT COLOURS. Legs olive-green. Iris brown or chestnut-brown. Bill black, paler horn below.

STOMACH CONTENTS. Mostly insects and wax, some pollen and a few seeds.

ANNUAL CYCLE. A March female was noted as having an enormously distended oviduct and two November females were in breeding condition, one with a very large ovary and the other with yolks to 8 mm. Single August, October and two November males had testes of 6 mm. A June bird was in an advanced stage of wing-moult (7th primary in pin), and two July birds were in wing-moult, one with the 5th and the other the 9th (outermost) primary growing.

HABITAT. Primary and lowland forest, in the denser parts as well as in clearings and at their edges.

Indicator conirostris Thick-billed Honeyguide

SPECIMENS. 12 ♂♂, Jun. 1967, Aug., Nov. 1968 (10). 5 ♀♀, Nov. 1968 (5). — *I. c. ussheri* (Liberia to southern Ghana).

IMPERMANENT COLOURS. Legs olive-grey. Iris brown. Bill black with a pinkish tinge to the base of the lower mandible. Bare skin around eye grey.

STOMACH CONTENTS. Green vegetable matter, scaly yellow wax, parts of fruits, insects, flying termites and one black seed 3 mm long.

ANNUAL CYCLE. A November female was noted as having a distended oviduct. Two November males had testes of 6 mm and two others of 5 and 4.5 mm, all the rest (June, Aug., Nov.) being 3–4 mm. A November female was finishing wing-moult (outer primaries growing), and the remaining birds were mostly in fresh plumage.

DISTRIBUTION. *Indicator conirostris* forms a superspecies with *I. minor*, the joint ranges of which cover much of sub-saharan Africa. *Indicator conirostris* occupies heavy, closed evergreen forest whereas *I. minor*, found only some 150 km NW. of Nimba, ranges mostly in savanna woodlands. There is only one other Liberian record of *I. conirostris*, a ♀ which was collected at Firestone Plantation (Rand, 1951) and which is shown as *minor* in Snow (1978).

HABITAT. Lowland forest and forest-grassland mosaics. Forbes-Watson records it from Yekepa and Grassfield, where it is not uncommon but seldom seen. Mostly found in the canopy or mid-levels. On 12 August 1978 the Oxford University Expedition netted a bird near the top of Mount Nimba (RW).

Indicator exilis Least Honeyguide

SPECIMENS. 12 ♂♂, Jun. 1967 (2), 1968, Nov. 1968 (9). 9 ♀♀, Mar., Aug. 1968 (2), Oct. 1967, Nov. 1968 (5). — *I. e. exilis* (Sierra Leone to eastern Zaire).

IMPERMANENT COLOURS. Legs olive-grey. Iris brown. Bill black, pale pink below.

STOMACH CONTENTS. Mostly insects with small amounts of wax, ? yellow pollen, fibres and small pink ? worms noted.

ANNUAL CYCLE. An August female was noted as having laid and two November birds have very large yolks of 7–8 mm. A June male had testes of 4 mm and 6 November birds testes of 3.0–3.5 mm. Two June males were in advanced stages of wing-moult and three November birds were finishing (outer primaries growing).

HABITAT AND STATUS. Forest-shrub-grassland mosaic. This is a new record for Liberia.

Indicator willcocksi Willcocks's Honeyguide

SPECIMENS. 2 ♂♂, Sept. 1968, Dec. 1967. 5 ♀♀, Aug. 1967, 1968 (2), Sept., Nov. 1968. — *I. w. willcocksi* (Ghana to Zaire).

IMPERMANENT COLOURS. Legs olive-grey to olive-green. Iris brown. Bill black, paler horn base to lower mandible.

STOMACH CONTENTS. Insects and wax.

ANNUAL CYCLE. Two August and the September female had ovaries of 7–9 mm, but males' testes were 1.5 mm or less. One August female was in worn condition and the rest were in fresh plumage.

HABITAT AND STATUS. Forest-shrub-grassland mosaic; seen at Yekepa and Grassfield. Forbes-Watson records it as an unobtrusive bird of the forest mid-levels, sometimes appearing at the forest edge. This is a new record for Liberia.

Melichneutes robustus Lyre-tailed Honeyguide

SPECIMENS. 4 ♂♂, Feb. (2), Mar., Dec. 1968. 2 ♀♀, Apr., Nov. 1968.

IMPERMANENT COLOURS. Legs dark grey tinged olive. Iris chestnut-brown. Bill brownish horn tinged pink below.

STOMACH CONTENTS. Insects, including fine chitin fragments in small balls of wax.

ANNUAL CYCLE. The April female had an ovary of 9 mm and the February–March males had enlarged gonads (6–8 mm). February–April birds were in worn condition and November–December birds were in fresh plumage.

DISTRIBUTION AND VARIATION. Nimba birds which are in fresh plumage are slightly paler below when compared with the female type from Bitye, Cameroon, and two old and rather worn and foxed specimens from Cameroon and Gabon in the BM(NH) collection. The species, which is new for Liberia, is known from south-east Nigeria to Zaire and north-west Angola.

FIELD OBSERVATIONS. The species was observed in several localities in lowland forest, up to 1000 m (AF-W). The remarkable sound produced by the male in what is presumed to be a display flight has made this bird famous. In March 1968 Forbes-Watson and Yallah guided Curry-Lindahl to a recently discovered locality at Nimba where a male was displaying. This area was characterised by scattered stands of tall trees, so that one could easily see the sky above the canopy. Curry-Lindahl returned there in later years and the male again performed aerial display, in January–April and once in November. During the 1970s and 1980s displaying males were found in two more localities in the lowland forest.

The sound has been described well by Chapin (1939), who believed it to be produced by the passage of air through the narrowed rectrices in much the same way as in the snipe *Gallinago gallinago*. However, the sound produced by *Melichneutes* is extremely loud in volume and far more impressive than in any snipe. It carries far, and both in Liberia and Zaire Curry-Lindahl has heard it at least 400 m from the site where the bird was displaying. Chapin's assumption of how the sound is produced has been fully confirmed (Rougeot, 1950, 1951; Chapin, 1954).

Melignomon eisentrauti   Coe's Honeyguide

SPECIMENS. 6 ♂♂, Jun. 1966 (2), Aug. 1968, Sept. 1968, 1970, Nov. 1968. 5 ♀♀, Feb. 1969, Apr. 1974, Jul. 1967, Aug. 1971, Oct. 1965.

IMPERMANENT COLOURS. Legs pale yellow tinged pinkish on the sides. Iris clear brown. Bill brownish, tinged yellowish below. Gape yellow.

STOMACH CONTENTS. Insects, yellow wax (or pollen ?), small fruits and some seeds.

ANNUAL CYCLE. Only four birds were examined, a July female and 3 males, collected August, September and November, and none of the birds was considered to be in breeding condition. Single April and October females were in worn condition and the remaining birds were in fresh plumage.

DISTRIBUTION. This is the second new species for science to be found at Nimba (see *Melaenornis annamarulae*). The genus *Melignomon* was long thought to consist of a single species, *M. zenkeri*. With the description of *eisentrauti* (Colston, 1981; Louette, 1981a), a species apparently endemic to the Upper Guinea forest, and as far as is known, allopatric with *zenkeri* (see Snow, 1978, map 374), it seems probable that the genus consists of two species in a single superspecies. In addition to the 11 Nimba specimens, there is a single specimen in the BM(NH) collected by Dr W. Serle, in secondary forest at Bakebe, Cameroon. It was previously thought by Serle to be an immature specimen of *M. zenkeri* (Serle, 1959). The bird is a male in fresh plumage and does not differ significantly from Nimba adult specimens of *eisentrauti*. There is also a recent sight record of *M. eisentrauti*, confirmed by a detailed field description given by Macdonald (1980), of a bird observed at Kakum F.R. in Ghana (5°20′N, 1°22′W), in closed secondary forest. The species has now been found in Liberia, Ghana and Cameroon, and it seems likely that it will be found in other areas of the Upper Guinea forest.

HABITAT AND HABITS. An uncommon forest species of mid-levels and the canopy, of rather more warbler-like habits than any of the preceding species. Occurs both at Yekepa and Grassfield (AF-W).

REMARKS. This species has been known much longer than the date of its description (1981) might suggest, and its history deserves to be recorded. On 2 August 1956 Serle collected a single specimen at Bakebe in the British Cameroons, which he and Friedmann determined as an immature *M. zenkeri* (1959). Another specimen was collected by Professor M. Eisentraut on 17 December 1957 at Malende near Mount Cameroon (Eisentraut, 1963); contrary to Louette (1981b), this was not the first specimen ever collected.

The species was seen alive, actually within the compound of the Nimba Research Laboratory, by Coe in 1964, and he wrote to Curry-Lindahl as follows: 'It flew from the forest edge where it appeared to be searching amongst the leaves and branches of a large climbing *Combretum* and then settled on the wire. I watched it several times during the day and felt sure it was a honeyguide, but one that was quite unknown to me, and even a look at Bannerman could get me no closer than *Melignomon*.' Three specimens, collected by Coe and Yallah in 1964 and 1966, were recognised by them and by Friedmann as belonging to a new species. Coe wrote a paper describing and discussing the new species, and gave it to Forbes-Watson in about 1968. The latter did nothing about it, and did not mention the question to other interested ornithologists, so that Curry-Lindahl knew nothing of Coe's draft until 1982. In his list of the birds of Liberia, Forbes-Watson (1970) listed the *Melignomon* as 'sp.nov.'.

On taking over responsibility for writing up the Nimba collection, Colston wrote a description of the new species based on the whole series, and submitted it in 1980 to the *Bulletin of the British Ornithologists' Club*. Shortly afterwards Louette requested, from the BM(NH), a loan of the Nimba series for comparison with a single specimen which he had collected in 1980 at Grassfield, close to the Nimba Research Station, though the staff were unaware of his visit. Instead, Colston sent him a copy of his own unpublished description. Without informing Colston or the Laboratory of his intention, Louette (1981a) published a description of the new species, under the name *M. eisentrauti*. Colston's description was published soon afterwards, since publication had progressed too far for the paper to be withdrawn or altered, beyond changing the name to *eisentrauti* and adding a footnote.

Malcolm Coe had so much to do with the discovery of *Melignomon eisentrauti* that Curry-Lindahl proposed for it the English name Coe's Honeyguide.

Prodotiscus insignis   Cassin's Honeyguide

SPECIMENS. 3 ♂♂, Aug., Nov., Dec. 1968. 3 ♀♀, May, Sept. 1968, Nov. 1972. 1 o, Aug. 1968. — *P. i. flavodorsalis* (Sierra Leone to south-east Nigeria).

IMPERMANENT COLOURS. Legs blue-grey. Iris brown. Bill black, pale bluish-horn below.

STOMACH CONTENTS. Insects, spiders, scale insects, bugs and yellow wax.

ANNUAL CYCLE. The May female had a moderately enlarged ovary of 7 mm and the September female 3 mm. Both were finishing wing-moult (outer primaries growing). Testes of the males were small (1.3 mm). The remaining August, November and December birds were in fresh plumage.

HABITAT AND HABITS. Lowland and montane forests up to about 1000 m as well as forest-shrub-grassland mosaics. This is a tree-top species which looks and behaves like a warbler, and often accompanies mixed bird flocks.

Prodotiscus regulus   Wahlberg's Honeyguide

SPECIMEN. 1 imm. o, Jan. 1968; fresh plumage.

IMPERMANENT COLOURS. Legs dark brown. Iris brown. Bill black. Gape whitish.

STOMACH CONTENTS. Fragments of honeycomb.

DISTRIBUTION. This is the first record for Liberia and it represents an important extension of range from the nearest known locality in Togo (de Roo *et al.*, 1971). The Nimba bird agrees with the BM(NH) type of *P. r. caurinus* from Enugu, Nigeria. This race extends eastwards to Cameroon.

HABITAT. Forest-shrub-grassland mosaic.

Family Picidae

Jynx torquilla   Wryneck

SPECIMEN. 1 ♂, Jan 1968; gonads small, in body moult.

IMPERMANENT COLOURS. Legs grey tinged olive. Iris clear brown. Bill pale grey.

STOMACH CONTENTS. Ants.

DISTRIBUTION. The Nimba bird is *J. t. torquilla* which is a wintering Palaearctic migrant widely recorded in West Africa. This is the first record for Liberia.

HABITAT. Lowland and montane forests to about 1000 m as well as forest-shrub mosaic.

Campethera maculosa
Golden-backed Woodpecker

SPECIMENS. 3 ♂♂, Jan., Sept. 1968, Nov. 1964. 1 ♀, Sept. 1967.

IMPERMANENT COLOURS. Legs dull green to olive-grey. Iris brown. Bill dark grey, paler below.

STOMACH CONTENTS. Black ants.

ANNUAL CYCLE. The specimens gave no evidence of breeding. Both September birds were finishing their wing-moult, outer primaries growing. January and November birds were slightly worn.

HABITAT. Primary and secondary forest as well as forest-shrub mosaic up to the ridge of Mount Nimba.

Campethera caroli   Brown-eared Woodpecker

SPECIMENS. 7 ♂♂, Jun. 1967 (2), Jul. 1970 (2), Aug. 1967 (3). 6 ♀♀, Jun. 1966, 1967 (2), 1968, Jul. 1967, Aug. 1968. 2 imm. ♀♀, Jun. 1968, Dec. 1969. — *C. c. arizelus* (Guinea Bissau to Liberia).

IMPERMANENT COLOURS. Legs pale olive-green. Iris brown. Bare skin around eye dull green. Bill blackish-grey, paler at the base.

STOMACH CONTENTS. Small black ants and larvae.

ANNUAL CYCLE. Gonad data incomplete for two July males and single June and August females. The remaining specimens gave no evidence of breeding. Three June birds were in a fairly advanced stage of wing-moult and a July female was finishing (outer primaries growing). August birds were in fresh plumage.

HABITAT. A pair was observed in primary lowland forest seeking insects on a dead and dry branch up in the canopy. Also seen and heard in the forest-shrub-grassland mosaic at Grassfield.

Campethera nivosa   Buff-spotted Woodpecker

SPECIMENS. 11 ♂♂, Mar. 1968 (2), Jun. 1967 (3), Jul., Aug. 1968 (3), Sept. 1965, 1968. 1 imm. ♂, Sept. 1968. 11 ♀♀, Jan. 1971, Apr. 1968 (2), May 1966, Jun. (2), Jul. 1967, Aug. 1967, 1968, Sept. 1968, Oct. 1970. 1 o, Jun. 1967. — *C. n. nivosa* (Senegal to south-east Nigeria).

IMPERMANENT COLOURS. Legs olive-green or yellowish-green. Iris brown. Bare skin around eye green. Bill blackish or dark grey.

STOMACH CONTENTS. Black ants, which are its main food source.

ANNUAL CYCLE. Two April females had moderately enlarged ovaries (8 and 10 mm) and the remaining June to October females showed no signs of breeding (ovaries 3–6 mm). Single March and August males had enlarged testes of 6 mm whilst seven males for June to September were 4 mm or less. Four June birds were in wing-moult, one of which was almost complete (outer primaries growing). The two July, six August and one September male were also in advanced stages of wing-moult.

HABITAT. Rather common at Nimba in primary and secondary lowland and montane forest up to about 950 m as well as in *Gmelina* woodlands, mosaic of forest patches, shrub, grassland and gardens.

Dendropicos gabonensis Gaboon Woodpecker

SPECIMENS. 4 ♂♂, Jan., Nov. 1968 (3). 6 ♀♀, Feb. 1966, Jul., Sept. 1967, Oct. 1968 (2), 1970. — *D. g. lugubris* (Sierra Leone to Ghana).

IMPERMANENT COLOURS. Legs olive-green. Iris chestnut-brown. Bill black, paler grey below.

STOMACH CONTENTS. Insects, ants and beetle larvae.

ANNUAL CYCLE. The specimens provide no evidence of breeding. A July female was completing wing-moult (outer primaries growing), and a September and two October birds were in advanced stages of wing-moult. November and January birds were in fresh plumage.

HABITAT. Rather open forest segments, clearings and *Gmelina* woodlands.

Dendropicos pyrrhogaster Fire-bellied Woodpecker

SPECIMENS. 6 ♂♂, Jan. (2), Mar. 1968, Apr., Jun. 1969, Nov. 1968. 1 ♀, Aug. 1968.

IMPERMANENT COLOURS. Legs olive-grey to olive-green. Iris brown or red-brown. Bare skin around eye grey. Bill dark grey-horn, paler below.

STOMACH CONTENTS. Mostly larvae of beetles and white ants. Also insect fragments.

ANNUAL CYCLE. The specimens provide no evidence of breeding. April, June and August birds were in wing-moult, and November and January birds in fresh plumage. Liberian birds in breeding condition have been reported in November; also nestlings in March (Mackworth-Praed & Grant, 1970).

HABITAT. Patches of isolated tall trees, clearings, forest edges and forest-grassland mosaic.

Family Eurylaemidae

Smithornis capensis African Broadbill

SPECIMEN. 1 ♂, Apr. 1968; in breeding condition (testes 8 mm), fresh plumage. — *S. c. delacouri* (Sierra Leone to Ghana).

IMPERMANENT COLOURS. Legs pale grey. Iris brown. Bill black, whitish below.

STOMACH CONTENTS. Beetles.

HABITAT. Primary and secondary lowland forest as well as forest shrub mosaic.

Smithornis rufolateralis Rufous-sided Broadbill

SPECIMENS. 12 ♂♂, Jan. 1970 (2), Feb., Mar., Apr. 1968, Jun., Jul., Aug. 1967, 1968, Sept. 1967 (2), Nov. 1968. 9 imm. ♂♂, Feb. 1968 (3), Jun. 1967, Jul. (2), Aug. 1967 (2), 1968. 2 ♀♀, Feb., Aug. 1968. 4 imm. ♀♀, Apr. 1968, Jun. 1966, Aug. 1967, Sept. 1968. — *S. r. rufolateralis* (Liberia to Cameroon and north-western Zaire).

IMPERMANENT COLOURS. Legs olive-green. Iris brown. Bill black, pinkish-horn below.

STOMACH CONTENTS. Insects, including ants, beetles and grasshoppers.

ANNUAL CYCLE. The August female was in breeding condition with an enlarged ovary of 12 mm. The ovary of the February female measured 7 mm. Four males' testes were moderately enlarged (5–7 mm) in March, April, September and November. Two January and a single June bird were in wing-moult, and July to September adults were in fresh plumage.

HABITAT. The shady interior of lowland and montane forests.

Family Pittidae

Pitta angolensis — African Pitta

SPECIMENS. 2 ♂♂, Mar., Nov. 1968. — *P. a. pulih* (Sierra Leone to Cameroon).

IMPERMANENT COLOURS. Legs pale pink. Iris dark brown. Bill black, pinkish-horn below.

STOMACH CONTENTS. Insects.

ANNUAL CYCLE. The March male was apparently in breeding condition, with testes of 8 mm, and in fresh plumage. The testes of the November bird were small (2 mm).

MIGRATION. Probably a migrant in Liberia, as breeding does not appear to have been recorded west of Cameroon.

Family Alaudidae

Mirafra africana — Rufous-naped Bushlark

SPECIMEN. 1 ♀, Jul. 1967; ovary 8.5 mm, slightly worn plumage.

IMPERMANENT COLOURS. Legs flesh-pink. Iris brown. Bill blackish with a pinkish-horn lower mandible.

STOMACH CONTENTS. Insects and beetles.

DISTRIBUTION. The Nimba bird is *M. a. henrici*, the type of which was collected at Bossou on the Guinea side of Nimba. The upper parts are very heavily marked with black, except for the crown. This is the first record of this species in Liberia. In West Africa it is a local species occurring in certain areas of montane grassland and upland savanna in Guinea, Ivory Coast, and on the Jos Plateau in Nigeria, Cameroon, and the grass savannas of south Gabon and Zaire.

HABITAT. This lark was first observed in October 1963 on the grassland savanna in Liberia stretching along the border to Guinea, at the foot of Mount Nimba. It was seen again at this site in 1966 and in several subsequent years.

Pinarocorys erythropygia — Red-tailed Bushlark

SPECIMEN. 1 ♂, Feb. 1968; testes 6 mm, very worn plumage.

IMPERMANENT COLOURS. Legs flaky-white. Iris brown. Bill blackish-brown, pinkish below.

STOMACH CONTENTS. Several large grasshoppers.

DISTRIBUTION AND STATUS. This is the first Liberian record of this species, which is found in savannas north of the forest from Senegal to Sudan and Uganda. It migrates in March–April from the Guinea savanna belt of eastern West Africa to the Sahel zone. It is possible that a similar migration occurs in western West Africa and that the Liberian bird was a straggler.

Isolated emergents rise above dense secondary vegetation on a track 5 km from Grassfield. Photograph Malcolm Coe.

Family Hirundinidae

Riparia riparia — Sand Martin

SPECIMEN. 1 ♂, Sept. 1968. — *R. r. riparia* (Palaearctic winter visitor).

IMPERMANENT COLOURS. Legs pinkish-brown. Iris brown. Bill black.

STOMACH CONTENTS. Black flying ants.

DISTRIBUTION. This is the first record of the species in Liberia. It is common in winter in Senegal, Mali, Nigeria and Ethiopia, and is widely recorded elsewhere in Africa as a passage migrant.

Hirundo rustica — Swallow

SPECIMENS. 5 ♂♂, Sept. 1968 (3), Nov. 1967 (2). 5 imm. ♂♂, Feb. 1968, Oct. 1967 (3), Nov. 1967. 1 imm. ♀, Nov. 1970. — *H. r. rustica* — (Palaearctic migrant and winter visitor to tropical and southern Africa).

IMPERMANENT COLOURS. Legs dark brown. Iris brown. Bill black.

STOMACH CONTENTS. Insects.

ANNUAL CYCLE. Most birds were in very worn plumage. One adult male had almost completed its moult by 29 November with the last primaries growing.

HABITAT AND MIGRATION. The Swallow utilizes all kinds of habitats at Nimba ranging from the cultivated and settled Yah Valley up to the top ridges of Mount Nimba. At migration time thousands of Swallows congregate on the wires around Yekepa and Grassfield. On 1–2 March 1980 there was an invasion of tens of thousands of Swallows at Nimba. They were widespread throughout the area, but by the following day they had all departed.

Verschuren (1979) reported that the Swallow was common during his stay at Nimba, with the same number of birds present every day from December to February. On his annual visits to Nimba Curry-Lindahl has found a somewhat different picture. He records peaks of passage and sometimes several days of sojourn at Nimba in September–November and again in late February and the beginning of March, but there are few or no birds present at all in the periods between these passages.

Hirundo nigrita White-throated Blue Swallow

SPECIMENS. 1 ♂, Aug. 1968. 1 ♀, Aug. 1968.

IMPERMANENT COLOURS. Legs black. Iris brown. Bill black.

STOMACH CONTENTS. Insects.

ANNUAL CYCLE. The male had gonads of 9 mm. Both were in fresh plumage.

DISTRIBUTION AND HABITAT. It frequents rivers and lakes with forested banks in the rain forest zone from Sierra Leone to Gabon and Zaire. This is a rare species at Nimba and may be migratory.

Hirundo abyssinica — Lesser Striped Swallow

SPECIMENS. 2 ♂♂, Aug. 1967, Nov. 1969. 3 imm. ♂♂, Jun. (2), Aug. 1968. — *H. a. puella* (Sierra Leone to western and northern Nigeria).

IMPERMANENT COLOURS. Legs black. Iris brown. Bill black.

STOMACH CONTENTS. Insects.

ANNUAL CYCLE. The August male was in non-breeding condition (testes 3 mm) and in worn plumage. The November bird was in an advanced stage of wing-moult. The June immature males were in fresh plumage, with broad buff edges to their scapulars.

HABITAT. Cultivated areas, gardens, buildings, forest-grass mosaic, along roads and other partly open sites, but utilising the whole Nimba airspace over which to hunt. They were also recorded perched on isolated trees on the highest ridges of Nimba at about 1300 m.

Hirundo fuligula — African Rock Martin

SPECIMENS. 1 ♂, 1 ♀, Apr. 1968. — *H. f. bansoensis* (Senegal to Cameroon).

IMPERMANENT COLOURS. Legs brown. Iris dark brown. Bill black.

STOMACH CONTENTS. Insects.

ANNUAL CYCLE. Both birds were in non-breeding condition and in an advanced stage of wing-moult.

HABITAT AND STATUS. Cliffs and outcrops of the higher parts of the denuded Nimba peak, both in the abandoned and current mining areas. This is a new record for Liberia.

Hirundo griseopyga — Grey-rumped Swallow

SPECIMENS. 1 ♂, 1 ♀, 1 o, Jun. 1968. — *H. g. melbina* (Gambia–Liberia).

IMPERMANENT COLOURS. legs black. Iris brown. Bill black.

STOMACH CONTENTS. Insects.

ANNUAL CYCLE. The birds were in non-breeding condition. All three were in moult and renewing their primary feathers.

HABITAT AND HABITS. This is the predominant swallow at Nimba, occurring from about 700 m upwards. It is particularly common around the higher ridges, where it hunts low over the ground or over tree tops, sweeping up from one slope and then diving down 30–50 m to the other side of the next slope and repeating the manœuvre again. When the upper parts of Nimba are covered in clouds and mists the Grey-rumped Swallows descend to hunt at lower levels of the mountain or at its base, even over grasslands.

The species may be a partial migrant at Nimba, because numbers seem to fluctuate somewhat from time to time, but it is difficult to discern a pattern.

Psalidoprocne nitens — Square-tailed Roughwing Swallow

SPECIMENS. 7 ♂♂, Jun. (3), Aug. (2), Sept. 1967 (2). 13 ♀♀, Jun. 1967 (6), 1968 (2), Jul. (2), Aug., Sept. 1967 (2). — *P. n. nitens* (Sierra Leone to Zaire).

IMPERMANENT COLOURS. Legs black. Iris brown. Bill black.

STOMACH CONTENTS. Insects.

ANNUAL CYCLE. One August male had testes of 5 mm, and the two September males 4.5 and 4.0 mm (max. 3 mm for all other males). The females' ovaries were small. Most of the birds had completed their moult and were in fresh plumage except for three June, two July and single August and September birds which still showed traces of brown juvenile feathers on their underparts.

HABITAT AND STATUS. This species was common in 1963–1966 (from 900 to 1300 m), even before Mount Nimba was altered by mining activities. Here it hunted actively both above and within the montane forests. Later the Square-tailed Roughwing Swallow occupied the damaged areas of Mount Nimba and is presently common there. It is a new record for Liberia.

Psalidoprocne obscura — Fantee Roughwing Swallow

This swallow, which ranges from Senegal and Guinea Bissau to western Cameroon, was observed at Nimba in 1967 or 1968 (AF-W), in June 1973 (KC-L) and in July 1976 (AF-W & DT). It was netted at several sites in July–September 1978 by the Oxford University Expedition (Wolton, *in litt.*). It occurs in savanna adjoining the forest and in extensive forest clearings. The species may be a migrant at Nimba; in Ivory Coast it is present from September to April.

Family Motacillidae

Motacilla flava — Yellow Wagtail

SPECIMENS. 18 ♂♂, Jan. 1970 (14), Sept., Oct. 1967, Nov. 1969 (2). 31 ♀♀, Jan. 1966, 1970 (22), Feb. 1968, Mar. 1970, Oct. 1967, 1969 (3), Nov. 1969 (2). 42 o, Feb. (38), Mar. 1968 (2), Oct. 1967 (2).

IMPERMANENT COLOURS. Legs black. Iris brown. Bill black.

STOMACH CONTENTS. Insects.

ANNUAL CYCLE. The birds were in winter plumage, worn condition, or in varying stages of moult.

STATUS AND RACIAL COMPOSITION. A widespread and abundant passage migrant and winter visitor from the Palaearctic region; earliest and latest dates of observation at Nimba 21 September and 4 April (KC-L). Nearly all of the specimens are in winter plumage and some are so dull in colour that racial determination is difficult if not impossible. About 20 are *M. f. flavissima*. Many of the remainder have some degree of grey or blue about the head and are either *M. f. flava* or *M. f. iberiae*. A few are so dark-headed as to approach the northern Scandinavian form, *M. f. thunbergi*. Curry-Lindahl (1964) observed small flocks of about 30–40 individuals on Nimba at the end of September 1963, of which a high proportion could easily be identified as belonging to the British race, *M. f. flavissima*. These appear to be the first definite Liberian records of this subspecies. Close examination of males in the field by Curry-Lindahl during January–April (when some individuals have more or less completed their moult) in 1966–1982 gave the result that racially identifiable birds were predominantly *flava*, but there were also many *flavissima* and *iberiae*. Only a few *thunbergi* and *cinereocapilla* could be identified.

The main mine site at Mount Alpha, where the overburden has been removed to reveal the iron rich itabirite beneath. In the distance the 'Knife edge' of Guinea Nimba is capped by remnants of the old laterite cap where the vegetation is dominated by grassland. Photograph Malcolm Coe.

HABITAT AND HABITS. A common wintering bird at Nimba as they are in the rest of Liberia, where there are short grassy areas. This is the prime factor and not, it seems, the presence of larger grazing mammals that attracts them. In Liberia, there are practically no domestic or wild ungulates utilizing the short grassy plains and meadows. The Yellow Wagtails visiting Nimba have increased in numbers during the late 1970s and 1980s, and have begun to utilise an abandoned paved mine road which zig-zags and makes a vertical cross section of the entire mountain from the foothills to the top ridge. This road, which is gradually being recolonized by encroaching vegetation, is visited by Yellow Wagtails for feeding. The birds are found all along the road right up to the highest areas. They are often accompanied by pairs of Long-billed Pipts (*Anthus similis*) and Blue-spotted Wood-doves (*Turtur afer*), which are almost lost amongst the flocks of wagtails. As early as 1963, a few years after mining operations had begun, different races of Yellow Wagtails started to visit the newly denuded rocky flats or 'moon landscape' at 1200–1400 m. Thus they exploited a completely new habitat as soon as it was created, and they have remained faithful to it ever since; though in the late 1970s and early 1980s the number of birds seen in the mine area had diminished, while those on the adjoining mine roads and the grassy habitats below the mountain had increased. Presumably the latter areas offered better feeding conditions.

Motacilla clara — Mountain Wagtail

SPECIMENS. 3 ♂♂, Jun. 1967 (3). 1 imm. ♂, Apr. 1968. 2 o, Apr. 1972, Jul. 1967. — *M. c. chapini* (Sierra Leone to western Uganda).

IMPERMANENT COLOURS. Legs pinky-grey. Iris brown. Bill black.

STOMACH CONTENTS. Insects.

ANNUAL CYCLE. Males' gonads were small (2–3 mm). The five adults were in fresh plumage. The young male had only the barest trace of a grey breast-band and was in heavy moult around the chin and throat.

HABITAT. Occurs in and along rocky streams as well as besides and behind waterfalls in both the lowland and montane forest.

Anthus leucophrys — Plain-backed Pipit

Since 1963 this Pipit has been observed at Nimba a number of times but has not been collected. Curry-Lindahl has observed it only within the period November–February. It was observed in February 1971 (AF-W, JK & SK), and also in July 1976 (AF-W & DT). It frequents open grassy areas, bare ground or roads, from the lowland, e.g. Yekepa, at 475 m up to about 1100 m. In southern Liberia it is a partial migrant, present in large numbers November–January and in smaller numbers April–July.

Anthus similis — Long-billed Pipit

SPECIMENS. 2 ♂♂, Sept. 1967 (2). 2 ♀♀, Jul., Sept. 1967. — *A. s. bannermani* (Sierra Leone to Liberia and adjacent Ivory Coast).

IMPERMANENT COLOURS. Legs pale brownish-flesh. Iris brown. Bill dark brown with a pinkish-horn base.

STOMACH CONTENTS. Insects, including metallic green beetles.

ANNUAL CYCLE. No direct evidence of breeding, but the September males had enlarged testes (6–7 mm), and the September female an ovary of 7 mm (*cf.* the July female, 2 mm). The September female was in a late stage of wing-moult.

HABITAT AND STATUS. Common on Mount Nimba and invariably found at the same localities (900–1100 m) along the closed, paved winding mine road that was mentioned under *Motacilla flava*. Since the 1970s the Long-billed Pipit has occupied the rocky road banks and borders which were created when the road was built around 1960. These sites, which are now slowly and sparsely being colonized by grassy vegetation, are eventually occupied by pairs of this pipit. A small plateau at about 1200 m, which was partially cleared of vegetation around 1960, has been occupied by a pair of Long-billed Pipits since 1975. The open area is about 40 m square and is entirely surrounded by montane high forest. It is also bordered by a bank of bulldozed rocks 1.5 m high. Thin grasses and bushes have begun to cover the bare ground in patches and it is here that a pair of Long-billed Pipits is present throughout the year. The male sings from the 'rock-wall'. At other sites along the road most males sing from nearby trees. This is a new record for Liberia.

Anthus trivialis — Tree Pipit

SPECIMENS. 3 ♂♂, Feb., Mar. 1968, Oct. 1967. 1 ♀, Jan. 1966. 1 o, Jan. 1968. — *A. t. trivialis* (breeds Palaearctic, winter visitor to Africa).

IMPERMANENT COLOURS Legs pale flesh. Iris brown. Bill dark grey-brown with a pinkish base.

STOMACH CONTENTS. Insects.

ANNUAL CYCLE. October and January birds were in worn condition and February–March males were in fresh plumage.

HABITAT AND STATUS. This species was first observed in 1966, and in subsequent years, often in open woodlands or where there are forest-grassland mosaics such as around Yekepa and Grassfield. The latest record was on 13 March. This is a new record for Liberia.

Macronyx croceus Yellow-throated Longclaw

SPECIMEN. 1 imm. ♂, Aug. 1968; gonads small, in unusual plumage, showing well developed black throat-band, but still retaining a buff throat — *M. c. croceus* (Senegal–Equatorial southern Sudan).

IMPERMANENT COLOURS. Legs pale brown. Iris brown. Bill blackish, bluish-horn below.

STOMACH CONTENTS. Grasshoppers.

HABITAT. Open patches or larger areas of short grass in the lowland.

Family Campephagidae

Coracina azurea Blue Cuckoo-Shrike

SPECIMENS. 10 ♂♂, Jan. 1968, Feb. 1969, Apr. 1972, May, Jun. 1971, Jul. 1968, Sept., Oct., Nov. 1967, Dec. 1970. 3 ♀♀, Jul., Sept., Oct. 1967. 1 o, Jul. 1967.

IMPERMANENT COLOURS. Legs black. Iris brown. Bill black.

STOMACH CONTENTS. Insects, including beetles, grasshoppers and caterpillars.

ANNUAL CYCLE. Gonad data (incomplete) gave no indication of breeding. The April, May and July males were in advanced stages of wing-moult (8th–10th primaries growing), and the December and January birds were also in wing-moult (7th and 6th primaries growing). The remaining June–October birds were in fresh plumage.

HABITAT. Lowland and montane primary and secondary high forest up to about 900 m; also in the forest-grassland mosaic at Yekepa and Grassfield.

Campephaga quiscalina Purple-throated Cuckoo-shrike

SPECIMENS. 9 ♂♂, Mar. 1968, Jul. 1965, Aug. 1968, Sept. 1967 (3), 1968, 1970, Oct. 1967. 1 imm. ♂, Nov. 1964. 4 ♀♀, Feb. 1968, May 1971, Jun. 1968, Nov. 1964. — *C. q. quiscalina* (Sierra Leone to Cameroon, Zaire and northern Angola).

IMPERMANENT COLOURS. Legs black. Iris brown. Bill black. Gape of male deep orange.

STOMACH CONTENTS. Insects, including caterpillars.

ANNUAL CYCLE. Gonad data incomplete and the only evidence of breeding is a February female noted as probably having laid, with an ovary of 10 mm and ova of 5 mm. Single February, March and September birds were in wing-moult, and June to September birds were mostly in fresh plumage.

HABITAT. Primary and secondary forests. Most often seen along their edges or in clearings, but this may be due to better visibility than inside the forest.

Campephaga lobata Wattled Cuckoo-shrike

SPECIMENS. 15 ♂♂, Apr. 1968, May 1971, Jul. 1965, 1967 (2), 1968, 1970, Aug. 1968, 1969, Sept. 1967 (2), 1968 (2), Oct. 1968, Nov. 1967. 3 imm. ♂♂, Apr. 1969, Jul. 1967, Aug. 1967. 2 ♀♀, Jul. 1967 (2). 1 imm. ♀, Jul. 1968.

IMPERMANENT COLOURS. Legs black. Iris dark brown. Bill black. Wattle at gape velvety-orange.

STOMACH CONTENTS. Caterpillars, grasshoppers, a green mantis and a few small black seeds.

ANNUAL CYCLE. No definite evidence of breeding but August–November males, with testes 6–8 mm, were probably in breeding condition (*cf.* April–July males, 1.5–3.0 mm). The two July females had ovaries measuring 6.5 mm. The April male was in an advanced stage of wing-moult (7th primary growing), three July birds were finishing (10th primary growing), the other July and August–September birds being in fresh plumage. The April immature male was in moult and acquiring the adult's chestnut underparts. The July and August immature males were yellow below similar to the adult female (see below), with white tipped primary and median coverts.

PLUMAGE. The female of *lobata*, which was not previously known, has the head and throat dullish black with yellowish-green fringes to the feathers of the forehead and crown, and the wattles are very much reduced. The underparts are yellow and the rump yellowish-green, concolorous with the back. In the adult male both of these areas are chestnut.

DISTRIBUTION. Nimba birds are *C. l. lobata*. This is a new record for Liberia, and represents an extension of range some 800 km west. It is found in the lowland forests of Liberia, Ivory Coast and Ghana. Also G.D. Field saw this species on several occasions in the 1970s in the Gola Forest in eastern Sierra Leone.

Campephaga phoenicea   Red-shouldered Cuckoo-shrike

SPECIMEN. 1 imm. ♂, Dec. 1967. — *C. p. phoenicea* (Senegal to Eritrea).

IMPERMANENT COLOURS. Legs black. Iris grey. Bill black.

STOMACH CONTENTS. Caterpillars.

DISTRIBUTION AND STATUS. There is only one other Liberian record of this species, a male collected at Ganta (Rand, 1951). It is known to be locally migratory; in Sierra Leone it is present December–April.

Family Pycnonotidae

Pycnonotus barbatus   White-vented Bulbul

SPECIMENS. 9 ♂♂, Jan. 1968, Aug. 1967 (2), 1968 (2), 1975, Sept. 1968 (2), 1970. 4 ♀♀, Jun. 1967, Jul. 1968, Aug. 1967, 1968. — *P. b. inornatus* (Senegal to Cameroon).

IMPERMANENT COLOURS. Legs black. Iris brown. Bill black.

STOMACH CONTENTS. Small fruits.

ANNUAL CYCLE. At Nimba *P. barbatus* apparently breeds throughout the year (KC-L). The specimens gave no definite evidence of breeding, but the June female, with an ovary of 11 mm, and the January and one August male, with testes (10–11 mm), were probably in breeding condition. The January male was very worn and the June–August birds were mostly in fresh plumage. Three August birds were renewing their tail-feathers.

HABITAT AND HABITS. This species has become ubiquitous at Nimba. Between 1963 and 1982 it successively invaded every type of habitat, from cultivated land to primary forest, and from the lowland to the top ridges of Nimba. It has occupied all strata of the montane forests, and is especially common in clearings and along forest edges. During this period it has increased enormously, and is probably now the most common bird in the Nimba region.

Andropadus curvirostris   Western Sombre Bulbul

SPECIMENS. 8 ♀♀, Feb. 1966, Jun. (3), Aug. 1967 (3), Oct. 1968. 7 ♀♀, Jun. (3), Aug., Sept. 1967 (2), Oct. 1968. 1 o, Jun. 1967. — *A. c. leoninus* (Sierra Leone to Ghana).

IMPERMANENT COLOURS. Legs olive-green. Iris chestnut-brown. Bill black.

STOMACH CONTENTS. Fruit, small seeds and insects.

ANNUAL CYCLE. The females show evidence of an increase of ovary size from June to September (June 5.5–6.5 mm, August 7.5 mm, September 7.0, 8.0 mm).

Gonads of the males were small. A February male was in very worn condition. June to September birds were in fresh plumage with the exception of an August male which was in an advanced stage of wing-moult.

Andropadus gracilis   Little Grey Bulbul

SPECIMENS. 2 ♂♂, Jul. 1967, Sept. 1968. 2 ♀♀, Jun., Sept. 1967. — *A. g. extremus* (Sierra Leone to southern Nigeria).

IMPERMANENT COLOURS. Legs olive-green. Iris brown. Bill black. Gape creamy-yellow. Eye-lid pale yellowish-green.

STOMACH CONTENTS. Small hard-stoned fruits. Insects, including black ants and a small beetle.

ANNUAL CYCLE. No definite evidence of breeding, but the July male, with testes 6 mm, may have been in breeding condition. All specimens were in fresh plumage.

HABITAT. Shrub-forest mosaic.

Andropadus ansorgei   Ansorge's Bulbul

SPECIMENS. 5 ♂♂, Jul. 1967, 1970, Oct. 1968 (2), Nov. 1964. 1 ♀, Jul. 1967. — *A. a. ansorgei* (Sierra Leone to Zaire).

IMPERMANENT COLOURS. Legs grey. Iris chestnut-brown. Bill black.

STOMACH CONTENTS. Small fruits; insects, including beetles.

ANNUAL CYCLE. No evidence of breeding. One July male was moulting its tail feathers and the others were mostly in fresh plumage.

Andropadus virens   Litttle Green Bulbul

SPECIMENS. 9 ♂♂, Jun. 1967 (6), 1974, Aug. 1968, Sept. 1967. 11 ♀♀, Jan. 1966, Mar. 1968, Jun. 1967 (3), Jul. 1966, 1967, Aug. 1968, Sept. 1967, Oct. 1968, Nov. 1964. — *A. v. erythropterus* (Gambia to Nigeria).

IMPERMANENT COLOURS. Legs brown tinged orange. Iris grey-brown. Bill black. Gape pale yellow.

STOMACH CONTENTS. Small fruits and insects.

ANNUAL CYCLE. The males' gonads were small (2–5 mm in June, 1 and 5 mm in August–September). Only two females had enlarged ovaries, one in June (9.5 mm) and August (12 mm), and were probably in breeding condition. The March–June birds were in fresh plumage and one September female was in worn condition.

HABITAT. A common bird at Nimba in bushes, thickets, young secondary forests and clearings, forest-grassland mosaics at Yekepa and Grassfield, and gardens. Found up to about 1000 m on Mount Nimba.

Andropadus gracilirostris   Slender-billed Bulbul

SPECIMENS. 9 ♂♂, Feb. 1966, Apr. 1968, 1969, Jun. 1970, Jul. 1965, Aug., Sept. (2), Oct. 1967. 4 ♀♀, Jul. 1967, 1970, Nov. 1964. — *A. g. gracilirostris* (Sierra Leone to southern Nigeria).

IMPERMANENT COLOURS. Legs black. Iris chestnut-brown. Bill black.

STOMACH CONTENTS. Mostly fruit with a few seeds and insects.

ANNUAL CYCLE. None of the birds examined was in breeding condition. An April male was in wing-moult and June to August birds were in fresh plumage. October–February birds were in worn condition.

HABITAT. Shrub.

Andropadus latirostris   Yellow-whiskered Bulbul

SPECIMENS. 10 ♂♂, Jun. 1967 (8), Oct. 1964, 1968. 6 imm. ♂♂, Jan. 1969, Jun. 1967 (2), Oct. 1968 (3). 12 ♀♀, Jun. 1967 (2), Jul. 1971, Oct. 1968 (8), Nov. 1964. 1 imm. ♀, Dec. 1968. — *A. l. congener* (Senegal to southern Nigeria).

IMPERMANENT COLOURS. Legs brown tinged yellow. Iris brown. Bill black tinged pinkish basally, paler in imm. Gape pale yellow.

STOMACH CONTENTS. Small fruits.

ANNUAL CYCLE. The males' gonads were small (June 1–4 mm, Oct. 1–5 mm). An October female had an enlarged ovary (12 mm) and was probably in breeding condition, and two other females had ovaries of 8 mm. Three June birds were in wing-moult: one in an early stage, 3rd primary growing; and two in an advanced stage, outer primaries growing. June to October birds were mostly in fresh plumage and the November female was worn. The immature bird lacked the yellow stripe down each side of the throat.

HABITAT. Dense undergrowth of lowland and montane forests, forest edges, and isolated thickets in the forest-grassland mosaic. Ascends to about 900 m on Mount Nimba.

Calyptocichla serina   Golden Bulbul

SPECIMENS. 3 ♂♂, Aug., Sept. 1967 (2). 9 ♀♀, Jan., Mar. 1968, Jul. 1967, 1968 (2), Aug. 1967, Sept. 1970, Oct., Dec. 1967.

IMPERMANENT COLOURS. Legs grey. Iris brown. Bill pale pinkish-horn, browner at tip.

STOMACH CONTENTS. Fruit pulp and some seeds.

ANNUAL CYCLE. The specimens gave no indication of breeding condition. A March bird, three July birds, and a December bird were in various stages of wing-moult. The January female was worn and August–September birds were in fresh plumage.

HABITAT. Lowland primary and secondary forest.

Baeopogon indicator   Honey-guide Bulbul

SPECIMENS. 12 ♂♂, Mar., Apr. 1968 (2), Jun. (4), Jul., Aug., Sept. 1967 (2), Nov. 1964. 8 ♀♀, Feb. 1968, Apr. 1968, 1969, Jun. 1967, 1971, Jul., Aug. 1967, Nov. 1964. — *B. i. leucurus* (Sierra Leone and Liberia to Togo).

IMPERMANENT COLOURS. Legs greyish-black. Iris pale cream. Bill black.

STOMACH CONTENTS. Small fruits.

ANNUAL CYCLE. Gonads of the males were small (1.0–4.5 mm). The February female had a moderately enlarged ovary (10 mm) and may have been in breeding condition. Single March and April males were in wing-moult, and June to September birds were in fresh plumage.

HABITAT. Tall second-growth and on the edges of clearings in lowland forest.

Ixonotus guttatus   Spotted Bulbul

SPECIMENS. 3 ♂♂, Apr. (2), Aug. 1968. 3 ♀♀, Apr., Aug., Nov. 1968. 1 o, Apr. 1968. — *I. g. guttatus* (Liberia to Zaire).

IMPERMANENT COLOURS. Legs grey. Iris pale creamy-brown. Bill grey, paler below.

STOMACH CONTENTS. Yellow or pink fruits.

ANNUAL CYCLE. The two August birds were in breeding condition (testes 8 mm; ovary 10 mm). The four April birds were in advanced stages of wing-moult (8th–10th primaries growing) as was the November female (7th primary growing).

HABITAT AND HABITS. Primary and secondary lowland forests. Often seen in flocks of 6–10 birds flying in and out of the canopy and below it.

Chlorocichla simplex   Simple Leaf-love

SPECIMENS. 9 ♂♂, Feb., Apr. 1968, Jun., Jul, 1967, Aug. 1968 (3), Sept. 1964, Oct. 1968. 7 ♀♀, Jan., Feb. 1968, Jun. 1966, Jul. (2), Sept. 1968, Oct. 1967.

IMPERMANENT COLOURS. Legs grey. Iris brown. Bill black.

STOMACH CONTENTS. Fruit pulp and some seeds.

ANNUAL CYCLE. A February female had an enlarged ovary of 15 mm, with ova to 8 mm, and was evidently breeding. A July female was noted as having recently laid, and the other July and the September female may also have been in breeding condition (ovaries 11 and 12 mm). The males' gonads were small (testes 1–4 mm) February to July, but enlarged (7–9 mm) in August birds. A February male was in an early stage of wing-moult, 7 old primaries, and the April male was in a more advanced stage, last 3 primaries old.

HABITAT. Rather common at Nimba in thickets, bushes, secondary lowland forest and forest-grassland mosaic. Less frequently observed in montane forests up to the ridge of Mount Nimba.

Thescelocichla leucopleura Swamp Palm Bulbul

SPECIMENS. 4 ♂♂, Apr. 1968, Jun. 1970, Aug. 1968, Oct. 1970. 3 ♀♀, Jun. 1970, Jul., Nov. 1967.

IMPERMANENT COLOURS. Legs dark grey-brown. Iris brown. Bill black, paler grey below.

STOMACH CONTENTS. Hard-stoned fruits.

ANNUAL CYCLE. Gonad data incomplete. A July female (ovary 10.5 mm) may have been approaching breeding condition (6 mm in a November female). The males' gonads for the April and August birds were small (3–5 mm). The April male was in an advanced stage of wing-moult, last 3 primaries old, and October–November birds were in worn condition.

HABITAT AND HABITS. The Swamp Palm Bulbul has a rather wide range of habitats at Nimba besides the preferred swamp vegetation of *Raphia* palms or other plants growing along water courses. It visits both primary and secondary forests, particularly where there are clearings, and also the forest-grassland mosaic, plantations, gardens and isolated stands of fruit trees. The bird is social and usually moves around in groups of 3–6 individuals.

Phyllastrephus scandens Leaf-love

SPECIMENS. 4 ♂♂, Mar., Apr. 1968, Jul. 1973, Sept. 1968. 1 ♀, Jul. 1973. 1 o juv., Mar. 1968. — *P. s. scandens* (Senegal to Cameroon).

IMPERMANENT COLOURS. Legs blue-grey, yellowish in immature. Iris chestnut-brown, pale greyish-brown in imm. Bill grey, yellowish below.

STOMACH CONTENTS. Insects, including beetles, grasshoppers and caterpillars. Also small black fruits and seeds.

ANNUAL CYCLE. Egg laying in January is indicated by the juvenile of 6 March. Only three males examined for March, April and September (all with testes 6 mm). An April male was in wing-moult (5 outer primaries old) and two July birds had almost finished (outer primaries growing). The September male was in fresh plumage.

HABITAT AND STATUS. This is a new record for Liberia. It is chiefly found outside the main body of the West African rain forest. At Nimba it is mostly heard and seen in thickets and undergrowth along water courses, and in outside lowland forests and woodlands. Small groups of 3–6 birds move around together announcing their whereabouts with much noise and a variety of calls.

Phyllastrephus baumanni Baumann's Greenbul

SPECIMENS. 5 ♂♂, Jan., Mar., Apr., Sept., Nov. 1968. 4 ♀♀, Apr. 1968, Sept. 1967 (2), Oct. 1968. 1 o, Jan. 1971. — *P. b. baumanni* (Sierra Leone to south-east Nigeria).

IMPERMANENT COLOURS. Legs blue-grey. Iris chestnut-brown. Bill black, pinkish-horn below.

STOMACH CONTENTS. Insects, including a large caterpillar. Also small hard seeds.

ANNUAL CYCLE. The October female had a moderately enlarged ovary (10 mm) and may have been in breeding condition (6.0–7.5 mm for April and September birds). The January, April and November males had enlarged gonads (8–10 mm) and were probably in breeding condition. A January male was in an early stage of wing-moult (6 outer primaries old) and an April female had almost completed its wing-moult (outer primaries growing).

Phyllastrephus icterinus Icterine Greenbul

SPECIMENS. 18 ♂♂, Jan. 1969, Jun. (6), Jul. (6), Aug., Sept. 1967, Oct. 1968 (2), Nov. 1964. 11 ♀♀, Jan. 1969, May 1965, Jun. (5), Jul. 1967 (3), Oct. 1968. — *P. i. icterinus* (Sierra Leone to southern Nigeria).

IMPERMANENT COLOURS. Legs blue-grey. Iris greyish-brown. Bill blackish with a yellow cutting edge, paler grey below.

STOMACH CONTENTS. Insects, including ants and beetles.

ANNUAL CYCLE. Gonad data lacking for January, May and November birds. The October female had a slightly enlarged ovary of 8 mm (2–6 mm for June–July birds). The males gonads were enlarged for one August (8 mm) and two October birds (both 9 mm), *cf.* 2–6 mm for June–July males. Four June and a July female were in advanced stages of wing-moult; the other June to August birds were mostly in fresh plumage.

HABITAT AND HABITS. Dense parts of lowland and 'slope' forests up to about 700 m, but also forest-shrub-grassland mosaics. This species may follow wandering bird parties to other habitats such as clearings and the outskirts of forests. It seems to have a regular habit of associating with other birds, but may also form wandering groups of its own.

Phyllastrephus albigularis — White-throated Greenbul

SPECIMENS. 2 ♂♂, Apr., May 1968. 4 ♀♀, Apr. 1968 (4). — *P. a. albigularis* (Sierra Leone to Uganda and Sudan).

IMPERMANENT COLOURS. Legs blue-grey. Iris creamy to pale grey. Bill dark horn, paler below.

STOMACH CONTENTS. Insects, including beetles and ants. Also a small conical gastropod.

ANNUAL CYCLE. None of the birds was in breeding condition. An April male was in wing-moult (last four primaries old) and the remainder were in fresh plumage.

Bleda syndactyla — Bristle-Bill

SPECIMENS. 8 ♂♂, Jan. 1966, Feb. 1969, Jun. (5), Jul. 1967. 9 ♀♀, Feb. 1966, May, Jun. 1967 (7). — *B. s. syndactyla* (Sierra Leone to western Nigeria).

IMPERMANENT COLOURS. Legs pale blue-grey. Iris red-brown. Bare skin round eye dull blue-grey. Bill dark grey, paler below.

STOMACH CONTENTS. Insects, including beetles and ants. Also some seeds.

ANNUAL CYCLE. No definite evidence of breeding. The June–July males' gonads were small (2.0–3.5 mm) and May–July females' ovaries were generally small (3.5–8.5 mm) except for two June females (10 mm). No gonad data was available for the January–February birds. Three June females were in an advanced stage of wing-moult (outer primaries growing) and many of the remaining May–July birds were in fresh plumage. The January and February birds were in a worn condition.

HABITAT AND HABITS. Isolated thickets and dense undergrowth in lowland and montane forests, but also the forest-grassland mosaics at Yekepa and Grassfield. Often a participant in mixed bird parties.

Bleda eximia — Green-tailed Bristle-bill

SPECIMENS. 5 ♂♂, Jan. 1969, Jun. (2), Jul. 1967 (2). 9 ♀♀, Feb. 1966, Jun. (4), Jul. (3), Aug. 1967. — *B. e. eximia* (Sierra Leone to Ghana).

IMPERMANENT COLOURS. Legs whitish-flesh, tinged blue. Iris chesnut-brown. Bill grey, paler below.

STOMACH CONTENTS. Insects, including beetles and ants. Also small frog bones found in one individual.

ANNUAL CYCLE. Four females had slightly enlarged ovaries in June (8, 9 mm) and July (9.5, 10.5 mm), and single males had enlarged gonads in June (10 mm) and July (8.5 mm). Two July and an August bird were in the early stages of wing-moult.

HABITAT. Dense lower parts of primary and secondary forests as well as forest-grassland mosaics.

Bleda canicapilla — Grey-headed Bristle-bill

SPECIMENS. 6 ♂♂, Jun. (3), Jul. (2), Aug. 1967. 10 ♀♀, Apr. 1965 (2), Jun. (4), Jul. (2), Aug., Dec. 1967. 1 o, Jul. 1967.

IMPERMANENT COLOURS. Legs blue-grey. Iris clear chestnut-brown. Bare patch behind eye blue-grey. Bill blackish, blue-grey below.

STOMACH CONTENTS. Insects, including black ants, and a small millipede. Also small seeds.

ANNUAL CYCLE. A July female, with an enlarged ovary of 10 mm, and an August male, with testes 7 mm, were the only birds indicating possible breeding activity. An April male was in an early stage of wing-moult and it was almost completed in a June male (outer primaries growing). Many of the June–August birds were in fresh plumage.

HABITAT AND HABITS. Lowland, montane and swamp forest as well as the forest-grassland mosaic at Yekepa and Grassfield. Usually seen and heard in small parties searching for food in vegetation just above the ground.

Criniger barbatus — Bearded Bulbul

SPECIMENS. 11 ♂♂, Jun. 1966, 1967 (9), Jul. 1965. 1 juv. ♂, Oct. 1968. 8 ♀♀, Jun. 1967 (7), Jul. 1971. — *C. b. barbatus* (Sierra Leone to Togo).

IMPERMANENT COLOURS. Legs blue-grey. Iris clear chestnut-brown. Bill black, blue-grey below.

STOMACH CONTENTS. Insects, including small beetles and a moth. Also some small seeds.

ANNUAL CYCLE. The only evidence of breeding activity relates to the juvenile (24 Oct.) which still retained a great deal of down on its underparts and was obviously still dependent on the adults for food. The males' gonads for June were small (1–3 mm) and the June females' ovaries were not enlarged (1.0–8.5 mm). Gonad data for July birds not available. Two June males were in middle stages of wing-moult and a June female had almost completed (outer primaries growing). Most of the other June birds were in fresh plumage.

HABITAT. Primary and secondary lowland forest as well as forest-grassland mosaics.

Criniger olivaceus — Yellow-throated Olive Bulbul

SPECIMENS. 8 ♂♂, Apr., May 1968, Jun. 1967 (2), Jul. 1967 (3), Oct. 1968. 6 ♀♀, Mar., May 1968, Jun. 1967, Aug. 1965, 1978, Nov. 1968.

IMPERMANENT COLOURS. Legs blue-grey. Iris chestnut-brown. Bill blue-grey with a paler cutting edge.

STOMACH CONTENTS. Mostly insects, and a few small hard-stoned fruits.

ANNUAL CYCLE. The only evidence for breeding is a November female which had an enlarged ovary (yolks to 12 mm) and had recently laid. An April male was renewing three inner primaries and two June birds were in more advanced stages of wing-moult with the 7th and 10th primaries growing. March and October birds were worn and the remainder were in fresh plumage.

DISTRIBUTION. This bulbul is known from only three or four localities in West Africa and is rare in collections. The Nimba birds do not differ from two B.M.(N.H.) specimens from Fantee and another collected by Bates near Nzerekore in Guinea. It is found in primary forest (Senegal to Ghana). This is a new species for Liberia.

Criniger calurus White-beared Bulbul

SPECIMENS. 10 ♂♂, Jun. (7), Jul. 1967 (2), Nov. 1964. 1 juv. ♂, Nov. 1970. 5 ♀♀, Jun. (3), Jul. 1967, Nov. 1970. — *C. c. verreauxi* (Sierra Leone to western Nigeria).

IMPERMANENT COLOURS. Legs blue-grey. Iris red-brown. Bill black, blue-grey below.

STOMACH CONTENTS. Insects.

ANNUAL CYCLE. The juvenile of 11 November, with traces of down remaining on the breast and belly, is the only clear indication of breeding activity. Two males had slightly enlarged gonads in June (6.0, 6.5 mm), and two females, one in June and the other in July (both 8 mm). None of the birds was in wing-moult. The majority of June–July birds were in fresh plumage and both November birds were in worn condition.

HABITAT AND HABITS. Primary and secondary lowland and montane forest up to the ridge of Mount Nimba as well as forest-grassland mosaic. Often a member of mixed bird parties.

Nicator chloris West African Nicator

SPECIMENS. 5 ♂♂, Jun. (3), Jul. 1967, Nov. 1964. 5 ♀♀, Jun. (2), Jul., Aug. 1967, Oct. 1970. 2 imm. ♀♀, Apr. 1970, Aug. 1967. 2 o, Jul., Aug. 1967.

IMPERMANENT COLOURS. Legs blue-grey. Iris greyish-brown. Eye rim yellow. Bill black. Gape yellow.

STOMACH CONTENTS. Insects, including grasshoppers and beetles. Also the remains of a small amphibian.

ANNUAL CYCLE. No evidence of breeding activity. Gonad data incomplete, only available for June birds (testes 2–4 mm, ovaries 7–9 mm), and single July and August females (ovaries 5–6 mm). An August female was in the final stage of wing-moult (outer primaries growing). A July female was in very worn condition and the remaining birds were in fresh plumage.

HABITAT. Lower strata of primary forest and in thick foliage of high second-growth. Heard at Nimba in dense thickets up to about 800 m.

Family Laniidae

Prionops caniceps Grey-headed Helmet Shrike

SPECIMENS. 1 ♂, Jul. 1967. 1 imm. ♂, Jul. 1967. 5 ♀♀, Mar. 1968, Jul. 1970 (2), Aug. 1967 (2). — *P. c. caniceps* (Sierra Leone to Togo).

IMPERMANENT COLOURS. Legs dark orange. Iris bright yellow, dark grey-brown in imm. Eye wattle orange. Bill dark red, blackish in imm.

STOMACH CONTENTS. Grasshoppers and beetles.

ANNUAL CYCLE. Gonad data incomplete. Little evidence of breeding; testes (4 mm) for July male, ovaries 5–6 mm for March and two August females. The March female was just starting wing-moult and the July male was at a more advanced stage (last 3 primaries old). Two July and the August birds were in fresh plumage.

HABITAT AND HABITS. Primary and almost mature secondary lowland forests. Flocks of 6–10 birds seen flying around and feeding in the canopy.

Dryoscopus gambensis Gambian Puff-back

SPECIMENS. 1 ♂, Jan. 1968. 3 ♀♀, Jan. 1968 (2), Feb. 1966. 1 imm. ♀, Jan. 1968. — *D. g. gambensis* (Senegal to Cameroon and Gabon).

IMPERMANENT COLOURS. Legs grey. Iris bright orange. Bill black.

STOMACH CONTENTS. Insects.

ANNUAL CYCLE. No indication of breeding activity. The two January females were renewing their tail feathers and the other two birds were in slightly worn condition.

HABITAT. Clearings within both primary and secondary forests, *Gmelina* woodland, forest-grassland mosaics, isolated thickets, bushes of the savanna along the Guinea border, and gardens.

Dryoscopus sabini — Sabine's Puff-back

SPECIMENS. 3 ♂♂, Jan. 1966, Jun., Sept. 1967. 2 imm. ♂♂, Nov. 1968, 1973. 3 ♀♀, Jun. 1967, Aug., Nov. 1968. — *D. s. sabini* (Sierra Leone to southern Nigeria).

IMPERMANENT COLOURS. Legs blue-grey. Iris dark brown. Bill pale bluish, sides black.

STOMACH CONTENTS. Insects, including grasshoppers and beetles.

ANNUAL CYCLE. No definite evidence of breeding, but gonads moderately enlarged June–November (no data for the January male). The September male had testes of 6.5 mm, and the June, August and November females had ovaries of 8.5, 6.0 and 7.0 mm respectively. The two June birds were in middle stages of wing-moult and the August–November birds were in fresh plumage.

HABITAT. Forest and the edges of clearings.

Tchagra minuta — Little Blackcap Tchagra

SPECIMENS. 2 ♂♂, Feb. 1968, Jul. 1966. 3 ♀♀, Feb., Oct., Nov. 1968. — *T. m. minuta* (Sierra Leone to Ethiopia, south to Kenya and western Tanzania).

IMPERMANENT COLOURS. Legs grey. Iris dull pink. Bill black.

STOMACH CONTENTS. Grasshoppers and caterpillars.

ANNUAL CYCLE. No evidence of breeding. The February female had an ovary of 10 mm, and was in a late stage of wing-moult (8th primary growing). The February male was in fresh plumage, the July and October birds in worn plumage, and the November bird in very worn condition.

HABITAT AND STATUS. This is a new record for Liberia. It is found in bushes, with a preference for moist areas where the grass is tall, or the damp edges of forest.

Tchagra australis — Brown-headed Tchagra

SPECIMENS. 1 ♂, Oct. 1968. 1 imm. ♂, Jan. 1968. 1 ♀, Apr. 1969. 1 imm. ♀, Jan. 1968. — *T. a. ussheri* (Sierra Leone to south-west Nigeria).

IMPERMANENT COLOURS. Legs blue-grey. Irish dark brown. Bill black.

STOMACH CONTENTS. Insects.

ANNUAL CYCLE. The October male was in fresh plumage with slightly enlarged gonads (5 mm). The April female (no gonad data) was moulting its rectrices.

HABITAT. Scrub and bush of the savannas bordering Guinea; also wooded plantations and gardens as well as clearings and edges in lowland and montane forests up to the ridge of Mount Nimba.

Laniarius leucorhynchus — Sooty Boubou

SPECIMENS. 5 ♂♂, Mar. (2), Aug. 1968, Nov. 1967 (2). 2 ♀♀, Mar. 1968, Nov. 1967. 1 imm ♀, Jul. 1968.

IMPERMANENT COLOURS. Legs black. Iris brown. Bill black; white tinged pink in imm. ♀.

STOMACH CONTENTS. Insects, including green and bronze metallic beetles, and many caterpillars.

ANNUAL CYCLE. The November males had moderately enlarged gonads (6.5, 8.5 mm; *cf.* 4–5 mm in March and August). Both females had enlarged ovaries (10.0 mm, Mar.; 11.5 mm, Nov.) and were probably in or approaching breeding condition. The March female was completing wing-moult, the 8th and 9th primaries growing, and a March male was renewing its inner primaries.

HABITAT. Heard duetting from the lower parts of primary and secondary forests as well as in thickets and clearings, up to an altitude of about 900 m.

Malaconotus cruentus — Fiery-breasted Bush-shrike

SPECIMENS. 7 ♂♂, Jan. 1971, Mar. 1968, Apr. 1969, Sept. 1975, Oct. 1968, Nov. 1967, Dec. 1972. 1 juv. ♂, Nov. 1967. 4 ♀♀, Mar. 1975, Jul. 1967, 1968, Nov. 1968.

IMPERMANENT COLOURS. Legs blue-grey. Iris pale blue-grey, brown in juv. Bill black.

STOMACH CONTENTS. Insects, including beetles, grasshoppers and caterpillars. Also a few small seeds.

ANNUAL CYCLE. The November female was in breeding condition with an enlarged ovary and yolks to 15 mm. A July female, with ovary 13 mm and ova to 1 mm, was probably approaching breeding condition. The juvenile, collected on 29 November, still retained much down on its head and underparts, and was obviously still very dependent on its parents for food. Male gonad data was incomplete; testes 2.0, 4.0 and 6.5 mm in the March, October and November males respectively. The April and October birds were in wing-moult.

HABITAT. Dense parts of lowland primary and secondary forests.

Malaconotus multicolor — Many-coloured Bush-shrike

SPECIMENS. 21 ♂♂, Feb. 1968, Mar. 1968 (2), 1970 (2), Apr. 1968, 1969, May 1973, Jun. 1971, 1973, Jul. 1967, 1968, 1970, Aug. 1971, Sept. 1969, Oct. 1967 (2), 1968, 1973, Nov. 1967 (2). 2 imm. ♂♂, Jan., Apr. 1968. 3 ♀♀, Mar. (2), Apr. 1968. 1 imm. ♀, Jul. 1970. 1 o, Jul. 1967. — *M. m. multicolor* (Sierra Leone to Mount Cameroon); the males include red, orange and black phase birds.

IMPERMANENT COLOURS. Legs blue-grey. Iris bright violet or purple. Bill black.

STOMACH CONTENTS. Insects, including beetles and caterpillars.

ANNUAL CYCLE. The females' ovaries were small (8–10 mm). Male gonad data was available for only half the specimens. One October male was probably in breeding condition (testes 13 mm), and males with moderately enlarged testes were recorded in February (10 mm) and November (9.5 mm). Gonads of five males, March–July measured 2–8 mm. Three birds in March, and one each in April and May were in wing-moult, and a July bird was completing (outer primaries growing). Most of the June–October birds were in fresh plumage.

HABITAT. Frequent calls given by this species revealed that it was not restricted to primary and secondary forests. Throughout the year it was heard in the forest-grassland mosaics of Grassfield and Yekepa, where it also visited gardens. On Mount Nimba it occurs up to about 750 m.

Malaconotus lagdeni — Lagden's Bush-shrike

SPECIMENS. 1 ♂, Dec. 1967. 1 o, Oct. 1967. — *M. l. lagdeni* (Liberia east to Ghana).

IMPERMANENT COLOURS. Legs blue. Iris grey. Bill black.

STOMACH CONTENTS. Insects.

ANNUAL CYCLE. The December male (testes 7.5 mm) was commencing wing-moult (inner primaries growing). The October bird was in very worn plumage.

DISTRIBUTION. This is a new record for Liberia. The Nimba specimens extend the species' range some 800 km west from Ghana where it is only known from the type specimen, which was collected in lowland forest at Kumasi. The Nimba birds agree with the type. Another subspecies, *centralis*, occurs in the montane forests of Zaire, from Ruwenzori in the north to Itombwe, north-west of Lake Tanganyika, in the south.

HABITAT. In the central African mountains the species occurs in montane forest, where it keeps to the tree tops; in Zaire it is recorded at 2000–2400 m. The altitude of the Nimba specimens was not recorded, but the West African race, *lagdeni*, must occur at much lower altitudes than *centralis*.

Lanius collaris — Fiscal Shrike

SPECIMENS. 4 ♂♂, Jan. 1968, 1969, Feb. 1968, Oct. 1967. 2 ♀♀, Jan., Mar. 1968. — *L. c. smithii* (Sierra Leone to western Tanzania).

IMPERMANENT COLOURS. Legs black. Iris brown. Bill black.

STOMACH CONTENTS. Grasshoppers and beetles.

ANNUAL CYCLE. The only evidence for breeding was a March female which was noted as having laid. January to February males had testes 3–5 mm and the January female an ovary of 5 mm. The October male was completing a wing-moult (8th primary growing). The January to March birds were in fresh plumage.

HABITAT. A common bird at Nimba found in savannas, grasslands and all kinds of well-cleared ground with scattered bushes and trees, also gardens, roadsides and around houses. The species has increased considerably since the opening up of the Nimba area.

Lanius senator — Woodchat Shrike

SPECIMENS. 1 imm. ♂, Jan. 1968; moulting into adult plumage. 1 o, Jan. 1968; in worn condition. — *L. s. senator* (breeds Europe and north-west Africa).

IMPERMANENT COLOURS. Legs black. Iris brown. Bill brownish, pale grey below.

STOMACH CONTENTS. Grasshoppers.

DISTRIBUTION. A common Palaearctic winter visitor to West Africa. Rand (1951) gives one other record of this species for Liberia.

Family Turdidae

Saxicola rubetra — Whinchat

SPECIMENS. 7 ♂♂, Jan., Mar. (2), Nov. 1968, Dec. 1967 (2), 1968. 2 ♀♀, Jan. 1970, Dec. 1965.

IMPERMANENT COLOURS. Legs black. Iris brown. Bill black.

STOMACH CONTENTS. Insects, including small beetles and black ants.

ANNUAL CYCLE. The March males (testes 1 mm) were in fresh spring plumage. The other birds were in winter plumage.

HABITAT. Since 1966 this Palaearctic species has been observed wintering in the same localities each year. It occupies bushes in the savanna and the golf course at Yekepa, and is also found in similar habitats on the Guinean side of the border.

Saxicola torquata — Stonechat

This species was observed at Nimba by Forbes-Watson in 1967 or 1968. In West Africa it is a bird of montane grassland and has since 1963 been observed on each visit made by Curry-Lindahl to the montane savannas of Guinean Nimba. The race there is *S. t. nebularum*, which is found only on Mount Nimba and the mountains of Sierra Leone at altitudes of 1200–1600 m.

Myrmecocichla nigra — Sooty Chat

A male was observed by Curry-Lindahl on a termite hill in the savanna along the Liberian–Guinean border at the foot of Mount Nimba on 9 January 1982. This would appear to be the first Liberian record of this species. In West Africa it is irregularly distributed in savanna, occurring in Guinea, Nigeria, Cameroon, the Central African Republic, Gabon and Zaire.

Monticola saxatilis — Rock Thrush

SPECIMEN. 1 ♂, Jan. 1968; moulting into spring plumage.

IMPERMANENT COLOURS. Legs brownish. Iris brown. Bill grey, paler below.

STOMACH CONTENTS. Black flying ants.

DISTRIBUTION. A wintering Palaearctic migrant to Africa. This is the first record for Liberia. It is recorded from Senegal to northern Nigeria and east to eastern Africa.

HABITAT AND HABITS. First observed by Curry-Lindahl in September–October 1963 among the exposed rocks in the mine area of Mount Nimba. Seen again there in 1966, and since then it has been present in this area every European winter. It would appear to be territorial in its winter quarters.

Monticola solitaria — Blue Rock-Thrush

This species was observed by Curry-Lindahl in October 1963, in 1965, and on each subsequent visit made by him to Nimba during October–April. In 1967 or 1968 it was also seen by Forbes-Watson. The Blue Rock Thrush is a Palaearctic migrant wintering in northern Africa, in the massifs of the Sahara, in Senegal and at least since the 1960s in Liberia. Where the forest-clad Nimba ridges have been dynamited, the exposed fragmented rocky surfaces have been favoured by this species. There are few records of this thrush south of the Sahara, but recently it has been recorded from Gambia (McGregor & Thomson, 1965) and Nigeria (Elgood, 1982). Field (1973) recorded several birds in early December 1965, and thought that the species may regularly winter in Sierra Leone, in suitable locations above 1550 m. It has also been recorded in Mali, Ghana and Chad.

Erythropygia leucosticta — Forest Scrub-Robin

SPECIMENS. 11 ♂♂, Jan., Apr. (4), Jun. 1968, Aug. 1967, 1968, Sept. 1968, Oct. 1968, 1970. 7 ♀♀, Jan. 1968, Feb. 1971, Jul. 1967, Aug. 1967, 1968, Sept., Oct. 1968. — *E. l. leucosticta* (Sierra Leone to Ghana).

IMPERMANENT COLOURS. Legs flesh-pink. Iris brown. Bill black.

STOMACH CONTENTS. Insects, including black ants and beetles; several small millipedes; and the remains of a small amphibian in one bird.

ANNUAL CYCLE. An August female had an enlarged ovary with a yolk of 10 mm, and the September female had an ovary of 12 mm. An August male had testes of 7 mm, *cf.* 2–5 mm in January–June males. Two April birds were in an early stage of wing-moult and another was renewing its tail feathers.

HABITAT. Forest and bushy forest undergrowth.

Alethe diademata — Fire-crest Alethe

SPECIMENS. 13 ♂♂, Jan. 1968, Feb. 1971, Jun. (4), Jul. 1967 (2), Aug. 1965, 1967 (2), Sept. 1967, Nov. 1970. 6 juv. ♂♂, Jan. 1970, Aug. (3), Sept., Oct. 1968. 7 ♀♀, Apr. 1968, Jun., Jul. (3), Aug., Sept. 1967. 2 juv. ♀♀, Sept. 1968, Nov. 1970. 2 imm. ♀♀, Mar., Oct. 1968.— *A. d. diademata* (Guinea Bissau to Togo).

IMPERMANENT COLOURS. Legs blue-grey. Iris chestnut-brown. Bill black.

STOMACH CONTENTS. Insects, including black ants; also the remains of a small amphibian in one bird.

ANNUAL CYCLE. Single July, August and September females had enlarged ovaries (9–10 mm) and were probably in breeding condition. Three juveniles (28 Aug.) were heavily spotted with brown and had only recently fledged; October and November juveniles were similar. Males had enlarged gonads for June (6.5–7.5 mm), July (5–7 mm), August (6,8 mm) and September (8 mm), *cf.* January male (1 mm). Single

June, July and August birds were in early stages of wing-moult, inner 2–3 primaries growing, and the November male with primaries 4–6 growing.

HABITAT. Lower parts of the vegetation in primary and secondary lowland forests as well as the forest-grassland mosaic.

Alethe poliocephala — Brown-chested Alethe

SPECIMENS. 9 ♂♂, Jan. 1969, May, Jun. 1967 (5), Nov. 1964 (2). 7 juv. ♂♂, Jul. 1967, 1968 (2), Aug. 1967, Sept. 1967, 1968, Oct. 1968. 7 ♀♀, Jan. 1969 (2), Jun. 1967 (5). 6 juv. ♀♀, Jan. 1971, Jun. 1970, Sept. 1965, 1968, Nov., Dec. 1968. — *A. p. castanonota* (Sierra Leone to Ghana).

IMPERMANENT COLOURS. Legs pinkish-flesh. Iris chestnut-brown. Bill black.

STOMACH CONTENTS. Insects, including beetles and ants.

ANNUAL CYCLE. Gonad data incomplete, no data available for the January or November birds. Two June females had moderately enlarged ovaries of 8.5 and 9.5 mm, and were probably in breeding condition. The males' gonads were enlarged for May (9 mm) and three June birds (8.0–8.5 mm). The majority of the brown-spotted juveniles were collected June–September, with singles also for October, November, December and even a very young January bird not long out of the nest, which may indicate an extended breeding season where more than one brood may occasionally be raised. Both November birds were in advanced stages of wing-moult (primaries 8–10 growing; primaries finished and secondaries 5 and 6 growing).

HABITAT AND HABITS. Lower levels of primary and secondary forests up to about 900 m, but also in forest-grassland mosaics, eg. Grassfield and Yekepa. The species feeds mostly on the ground or on tree trunks, and especially where there are ant columns.

Sheppardia cyornithopsis — Akalat

SPECIMENS. 9 ♂♂, May, Jun. (4), Jul., Aug., Sept. 1967, Dec. 1968. 1 imm. ♂, Jul. 1968. 3 juv. ♂♂, Jun. 1967 (2), Oct. 1968. 3 ♀♀, Jan. 1969, Jun. 1967 (2). 1 juv. ♀, Nov. 1965. 2 o, Jun., Sept. 1967. — *S. c. houghtoni* (Sierra Leone to Liberia).

IMPERMANENT COLOURS. Legs grey. Iris brown. Bill black, paler at the base.

STOMACH CONTENTS. Insects, including small beetles and ants.

ANNUAL CYCLE. Gonads were enlarged in one June male (6 mm) and in the July, August and September males (6.0, 8.0 & 7.5 mm respectively). Ovaries of the two June females were small (4.0–4.5 mm). The October juvenile was the youngest and had apparently recently fledged. A June female was completing wing-moult, the outer two primaries old, and the December bird was just beginning to renew inner primaries.

HABITAT. Lower vegetation of primary lowland forest. Also recorded in a clearing and frequently in the forest-grassland mosaic at Grassfield. Occasionally in montane forests up to about 900 m.

Stiphrornis erythrothorax — Forest Robin

SPECIMENS. 17 ♂♂, Jan. 1966, 1968, Feb. 1969 (2), Jun. 1966, 1969 (9), Aug. (2), Sept. 1967. 5 imm. ♂♂, Jan., Feb., Aug. 1968 (2), Nov. 1967. 3 juv. ♂♂, Aug. 1967 (2), 1968. 7 ♀♀, Apr. 1965, Jun. 1966, 1967 (5). 1 imm. ♀, Feb. 1968. — *S. e. erythrothorax* (Sierra Leone to Nigeria).

IMPERMANENT COLOURS. Legs greyish flesh. Iris brown. Bill black.

STOMACH CONTENTS. Insects.

ANNUAL CYCLE. Gonad data was incomplete for the January–April birds. Three June females had enlarged gonads (7.0–7.5 mm) and the August male (5.5 mm), *cf.* 2 January males with testes 1.5–2.0 mm. A June female had an enlarged ovary with ova 5 mm, and two other June birds had ovaries 6–9 mm. The youngest juvenile (22 Aug.) was brown and speckled, with wings and tail not fully grown, and the other two (24 Aug.) appeared to be not long out of the nest.

HABITAT. A rather common species at Nimba in primary and secondary lowland and montane forest up to about 900 m; also in the forest-grassland mosaics.

Cossypha cyanocampter — Blue-shouldered Robin-chat

SPECIMENS. 3 ♂♂, Jul., Aug. 1968, Oct. 1967. 1 ♀, Sept. 1968. 1 o, no date. — *C. c. cyanocampter* (Sierra Leone to Cameroon and Gabon).

IMPERMANENT COLOURS. Legs brown. Iris brown. Bill black.

STOMACH CONTENTS. Insects, including small beetles.

ANNUAL CYCLE. The August male had gonads of 8 mm, and the October male 5 mm. The September female had an enlarged ovary of 8 mm with ova to 5 mm and was probably approaching breeding condition. All birds were in fresh plumage.

HABITAT. Seen and heard in thickets or dense undergrowth in primary and secondary lowland and montane forests up to about 900 m.

Cossypha polioptera White-browed Robin-chat

SPECIMENS. 6 ♂♂, Jan. (4), Oct., Nov. 1968. 4 ♀♀, Jan. (4) 1968. 2 o, Jan., Nov. 1968. — *C. p. nigriceps* (Sierra Leone to Cameroon).

IMPERMANENT COLOURS. Legs dusky-flesh. Iris brown. Bill black.

STOMACH CONTENTS. Insects, including beetles and ants.

ANNUAL CYCLE. Two January males had testes of 6 and 7 mm, *cf.* 1–2 mm in October–November males. Females ovaries measured 4–8 mm. Most of the birds were in fresh plumage, none in wing-moult.

HABITAT AND STATUS. This robin-chat was observed in the Iti valley in 1963, 1964 and several subsequent years. It frequented small open patches in the forest on both sides of the stream. This is a new record for Liberia.

Cossypha niveicapilla Snowy-crowned Robin-chat

SPECIMEN. 1 ♂, Mar. 1968; gonads 3 mm, fresh plumage. — *C. n. niveicapilla* (Senegal to Sudan and south-west Ethiopia).

IMPERMANENT COLOURS. Legs dark brown. Iris brown. Bill black.

STOMACH CONTENTS. Insects.

HABITAT. Observed in 1964 and 1966 in secondary forests, but in later years also noted in clearings, forest edges, banana plantations and smaller areas surrounded by forest in both lowland and highland areas up to about 700 m.

Neocossyphus finschi Finsch's Rufous Ant-Thrush

SPECIMENS. 9 ♂♂, Feb. 1968, Mar. 1974, Jun. 1967 (5), Aug. 1967, 1970. 5 ♀♀, Feb. 1968, Jun. (2), Aug., Sept. 1967.

IMPERMANENT COLOURS. Legs pale flesh or brownish. Iris brown. Bill black, paler brown below.

STOMACH CONTENTS. Insects, including beetles and ants.

ANNUAL CYCLE. An August male had testes of 11 mm, *cf.* 1 mm in the February male and 1–3 mm in five June males. The September females had an enlarged ovary of 8.5 mm, *cf.* 3 mm in the February female and 4.5–5.0 mm in the two June females. The March male was very worn, and the remaining birds were in fresh plumage.

HABITAT AND STATUS. A lowland forest species which is found from Sierra Leone to Ghana and southern Nigeria. It is replaced by *N. fraseri* in central West Africa with which it forms a superspecies (PRC).

Neocossyphus poensis White-tailed Ant-Thrush

SPECIMENS. 10 ♂♂, Apr. 1968, Jun., Jul. (3), Aug. (3), Sept. (2) 1967. 9 ♀♀, May, Jun. (2), Jul. 1967 (3), Aug. 1965, 1967, Nov. 1964. — *N. p. poensis* (Sierra Leone to Gabon).

IMPERMANENT COLOURS. Legs pale pink. Iris brown. Bill blackish.

STOMACH CONTENTS. Black ants.

ANNUAL CYCLE. April and June males had enlarged gonads (11 mm), *cf.* 7.0–8.5 mm in July males and 2.0–7.5 mm in August–September males. A May female had an enlarged ovary (11 mm) and two very large yolks, and was evidently breeding. The females' ovaries for June measured 7.5–9.0 mm, for July 6–10 mm, and for one August bird 8 mm. One June, two July and three August birds were in the early to middle stages of wing-moult.

HABITAT. A wide variety of habitats within lowland primary and secondary forests, including dense undergrowth, more open vegetation in clearings, forest edges and forest-grassland mosaics.

Luscinia megarhynchos Nightingale

SPECIMENS. 4 ♂♂, Feb. 1968 (2), Nov. 1967, 1970. 3 ♀♀, Feb., Mar. 1968, Nov. 1967. — *L. m. megarhynchos* (winter visitor from Palaearctic).

IMPERMANENT COLOURS. Legs brown. Iris brown. Bill dark blackish-brown. Gape yellow.

ANNUAL CYCLE. The heaviest bird was a female collected on 20 March and noted as being exceedingly fat. Its pre-migration weight of 33.5 g was almost double that of an early November female weighing only 17 g. The birds were in fresh plumage.

HABITAT AND STATUS. This species was first observed in 1965 in Grassfield in a hedge close to a house (KC-L). Since then it has been recorded a number of times both in Grassfield and Yekepa. At Nimba the species definitely prefers cultivated habitats within the forest-grassland mosaic. Gardens and even parking areas surrounded by hedges are favourite sites, from where the song is often heard. At Yekepa, on 8–14 January 1982, a Nightingale was heard singing vigorously every morning in a hedge (1.3 m high) close to Curry-Lindahl's room and adjacent to a huge, paved parking area. The bird invariably kept to the hedge in which it moved between song phrases. It began singing regularly at 07.30 and continued until about 09.30, but was always silent at night, as are most Nightingales in Africa.

The Nightingale generally appears at Nimba in late October or the first half of November, and remains until the second half of March (latest observed, 16 March; specimen, 20 March). This is a new record for Liberia.

Turdus pelios — West African Thrush

SPECIMENS. 3 ♂♂, Jan. 1972, Feb. 1968 (2). 2 ♀♀, Jan. 1972, Nov. 1967. 1 imm. ♀, Jun. 1966. — *T. p. chiguancoides* (Senegal to northern Ghana).

IMPERMANENT COLOURS. Legs pale brown. Iris brown. Bill dull yellowish-brown.

STOMACH CONTENTS. Fruit pulp and a few seeds.

ANNUAL CYCLE. No evidence of breeding (testes 1.5 mm; ovary 2.5 mm); no gonad data for the January birds. The specimens were mainly in fresh plumage; no wing-moult.

HABITAT. It inhabits savanna and forest and is partial to cultivation and human habitation, including gardens where it is now common. At Nimba it is found at all elevations between 450 and 1000 m and is apparently sedentary.

Turdus princei — Grey Ground-Thrush

SPECIMENS. 2 ♂♂, Jun. 1967 (2). 1 imm. ♂, Aug. 1967. 3 ♀♀, Jan. 1969, Jun. 1968, Aug. 1968. 1 o, Nov. 1964. — *T. p. princei* (Liberia to Nigeria).

IMPERMANENT COLOURS. Legs dull pinkish-flesh, tinged grey. Iris dark brown. Bill black, pinkish below.

STOMACH CONTENTS. Insects, including beetle larvae and grasshoppers.

ANNUAL CYCLE. A June female had an enlarged ovary (10 mm with ova to 8.5 mm) and an August female had recently laid two eggs. No specimens in wing-moult.

STATUS. A rare and shy species and the nominate form has only been recorded from a few localities in the lowland rain forests in West Africa.

Family Timaliidae

Trichastoma fulvescens Brown Thrush Babbler

SPECIMENS. 9 ♂♂, Jun., Jul. (3) 1967, Aug. 1967, 1968, Sept. 1967, 1968, Oct. 1968. 2 juv. ♂♂, Sept. (2) 1968. 8 ♀♀, Mar. 1969, Jun. 1966, 1967, Jul., Aug. 1967, Sept. 1968, Oct. 1968, 1970. — *T. f. gularis* (Sierra Leone to Ghana).

IMPERMANENT COLOURS. Legs dusky-grey. Iris clear brown. Bill black, blue-horn below.

STOMACH CONTENTS. Insects and a few hard brown seeds.

ANNUAL CYCLE. A June female had an enlarged ovary (10 mm), and the October female was noted as having recently laid. The males' gonads were enlarged in June (6 mm), July (7–9 mm), August (6–9 mm), one September bird (7 mm), and October (9 mm). Single August and October birds were in early stages of wing-moult, and a September male was in an advanced stage (7th primary growing).

HABITAT. Forests and shrub-forest mosaic.

Trichastoma rufipennis — Pale-breasted Thrush Babbler

SPECIMENS. 12 ♂♂, Jun. (5), Jul. (4), Aug. 1967, Sept. 1967, 1968. 15 ♀♀, Jan. 1966 (2), May 1968, Jun. (7), Jul. (3), Aug. (2) 1967. — *T. r. extrema* (Sierra Leone to Ghana).

IMPERMANENT COLOURS. Legs blue-grey to dusky-grey. Iris brown. Bill black, pale horn below.

STOMACH CONTENTS. Insects, including beetles, ants and caterpillars; also a small gastropod.

ANNUAL CYCLE. Two June females had enlarged ovaries and one had laid. An August female was also noted as having laid. Gonads were enlarged in four June males (7.5–10.0 mm), two July (8, 9 mm), August (9 mm) and two September males (9, 10 mm). A January female was just beginning a wing-moult, and the May to August birds were in fresh plumage.

HABITAT AND STATUS. Thickets in secondary forest along roads and paths, dense bush in clearings in both lowland and montane forests up to about 800 m. Also forest-grassland mosaics, as at Grassfield and Yekepa. This is a new record for Liberia.

Trichastoma cleaveri Black-cap Thrush Babbler

SPECIMENS. 15 ♂♂, May 1968, Jun. 1967 (2), Jul. 1967 (2), 1968 (2), Aug. 1967, Sept. 1967 (2), 1968, Nov. 1968 (2), 1970, Dec. 1968. 1 juv. ♂, Sept. 1968. 6 ♀♀, Apr. 1968, Jun., Jul. 1967, Aug. 1968, Sept. 1967, Oct. 1970. — *T. c. johnsoni* (Sierra Leone to Liberia).

IMPERMANENT COLOURS. Legs pinkish-flesh. Iris chestnut-brown. Bill black, whitish below.

STOMACH CONTENTS. Insects.

ANNUAL CYCLE. The juvenile (8 Sept.) had barely left the nest. The April, July and August females had moderately enlarged ovaries (8–10 mm). The males' gonads were generally small: May–June 3.0–4.5 mm, July–August 2–5 mm, September 4.5–6.0 mm, November 1.5–7.0 mm and December 3 mm. The April, May, and two June birds were in early to middle stages of wing-moult, and a July bird was completing (10th primary growing). The remainder were mostly in fresh plumage.

HABITAT. Forest, shrub and forest-shrub mosaic.

Trichastoma rufescens Rufous-winged Thrush Babbler

SPECIMENS. 10 ♂♂, Jan., Apr. 1968 (2), Jun. 1966, 1968 (2), Jul., Aug. 1967 (2), Sept. 1968. 8 ♀♀, Feb. 1969, Apr., May 1968, Jun. 1967 (2), 1968, Jul., Nov. 1968.

IMPERMANENT COLOURS. Legs pale whitish-flesh. Iris clear tawny-brown. Bill black, paler horn below.

STOMACH CONTENTS. Insects, including beetles and grasshoppers. Bones of a small amphibian also recorded.

ANNUAL CYCLE. One April male and all July–September males had enlarged gonads (5–8 mm). The females' ovaries were enlarged in April (12 mm) and November (10 mm, ova 1.5 mm). Two April and a May bird were in early to middle stages of wing-moult and two June birds were completing (outer primaries growing).

DISTRIBUTION. The species is known from only a half a dozen localities in West Africa and is a rare bird in collections. In Sierra Leone it has been collected at York Pass and Bintumane Peak (535–925 m), and in Ghana at Mampong and in Fantee. It was originally found at some unspecified locality in Liberia.

HABITAT. Forest undergrowth and dense high bush.

Trichastoma puveli Puvel's Thrush Babbler

SPECIMENS. 1 ♂, Aug. 1967. 2 ♀♀, Feb., Aug. 1968. — *T. p. puveli* (Guinea Bissau to Liberia).

IMPERMANENT COLOURS. Legs pale flesh. Iris brown. Bill black, paler horn below.

STOMACH CONTENTS. Insects.

ANNUAL CYCLE. Gonads were enlarged in the August birds (♂ 6.5 mm, ♀ 8.0 mm). All were in fresh plumage.

HABITAT AND STATUS. Forest. This is a new record for Liberia.

Phyllanthus atripennis Capuchin Babbler

SPECIMENS. 8 ♂♂, Apr. 1968, Jul. 1967, Aug. (4), Nov. 1968, Dec. 1967. 7 ♀♀, Jun. 1968, Jul. 1967, Aug. 1965, Nov. 1967, 1968, 1969, Dec. 1967. — *P. a. atripennis* (Guinea Bissau to Liberia).

IMPERMANENT COLOURS. Legs greenish grey. Iris brown. Bill creamy or yellowish, tinged green.

STOMACH CONTENTS. Insects, including ants, beetles, cockroaches and grasshoppers; also a small amphibian.

ANNUAL CYCLE. Four July–August males had testes of 8–10 mm, *cf.* 2 mm in April, 6 mm in November, and 3.5 mm in December. The June female had an ovary of 10 mm, *cf.* a maximum of 7 mm in other months. The April male was in an advanced stage of wing-moult (8th primary growing). November–December birds were in worn condition and the remainder were in fresh plumage.

HABITAT AND HABITS. Dense secondary forest or forest edge along roads and close to clearings, from where their chattering calls may often be heard. Although the species is social, forming groups of 5–7 birds, they are hardly seen except when travelling with mixed bird parties.

Family Picathartidae

Picathartes gymnocephalus Bare-headed Rockfowl

SPECIMENS. 2 ♀♀, May 1968, Nov. 1967.

IMPERMANENT COLOURS. Legs pale blue-grey. Iris brown. Bill black. Bare skin of head bright yellow. Ears black.

STOMACH CONTENTS. Insects.

ANNUAL CYCLE. The May female was noted as having recently laid and was in worn plumage. The November female was in fresh plumage, with an ovary of 12.5 mm. In the Ivory Coast sector of Mount Nimba eggs have been found in April (see below).

The Rockfowl (*Picathartes gymnocephalus*) was found nesting in a cave, situated on a steep slope in montane forest at about 1000 m — Mount Nimba, Liberia, March 1968. Photograph Alec Forbes-Watson.

HABITAT AND BREEDING. A nest, found by Forbes-Watson and Edward Yallah and visited by Curry-Lindahl, was located within a cave and attached to the upper part of the rock wall and the roof (see above). The cave was situated on a steep slope in the montane forest at about 1000 m. Another site with two nests in use was found by Edward Yallah in the lowland forest. Both nests were on the underside of a rock overhang. These nests were shown to Robert Wolton on 8 July 1978, when at least one of them contained eggs.

Brunel & Thiollay (1969) mention the presence of a small colony at the foot of Nimba in the Ivory Coast sector. They say that the local natives have always known of the colony's existence and capture the birds in specially made traps. Six nests were found in April 1968, of which two contained two incubated eggs each. The nests were sited under the overhang of porch-like recesses among moss-covered boulders in primary forest.

Family Sylviidae

Acrocephalus schoenobaenus   Sedge Warbler

This species was heard singing, somewhat hesitantly, from a cluster of aquatic vegetation in a small area of stagnant water at Yekepa on 3 March 1981 (KC-L). The bird was seen there again the following day. The Sedge Warbler was first recorded in swamp vegetation at Monrovia in December 1964 (Curry-Lindahl, 1981). It was found also at Buchanan in 1971 (AF-W, JK & SK). These are the first records of this species for Liberia.

Acrocephalus scirpaceus   Reed Warbler

SPECIMENS. 1 ♂, Feb. 1968. 2 ♀♀, Jan. 1970, Dec. 1968. — *A. s. scirpaceus* (breeds Europe and north-west Africa).

IMPERMANENT COLOURS. Legs dusky tinged greenish. Iris brown. Bill black, pinkish-horn below.

STOMACH CONTENTS. Insects.

ANNUAL CYCLE. The December female was in very worn condition and the January female was in fresh plumage. The male (10 Feb.) was in an advanced stage of wing-moult (outer primaries growing).

DISTRIBUTION. A common wintering Palaearctic visitor to tropical and southern Africa. Recorded near Monrovia in 1964 (Curry-Lindahl, 1981). This record and those from Nimba are the first ones of this species for Liberia. In West Africa the species has been found from Senegal to Nigeria and Cameroon.

Acrocephalus arundinaceus   Great Reed Warbler

SPECIMENS. 1 ♂, Feb. 1968. 2 ♀♀, Jan. 1970, Feb. 1968. — *A. a. arundinaceus* (breeds western Palaearctic).

IMPERMANENT COLOURS. Legs grey tinged green. Iris clear pale brown. Bill black, pinkish-horn below.

STOMACH CONTENTS. Insects, and some small amphibian bones in one bird's stomach.

ANNUAL CYCLE. The birds were in non-breeding condition and in fresh plumage.

HABITAT. This species seems to be an irregular visitor to Nimba during the European winter. It has been found there in rank high grass, such as *Pennisetum* or *Papyrus*, standing either on dry ground or close to water.

Melocichla mentalis   Moustached Grass Warbler

SPECIMEN. 1 ♂, Jun. 1968; gonads enlarged (9 mm), worn tail. — *M. m. mentalis* (Senegal to Zaire).

IMPERMANENT COLOURS. Legs dull whitish-brown. Iris pale creamy. Bill black, whitish below.

STOMACH CONTENTS. Insects.

HABITAT. Dense low cover or rank herbage.

Hippolais icterina   Icterine Warbler

This species was observed at Nimba on 10 March 1971 (AF-W, JK & SK). This is the first record for Liberia. The Icterine Warbler is a Palaearctic migrant to tropical and southern Africa. The main wintering area seems to be Zambia, Zimbabwe, Botswana and South West Africa, but the species migrates on a broad front from the Ivory Coast in the west to Ethiopia in the east.

Hippolais polyglotta   Melodious Warbler

SPECIMENS. 2 ♂♂, Jan., Dec. 1968. 2 ♀♀, Jan. 1966, 1968. 1 o, Jan. 1968.

IMPERMANENT COLOURS. Legs olive-grey. Iris brown. Bill brown, pinkish-horn below.

STOMACH CONTENTS. Insects.

ANNUAL CYCLE. The birds had completed their moult and were in fresh plumage.

DISTRIBUTION. A common wintering Palaearctic migrant to West Africa. These are the first records of this species for Liberia. In West Africa it is widespread in savannas north of the rain forest from Senegal to Cameroon.

FIELD NOTES. This species has been observed in the forest-grassland mosaics of Grassfield and Yekepa. Here it kept to the outskirts of isolated forest patches and was present for six consecutive days in a garden. Several times in February–March it was heard singing. The latest observation, prior to departure, was on 16 March.

Sylvia borin   Garden Warbler

SPECIMENS. 6 ♂♂, Jan. 1968, Oct. 1967 (2), Nov. 1964, 1967 (2). 1 ♀, Feb. 1966. 2 o, Jan. 1968 (2). — *S. b. borin* (breeds western Palaearctic).

IMPERMANENT COLOURS. Legs grey. Iris brown. Bill black, paler grey below.

STOMACH CONTENTS. Insects and fruit pulp.

ANNUAL CYCLE. October and November birds showed some wear to their plumage and two January birds were in very worn condition. Single January and February birds were in advanced stages of wing-moult.

FIELD NOTES. Found along forest edges, in bushes and secondary growth, the forest-grassland mosaic at Grassfield and Yekepa, and sometimes gardens. The latest observation, prior to spring migration, was on 8 April.

Sylvia atricapilla   Blackcap

SPECIMENS. 3 ♂♂, Jan. 1968 (3). 1 imm. ♂, Nov. 1964. 4 ♀♀, Jan. 1968 (3), Nov. 1964. — *S. a. atricapilla* (breeds western Palaearctic).

IMPERMANENT COLOURS. Legs dusky grey. Iris brown. Bill black.

STOMACH CONTENTS. Insects and fruit pulp.

ANNUAL CYCLE. A January male was in worn condition and the remainder were in fresh plumage.

STATUS AND HABITAT. The species was first observed at Nimba in 1964 and on later occasions by Curry-Lindahl. This is a new record for Liberia. Birds have been seen or collected in the past near the Nimba peak on the Ivory Coast side (Brunel & Thiollay, 1969). In the Nimba area Blackcaps occupy a wide range of habitats, including lowland and montane secondary forests, clearings and isolated stands of relic primary forest as well as forest-grassland mosaics. On Mount Nimba they ascend up to the ridge forests at 1000–1200 m. The latest observation, prior to spring migration, was on 13 April.

Phylloscopus trochilus　　　Willow Warbler

SPECIMENS. 6 ♂♂, Jan. 1966, 1968 (2), Feb. 1966, 1968, Oct. 1968. 3 ♀♀, Feb. 1966 (3). 1 o, Jan. 1968. — *P. t. trochilus* (breeds western Europe), except for one *P. t. acredula* (breeds Scandinavia to western Siberia).

IMPERMANENT COLOURS. Legs dusky-yellow. Iris brown. Bill brown, yellow-horn below.

STOMACH CONTENTS. Insects, including small caterpillars.

ANNUAL CYCLE. Of the nine specimens assigned to *P. t. trochilus* the October bird was in worn condition, seven birds (25 Jan.–1 Feb.) were in advanced stages of wing-moult (primaries 7–10 growing), and one had completed its moult (11 Feb.). The single bird assigned to *P. t. acredula* (♂, 27 Jan.) was at a less advanced stage of moult, with the 5th primary growing.

HABITAT. Montane secondary forest and, especially, the *Parinari* ridge forest but occasionally found in the forest-grassland mosaic.

Phylloscopus sibilatrix　　　Wood Warbler

SPECIMENS. 1 ♂, Dec. 1968. 2 ♀♀, Feb., Mar. 1968.

IMPERMANENT COLOURS. Legs dusky-yellow. Iris brown. Bill black, yellow-horn below.

STOMACH CONTENTS. Insects.

ANNUAL CYCLE. The December male was in worn plumage, and the February and March birds were in advanced stages of wing-moult (9th and 10th primaries growing).

STATUS AND HABITAT. A Palaearctic winter visitor, widely recorded in West Africa. The species was first recorded at Nimba in 1963 and 1965, and since then regularly during the European winter (KC-L). These are the first records for Liberia. In the Nimba area it is found in primary and secondary lowland forests, where it is a canopy dweller, but also along forest edge and in clearings. It is occasionally found in the *Parinari* ridge forest. The latest observation, prior to spring migration, was on 2 April.

Cisticola erythrops　　　Red-faced Cisticola

SPECIMENS. 8 ♂♂, Feb. (3), May 1968, Jun. 1966, Jul. 1968, Oct. 1967, 1969. 2 juv. ♂♂, Oct. 1967 (2). 4 ♀♀, Feb., Apr., Jul., Aug. 1968. — *C. e. erythrops* (widespread in West Africa).

IMPERMANENT COLOURS. Legs pale pinkish-flesh. Iris brown. Bill dark brown, pinkish-horn below.

STOMACH CONTENTS. Insects.

ANNUAL CYCLE. One juvenile of 18 October (with a half-grown tail) was evidently just out of the nest. The July female was noted as having laid, and the August female had an enlarged ovary (8 mm, ova 1 mm). The males' gonads were small in February (1 mm), and larger (3.0–3.5 mm) in May, July and October (not recorded in the June and one October ♂). Two February birds were in advanced stages of wing-moult (9th and 10th primaries growing). The May and June males had worn rectrices and the October birds were in very worn plumage.

HABITAT AND STATUS. Grass savanna and rank undergrowth. A new record for Liberia.

Cisticola cantans　　　Singing Cisticola

This species was heard and seen in February 1980 (KC-L) at the foot of Mount Nimba, in a cleared flat area where grasses and bush have been regenerating over several years. This would appear to be the first record of the species for Liberia. In West Africa it ranges in the savanna north of the forest from Senegal and Guinea Bissau to northern Cameroon.

Cisticola lateralis　　　Whistling Cisticola

SPECIMENS. 2 ♂♂, Jun., Nov. 1967. 5 ♀♀, Mar. 1974, Jun. 1967, Sept. 1965, Oct. 1964, Nov. 1967. — *C. l. lateralis* (Gambia to Cameroon and Ubangi).

IMPERMANENT COLOURS. Legs pinkish-brown. Iris brown. Bill black, pinkish below.

STOMACH CONTENTS. Insects, including grasshoppers.

ANNUAL CYCLE. Gonad data incomplete. The June female had an enlarged ovary (8.5 mm) and had recently laid. The March female was in the foxy non-breeding plumage. June birds were in fresh plumage and September–November birds were in worn condition.

HABITAT. At Nimba a wide range of elevations from the lowland up to the top of the highest ridge.

Cisticola natalensis　　　Croaking Cisticola

SPECIMENS. 2 ♂♂, Apr. 1968, Jul. 1966. 1 ♀, Apr. 1968. — *C. n. strangei* (Guinea Bissau to Gabon and Uganda).

IMPERMANENT COLOURS. Legs pinkish. Iris tawny. Bill black, whitish-horn below.

STOMACH CONTENTS. Insects, including beetles and grasshoppers.

ANNUAL CYCLE. The April female had an enlarged ovary (10 mm, ova 1 mm) and was in breeding condition. The April male had gonads of 5 mm; no data for the July male, which was in worn plumage.

HABITAT AND STATUS. This cisticola is found in grassland with bushes, clearings or the edge of cultivated land. These are the first records of this species for Liberia.

Cisticola brachyptera   Shortwing Cisticola

SPECIMENS. 8 ♂♂, Feb. 1968 (3), Jul. 1967, Sept. 1968, Oct. 1967, Nov. 1968 (2). 2 juv. ♂♂, Sept. 1967, 1968. 4 ♀♀, Feb. 1968, Jun. 1966, Sept., Nov. 1968. 1 imm. o, Nov. 1968. — *C. b. brachyptera* (Senegal to Gabon and Zaire).

IMPERMANENT COLOURS. Legs brownish-pink. Iris tawny. Bill black, paler horn below.

STOMACH CONTENTS. Insects.

ANNUAL CYCLE. Breeding in August and September is indicated by the two September juveniles and a September female with an enlarged ovary and yolks to 6 mm, cf. ovaries of 2 mm in February and 1.5 mm in November (no data for June). Gonads were moderately enlarged (4–5 mm) in the two February males, the July male, and one September male (cf. 2.0–2.5 mm in other ♂♂). February to September birds were in fresh plumage and November birds were worn.

HABITAT. The savanna found along the Liberian Guinea border at the foot of Nimba, and the forest-grassland mosaic at Grassfield and Yekepa.

Prinia subflava   Tawny-flanked Prinia

SPECIMENS. 8 ♂♂, Apr. (3), Jun. 1968, Jul. 1965, 1968, Sept., Oct. 1968. 3 juv. ♂♂, Jun. 1968, Oct. 1967, Nov. 1968. 2 ♀♀, Aug., Oct. 1968. — *P. s. melanorhyncha* (Sierra Leone to south-west Nigeria and Zaire).

IMPERMANENT COLOURS. Legs flesh-pink. Iris orange-brown. Bill black.

STOMACH CONTENTS. Insects.

ANNUAL CYCLE. Evidence for breeding during the period June to October is provided by the three juveniles. The August female had an enlarged ovary (8 mm) and the October female was laying (had recently laid, and ovary contained yolk to 3 mm). Males had moderately enlarged gonads in April (2.5–4.0 mm), June (3.5 mm), July (3 mm), September (3 mm) and October (4 mm). An April male was completing wing-moult (10th primary growing), and single April, June and July birds were in mid wing-moult (primaries 3–5 growing).

HABITAT. This species was common at Nimba in 1963–1966, even before the great upheaval. During the last decade it has greatly increased probably due to the alterations in the landscape. It occupies a wide range of habitats, from bushes and thickets on more or less open ground to edges and clearings in secondary forest, and may reach 1100 m.

Prinia leontica   Sierra Leone Prinia

SPECIMENS. 4 ♂♂, May 1968, Sept. 1967, Oct. 1968 (2). 1 ♀, Sept. 1967.

IMPERMANENT COLOURS. Legs pinkish flesh. Iris silvery-white. Bill black.

STOMACH CONTENTS. Insects, including small black beetles.

ANNUAL CYCLE. The September female had a moderately enlarged ovary (6.5 mm). The males' gonads were small (2–3 mm). The May male was completing wing-moult (10th primary growing).

DISTRIBUTION. This is a new record for Liberia. It has a restricted range in wooded highland areas from Sierra Leone to Ivory Coast.

Apalis nigriceps   Black-capped Apalis

SPECIMENS. 8 ♂♂, May 1970, Jul. 1967, Sept. 1967, 1968 (3), Nov. 1968 (2). 1 imm. ♂, Jul. 1967. 3 ♀♀, Apr. 1968, Jul. 1967, 1968. — *A. n. nigriceps* (Sierra Leone to Cameroon and the Central African Republic).

IMPERMANENT COLOURS. Legs bright pink. Iris brown. Bill black.

STOMACH CONTENTS. Insects, including caterpillars.

ANNUAL CYCLE. No evidence of breeding activity. The males' gonads were small in July (4 mm), September (3.5–4.5 mm) and November (3.5 mm). The ovaries of the April and one July female were small (4 mm), and that of the other July female slightly enlarged (6 mm). The April and May birds were both in wing-moult (7th and 6th primaries growing), and July and September birds were in fresh plumage.

HABITAT AND STATUS. Primary forest, and inhabits the foliage of old second-growth, also creepers and tree ferns. This is a new record for Liberia.

Apalis sharpii   Sharpe's Apalis

SPECIMENS. 14 ♂♂, Jun. (4), Jul. (5), Aug. (2) 1967, Sept., Oct. 1968, Nov. 1967. 4 imm. ♂♂, May 1968, Jun. 1967 (3). 2 juv. ♂♂, Aug. 1968 (2). 7 ♀♀, Apr. 1968, Jun. (2), Jul. 1967 (2), Aug. 1970, Oct. 1968. 1 imm. ♀, Jul. 1967. 1 juv. ♀, Jul. 1967.

IMPERMANENT COLOURS. Legs pinkish flesh. Iris chestnut brown. Bill black.

STOMACH CONTENTS. Insects, including small beetles, grasshoppers and caterpillars.

ANNUAL CYCLE. The three juveniles indicate that the species breeds around May–June. The April female, which had almost completed a wing-moult (outer primary growing), had a moderately enlarged ovary (7 mm), but the ovaries of four June–July females were relatively small (2–5 mm; no data for the Aug. ♀). Four males had enlarged gonads in June–July (5.0–5.5 mm), as had the September and November males (5.0, 5.5 mm), the others all being 1–3 mm. In addition to the April female, single August and October birds were in advanced stages of wing-moult (8th primaries growing). Many of the June–September birds were in fresh plumage.

PLUMAGE. The adult male has a dark sooty-grey throat and breast and a grey abdomen. The female (formerly known as *A. hardyi*), has a pale rufous throat, grey breast and whitish abdomen. The young bird, hitherto undescribed, is suffused with pale yellow on the throat and pale yellowish-green on the breast and belly. The immature male is similar in plumage to the adult female, but it has a buffy throat and the greyish underparts have a pale yellowish-green ventral patch.

DISTRIBUTION. *A. s. sharpii* was previously known from only four specimens: from a ravine on the Birwa Plateau, Sierra Leone; from forest in the Ivory Coast; and from an unspecified locality in Ghana. It is very gratifying to have such a comprehensive series of this rarely collected bird. This is a new record for Liberia.

HABITAT. Forest.

Bathmocercus cerviniventris
Black-capped Stream Warbler

SPECIMENS. 7 ♂♂, Feb. (3), Mar., Apr., Aug. 1968 (2). 1 imm. ♀, Feb. 1968. — *B. c. cerviniventris* (Sierra Leone to Ghana).

IMPERMANENT COLOURS. Legs blue-grey. Iris chestnut. Bill black.

STOMACH CONTENTS. Insects, including small beetles and grasshoppers. Also a small gastropod.

ANNUAL CYCLE. No evidence of breeding activity. The males' gonads were small, 1–4 mm in February–April and 4–5 mm in August. An August bird was in wing-moult. The immature female was in moult around the chin and throat, with black feathers replacing white.

DISTRIBUTION. This warbler is known only from a few specimens which have been collected in thick undergrowth, often near streams. These are the first records of the species for Liberia.

Camaroptera superciliaris
Yellow-browed Camaroptera

SPECIMENS. 8 ♂♂, Feb., Mar. (3), Apr. 1968, Jun., Oct. 1967, Nov. 1970. 1 imm. ♂, Jun. 1968. 4 ♀♀, Apr. 1968, Jun. 1967, 1968, Sept. 1968.

IMPERMANENT COLOURS. Legs brownish-flesh. Iris brown. Bill black. Bare skin at sides of neck blue.

STOMACH CONTENTS. Insects, including beetles and caterpillars.

ANNUAL CYCLE. The September female had an enlarged ovary (9 mm, ova 1 mm) and single April and June females (7 and 8 mm resp.). The males had enlarged gonads in February (4 mm), March (3–5 mm), April (6 mm) and June (5 mm); no data for the October–November birds. March to June birds were in fresh plumage.

HABITAT. Mainly the undergrowth of primary and secondary forests up to about 700 m.

Camaroptera chloronota
Olive-green Camaroptera

SPECIMENS. 16 ♂♂, Jan. 1971 (2), Feb. (2), Mar., Apr. 1968, Jun., Jul. 1967 (3), Aug. 1965, 1967 (2), Sept. 1965, 1967, Oct. 1968. 11 imm. ♂♂, Jan. (2), Apr. 1968, Jun. 1967, 1968, Jul. (2), Aug. (2), Sept. 1967, Nov. 1970. 9 ♀♀, Apr. 1968 (2), Jul. 1965, 1967, Sept. 1967 (4), Oct. 1968. — *C. c. kelsalli* (Senegal to Ghana).

IMPERMANENT COLOURS. Legs orange-brown. Iris tawny. Bill black.

STOMACH CONTENTS. Insects, including small beetles and caterpillars.

ANNUAL CYCLE. Two April females had enlarged ovaries (yolks to 5 mm; 7 mm). A September female was noted as having recently laid, and an October female had an ovary measuring 8 mm with ova of 1 mm. Two males had enlarged testes in February (5 mm), and single males in April, August and September (8, 4.5 & 6 mm resp.). An October male was just starting a wing-moult (primaries 1–2 growing); single June and July birds were in advanced stages (primaries 6–7 growing); and two July and an August bird were completing their wing-moult.

HABITAT. From its readily identifiable calls it is clear that this bird prefers dense undergrowth in secondary lowland forests, as well as the edges of clearings.

Camaroptera brachyura
Grey-backed Camaroptera

SPECIMENS. 11 ♂♂, Feb. 1968, Jun. (5), Aug. 1967, Sept. 1968, Oct. 1967 (3). 2 imm. ♂♂, Jan., Mar. 1968. 3 ♀♀,

Feb. 1966, Mar. 1968, Jun. 1967. — *C. b. tincta* (Sierra Leone to Cameroon and southern Zaire).

IMPERMANENT COLOURS. Legs fleshy-pink. Iris brown. Bill black.

STOMACH CONTENTS. Insects.

ANNUAL CYCLE. The June female had an enlarged ovary (7.5 mm). Testes were moderately enlarged in the February male (6 mm), three June males (4.5–5 mm), the August male (4 mm), and one October male (5 mm); the rest being 1–2.5 mm. The February female was finishing wing-moult and the single March, June and August birds were in advanced stages of wing-moult (primaries 7–9 growing). October birds were in very worn plumage.

HABITAT. Common at Nimba in dense thickets on more or less open ground, and in the bush of forest-grassland mosaics.

Eremomela badiceps Rufous-crowned Eremomela

SPECIMENS. 7 ♂♂, Jul. 1968, Aug. 1967, Sept. 1967, 1968 (2), Oct. 1968 (2). 3 ♀♀, Aug. 1967 (2), Sept. 1968. — *E. b. fantiensis* (Sierra Leone to Ghana).

IMPERMANENT COLOURS. Legs yellow or orange flesh. Iris brown. Bill black.

STOMACH CONTENTS. Insects, including beetles and caterpillars.

ANNUAL CYCLE. The September female had an enlarged ovary with a yolk to 6 mm. The males' testes were enlarged in four September–October birds (5.5–8 mm). A September male was completing wing-moult (outer primaries growing), and another September male was in an advanced stage, (3 outer primaries old).

HABITAT. Secondary lowland forests, but also observed on three occasions in more open woodlands. Usually found in the tree tops.

Sylvietta virens Green Crombec

SPECIMENS. 6 ♂♂, Mar., Apr. 1968 (2), Sept. 1967, 1968 (2). Imm. ♂ Jul. 1967. 9 ♀♀, Feb. (2), Mar. 1968, Jun. 1968, 1970, Aug. 1968, Oct. 1967, 1968, Nov. 1968. 1 o, Apr. 1968. — *S. v. flaviventris* (Sierra Leone to western Nigeria).

IMPERMANENT COLOURS. Legs pink. Iris tawny. Bill brown.

STOMACH CONTENTS. Insects, including black ants.

ANNUAL CYCLE. No definite evidence of breeding activity. Single females had moderately enlarged ovaries (4–6 mm) in February, March, June and October. March–April males had testes measuring 1–3 mm, and September males, 1.5–3.5 mm. A February female was in wing-moult (6th primary growing), a March male was finishing wing-moult (outer primaries growing), and two September and an October bird were in early to mid stages (primaries 2–6 growing).

HABITAT. Forest edge and clearings, open patches in gallery forest, and forest-grassland mosaics.

Sylvietta denti Lemon-bellied Crombec

SPECIMENS. 1 ♂, Oct. 1968. 1 ♀, Sept. 1968. — *S. d. hardyi* (Sierra Leone to Ghana).

IMPERMANENT COLOURS. Legs dusky pink. Iris orange-brown. Bill black.

STOMACH CONTENTS. Insects, including caterpillars and beetles.

ANNUAL CYCLE. The testes of the male measured 4 mm, and the female was noted as having recently laid. Both were in fresh plumage.

STATUS. This is a new record for Liberia. It is mainly found in secondary forest.

Macrosphenus concolor Olive Longbill

SPECIMENS. 9 ♂♂, Mar. 1968, 1976, Jun. 1967, Jul. 1965, 1967 (2), Aug. 1967, 1968, Oct. 1968. 6 ♀♀, Mar. 1968, Jun., Jul. (2), Aug., Oct. 1967.

IMPERMANENT COLOURS. Legs dusky-pink. Iris brown. Bill brown, pinkish below.

STOMACH CONTENTS. Insects.

ANNUAL CYCLE. No definite evidence of breeding activity. The March, June and October females had ovaries measuring 5 mm, and single July and October males' testes of 6.0–6.5 mm. The June female was completing wing-moult (outer primaries growing), and the June male and one July bird were in advanced stages with the 7th to 8th primaries growing. The other July, August and October birds were in fresh plumage.

HABITAT. Dense tangles of vines or creepers in primary or secondary forest.

Macrosphenus kempi Kemp's Longbill

SPECIMENS. 16 ♂♂, Jan. 1971, May 1968 (2), Jun. 1967, 1968 (3), Jul. 1968, Aug. 1967 (2), 1968, Sept. 1967 (2), 1968, Oct. 1967, Nov. 1968. 4 imm. ♂♂, Jul., Sept. 1967, Oct. 1967, 1968. 5 ♀♀, Jan. 1970, 1971, Jun. 1967, Sept., Dec. 1968. 3 imm. ♀♀, Apr., Jul., Sept. 1968. 1 o, Jul. 1967. — *M. k. kempi* (Sierra Leone to western Nigeria).

IMPERMANENT COLOURS. Legs dusky-grey. Iris yellow and pale grey. Bill black, pinkish horn below.

STOMACH CONTENTS. Insects, including beetles and ants.

ANNUAL CYCLE. The December female had an enlarged ovary with two yolks (6, 8 mm). One May male, two June males and one August male had moderately enlarged testes (5–6 mm). Single January, May and June birds were completing wing-moult (outer primaries growing), and single June and July birds were in advanced stages (7th primaries growing).

PLUMAGE. The young birds were olive-green above while the underparts were pale yellowish-green with an olive wash across the breast. Further knowledge of the dress of the young *kempi* confirms the view held by Hall & Moreau (1970), that the unique type of *M. leoninus* from Sierra Leone is not a form of *M. flavicans* (which forms a superspecies with *M. kempi*), but a juvenile *kempi*. *Macrosphenus leoninus* was described as olive-green above and yellow below with some olive on the breast. It is unlikely that, after an apparent gap of 2250 km *flavicans* should occur alongside *kempi* in Sierra Leone.

HABITAT. The edge of secondary lowland forest.

Hylia prasina   Green Hylia

SPECIMENS. 10 ♂♂, Jan. 1971, Mar. 1968, Jun. 1967 (4), Jul. 1965, 1967 (2), Sept. 1967. 6 imm. ♂♂, Feb., Jun. 1968, Jul. (2), Aug. 1967 (2). 11 ♀♀, Jan. 1966, Apr. 1968, Jun. (3), Jul., Aug. 1967, Sept. 1967, 1968, Oct. 1968, Nov. 1964. 2 imm. ♀♀, Jan. 1971, Feb. 1966, 2 o, July, Aug. 1967. — *H. p. superciliaris* (Guinea Bissau to Ghana).

IMPERMANENT COLOURS. Legs olive-green. Iris brown. Bill black, yellowish-horn in young birds.

STOMACH CONTENTS. Insects, including beetles and grasshoppers.

ANNUAL CYCLE. A September female had an enlarged ovary with a 10 mm yolk. The remaining females' ovaries did not exceed 5 mm and males' testes were generally small (1–4 mm). Single June and July birds were completing wing-moult (outer primaries growing) and another June male was at an earlier stage (4th primary growing).

HABITAT. Undergrowth and tangles of lianas in primary and secondary lowland forest as well as the grassland-forest mosaic.

Family Muscicapidae

Muscicapa striata   Spotted Flycatcher

SPECIMENS. 1 ♂, Oct. 1967. 2 ♀♀, Oct. 1965, 1968. 1 imm. ♀, Nov. 1967. — *M. s. striata* (Palaearctic winter visitor).

IMPERMANENT COLOURS. Legs dark brown. Iris brown. Bill black.

STOMACH CONTENTS. Insects.

ANNUAL CYCLE. October adults were in worn condition and the November bird was in fresh plumage.

HABITAT. Primary and secondary lowland forests including clearings and edges; forest-grassland mosaics, and isolated patches of trees on open ground.

MIGRATION. Last observation prior to spring migration, 26 April.

Muscicapa gambagae   Gambaga Dusky Flycatcher

This flycatcher was observed at Nimba (AF-W, JK & SK). This is the first record for Liberia and represents an extension of range some 900 km southwest. In West Africa the species is also found in wooded savanna in northern Ghana, northern Nigeria and Cameroon.

Muscicapa aquatica   Swamp Flycatcher

This flycatcher, which is found in vegetation fringing swamps and pools, was observed at Nimba (AF-W). This is the first record for Liberia. In West Africa it is recorded from Senegal, Gambia, Ghana, southern Mali and Nigeria.

Muscicapa cassini   Cassin's Grey Flycatcher

This flycatcher, which is associated with wooded river banks and the margins of lakes in the forest region, was observed at Nimba in February 1971 (AF-W, JK & SK). In West Africa it is found from Liberia east to Gabon, Zaire and the Central African Republic.

Muscicapa epulata   Little Blue Flycatcher

SPECIMENS. 2 ♂♂, Aug. 1967 (2). 1 ♀, Jan. 1968. 1 imm. ♀, Sept. 1968.

IMPERMANENT COLOURS. Legs black. Iris brown. Bill black, yellow below.

STOMACH CONTENTS. Insects, including flying ants and small beetles.

ANNUAL CYCLE. The January female had an enlarged ovary (6 mm) and was in fresh plumage. The two males had small testes (1 mm), and were both in an early stage of moult (2nd primary growing). The young bird had buffy edges to the inner secondaries and wing-coverts.

DISTRIBUTION. This is a new record for Liberia and represents an important extension of range some 700 km west. It has an apparently discontinuous distribution in both the Upper and Lower Guinea lowland forest.

HABITAT. Primary and secondary lowland forest, including clearings and edges as well as relict stands of isolated groups of tall trees.

Muscicapa olivascens   Olivaceous Flycatcher

SPECIMENS. 8 ♂♂, Apr. 1968, Jun. 1967 (2), Aug. 1967 (3), 1968, Sept. 1968. 1 juv. ♂, Oct. 1968. 3 ♀♀, May 1971, Jun., Aug. 1967. 1 imm. o, Jun. 1967.

IMPERMANENT COLOURS. Legs grey. Iris brown. Bill black, pale pinkish below.

STOMACH CONTENTS. Insects, including ants, small beetles and caterpillars.

ANNUAL CYCLE. The juvenile of 14 October was the only definite evidence of breeding activity. The August female had a moderately enlarged ovary of 7.5 mm. The April male, which was in an early stage of wing-moult, had testes measuring 8 mm. June males' measured 1–3 mm, and August–September males 4.5–5.5 mm. The May female was completing wing-moult and June–August birds were in fresh plumage.

DISTRIBUTION AND GEOGRAPHICAL VARIATION. This is a new record to Liberia. It also represents an important extension of range, some 800 km west, previous records being from Ghana to Gabon, east to eastern Zaire. This is a rare bird, found only in deep lowland forest.

Nimba birds differ in being more rufous-brown above, whiter on the chin and belly with a more pronounced breast-band, paler sides to the face and paler whitish-grey lores, when compared with four BM(NH) specimens collected by Bates & Serle in Cameroon, and a single bird from Ghana collected by Ussher. White (1963) gives no races. M.A. Traylor (*in litt.*), who examined the Nimba birds, was of the opinion that they were distinct from those of Cameroon, but wished to see further material from Gabon and Zaire before naming them. However, in view of the significant differences mentioned above, we feel that the Nimba birds are sufficiently distinct to warrant recognition and we therefore propose the following name.

Muscicapa olivascens nimbae subsp. nov.

HOLOTYPE. Male, Grassfield, Mount Nimba, Liberia, 7°30′N, 8°35′W, altitude 550 m, 1 August 1968. Collected by A.D. Forbes-Watson. Lodged in British Museum (Natural History), B.M. No: 1977-20-2040.

DESCRIPTION. The head, back and rump are a warmer rufous-brown when compared with nominate *olivascens*, which has these areas more olive-brown. The primaries and wing-coverts are narrowly edged rufous-brown, whereas *olivascens* has these areas edged more olive-brown, and the tail is also more rufous-brown and less olive-brown than in *olivascens*. The sides of the head are paler greyish-brown and the lores are a distinctly paler greyish-white. The underparts also differ in having a much greater area of pure white extending from the lower breast to the vent and undertail coverts. The whitish throat is similar to *olivascens*, but the chin is purer white and there is a better defined olive-brown breast band, some 20 mm wide. In *olivascens* the underparts are very much more suffused with greyish-olive, with less white on the belly.

COLOUR OF SOFT PARTS AT TIME OF COLLECTION. Legs grey. Iris brown. Bill black, lower mandible whitish.

MEASUREMENTS OF TYPE. Wing (flattened) 76.0 mm, tail 59.0 mm, culmen from base 14.5 mm, tarsus 18.0 mm, weight 18.6 g.

Comparative measurements of *M. o. nimbae* and *M. o. olivascens*.

M. o. nimbae
Wing	8 ♂♂	72–78	(mean 74.9)	3 ♀♀	67–70	(mean 68.7)
tail	„	56–62	(mean 58.6)	„	55	(mean 55.0)
bill	„	14.5–16.0	(mean 15.4)	„	15	(mean 15.0)
tarsus	„	18–20	(mean 18.8)	„	18	(mean 18.0)

M. o. olivascens
Wing	3 ♂♂	73–79	(mean 76.0)	1 ♀		69.0
tail	„	56–59	(mean 57.3)	„		51.0
bill	„	15–16	(mean 15.3)	„		14.5
tarsus	„	17–19	(mean 18.0)	„		16.0

HABITAT. Lowland forest and shrub.

RANGE. Known only from the type-locality.

Muscicapa caerulescens   Ashy Flycatcher

This flycatcher was observed at Nimba (AF-W & SK). It is found in a wide variety of habitats, from clearings in heavy forest in Zaire to thorn scrub in East Africa. In West Africa it is rather uncommon and ranges in the forest from Guinea to Gabon.

Muscicapa comitata   Dusky blue Flycatcher

This species was observed at Nimba (KC-L) on several occasions in different years in secondary lowland forests. In West Africa it ranges in forest from Sierra Leone to Gabon and Zaire. In Cameroon it ascends to 1550 m.

Muscicapa ussheri Ussher's Dusky Flycatcher

SPECIMENS. 3 ♂♂, Apr. 1968, Jul., Aug. 1967. 3 ♀♀, Jul., Sept. 1967 (2). 1 o, Dec. 1964.

IMPERMANENT COLOURS. Legs dark brown. Iris brown. Bill black.

STOMACH CONTENTS. Insects.

ANNUAL CYCLE. No evidence of breeding activity. The April male (testes 7 mm) was in an early stage of wing-moult (inner primaries growing). Testes for July and August males, 2 and 5 mm respectively. The females' ovaries were not enlarged (2–6 mm). The September female was in wing moult (4th primary growing).

HABITAT. Forest clearings with a few scattered dead trees or the edges of the high forest are its favourite terrain.

Muscicapa griseigularis Grey throated Tit-flycatcher

SPECIMENS. 1 ♂, Sept. 1967. 1 imm. ♂, Sept. 1968. 4 ♀♀, Aug. (2), Sept. 1967 (2).

IMPERMANENT COLOURS. Legs grey. Iris chestnut-brown. Bill black, lower mandible paler horn, darker towards the tip.

STOMACH CONTENTS. Insects.

ANNUAL CYCLE. The September male (testes 4.5 mm) and one of the September females (ovary 7 mm) were a pair and had a nest containing 2 eggs on 19 September. The nest, appropriated by the flycatchers, was identified by Forbes-Watson as built by *Nectarinia cyanolaema*. One August female and the other September female also had enlarged ovaries (7–8 mm) and were probably in breeding condition. All birds were in fresh plumage. The immature male had buff-tipped wing-coverts and was moulting into adult plumage.

DISTRIBUTION AND GEOGRAPHICAL VARIATION. Traylor (1970) described a new race from a male collected at Duékoué, Ivory Coast. Recently he examined the Nimba birds and confirmed that they are similar to the Ivory Coast specimen, and are *M. g. parelli*. It differs from nominate *griseigularis* in having the lower mandible black with a trace of pale horn at the base, instead of being wholly pale. It also has a shorter wing, a longer tail and is more bluish-slate in colour. This is a new species for Liberia, and the Ivory Coast and the Nimba birds represent a considerable extension of range. Previously the species was known from the lowland forests of south-east Nigeria to Gabon and east to eastern Zaire and western Uganda and south to the Kasai.

HABITAT. Shrub.

Ficedula hypoleuca Pied Flycatcher

SPECIMENS. 2 ♂♂, Jan., Apr. 1968. 1 ♀, Dec. 1967. 1 o, Jan. 1968. — *F. h. hypoleuca* (Palaearctic winter visitor).

IMPERMANENT COLOURS. Legs black. Iris brown. Bill black.

STOMACH CONTENTS. Insects.

ANNUAL CYCLE. The April male (testes 1 mm) had almost completed its moult into fresh spring plumage. The remainder were in winter plumage.

DISTRIBUTION. Observed at Nimba in October 1963 (KC-L), and seen several times in later years during the European winter. These are the first records of the species for Liberia. In West Africa it occurs from Senegal and Gambia to Cameroon.

HABITAT. Primary and secondary lowland forest, where the species often keeps to the canopy and edges along glades; on Mount Nimba up to about 700 m.

Fraseria ocreata Fraser's Forest Flycatcher

SPECIMENS. 9 ♂♂, Mar. 1968, Jun. (2), Jul. (4), Aug., Sept. 1967. 2 imm. ♂♂, Mar. 1968, Jul. 1965. 8 ♀♀, Jan. 1968, Jun. 1967, Jul. 1967 (2), Aug. 1967 (2), Oct. 1974, Dec. 1971. — *F. o. phosphora* (Liberia to Ghana).

IMPERMANENT COLOURS. Legs grey. Iris brown. Bill black.

STOMACH CONTENTS. Insects, including flying ants, small beetles, and a grasshopper; and a few small seeds.

ANNUAL CYCLE. The January female had an enlarged ovary measuring 9.5 mm, and the June, two July and single August birds had moderately enlarged ovaries (6.5–7.0 mm). No gonad data available for the October–December birds. One March male and one June male had moderately enlarged testes (7.0, 6.5 mm), and they were fully enlarged in the August and September birds (10.0, 9.5 mm resp., *cf.* four July males, 2.0–3.5 mm). October and December birds were in worn condition and a July female was in wing-moult (6th primary growing). The remaining birds were mostly in fresh plumage.

HABITAT AND HABITS. The species occurs in a wide range of habitats from rather open ground with trees to woodlands and edges of primary and secondary forests up to 800 m. It is almost always seen in tree-tops, often in small groups of 3–4 birds.

Fraseria cinerascens White-browed Forest Flycatcher

SPECIMENS. 1 ♂, Jul. 1968. 3 ♀♀, Jul. 1968, Nov. 1970, Dec. 1967.

IMPERMANENT COLOURS. Legs lead grey. Iris brown. Bill black.

STOMACH CONTENTS. Insects.

ANNUAL CYCLE. The July female had an enlarged ovary of 10 mm and was probably in breeding condition. The ovary of the December female measured 7 mm; no gonad data available for the November female. Testes of the July male were small (3 mm). July birds were in fresh and November–December birds in worn plumage.

DISTRIBUTION AND HABITAT. This is a riverine forest species, distributed from Guinea Bissau to Gabon and Zaire.

Melaenornis annamarulae Anna's Forest Flycatcher

SPECIMENS. 9 ♂♂, Jan. 1968 (2), Jun. 1968, 1971, Aug. 1967, 1968 (2), Oct. 1968 (2). 3 ♀♀, Jan., Jul., Aug. 1968.

IMPERMANENT COLOURS. Legs black. Iris brown. Bill black.

STOMACH CONTENTS. Insects, mostly black flying ants, metallic beetles and a caterpillar.

ANNUAL CYCLE. The July female had an enlarged ovary (10 mm, ova to 1 mm); the other two females had small ovaries (2 mm). One January and the two October males had enlarged testes of 7.0–8.5 mm; the remainder were small (1.0–2.5 mm). An August female was completing wing-moult (two outer primaries growing).

FIELD NOTES. This flycatcher was collected (AF-W) on 12 August 1967 (Forbes-Watson, 1970). It is a large robust species, uniform plumbeous in colour with a paler bluish cast than other *Melaenornis* spp., from which it also differs in structure and ecology. The species at present is only known from Nimba and the Tai National Park, Ivory Coast, where one was collected in 1976 by Chappius & Vielliard (specimen in Paris Museum). It has been found in the interior of lowland forest at the foot of Nimba, but never observed (KC-L, AF-W & DT) on its slopes, although the forest was similar. Most of the time this species frequented the tree tops and was rarely less than 20 metres from the ground. Forbes-Watson records them as usually silent, but at times they would utter rather strident calls reminiscent of other members of the genus, and not unlike certain calls of *Fraseria ocreata* and drongos *Dicrurus* spp.

Hyliota violacea   Violet-backed Flycatcher

SPECIMENS. 4 ♂♂, Jun. 1970, Jul. 1967, Nov. 1964 (2). 4 ♀♀, Jul., Aug. 1967, Oct., Nov. 1968. 1 imm. ♀, Jul. 1967. — *H. v. nehrkorni* (Liberia to Ghana).

IMPERMANENT COLORS. Legs black. Iris brown. Bill black, bluish below.

STOMACH CONTENTS. Insects, including beetles and caterpillars.

ANNUAL CYCLE. No evidence of breeding activity. Ovaries of the females measured 4.6 mm, and testes of the July male, 2 mm (no gonad data for June and November males). A July female was in the early stages of wing-moult, and the June male, August female and November female were completing (outer primaries growing).

HABITAT AND STATUS. This species, which Curry-Lindahl knows well from Zaire, was found in October 1963, and several times subsequently, travelling with mixed bird parties within the lowland forest. This is a new record for Liberia.

Megabyas flammulatus   Shrike Flycatcher

SPECIMENS. 7 ♂♂, Apr., May 1968, Jul. 1965, 1967, 1970, Oct. 1967 (2). 1 imm. ♂, Aug. 1968. 5 ♀♀, Jul. 1967, 1970, Aug. 1968, Oct. 1967 (2). — *M. f. flammulatus* (Sierra Leone to Zaire).

IMPERMANENT COLOURS. Legs brown. Iris red. Bill black.

STOMACH CONTENTS. Insects, including grasshoppers and a large bug.

ANNUAL CYCLE. An October male had enlarged testes of 7.5 mm (*cf*. 3.0–4.5 mm in other ♂♂, but data for only one July ♂). One October female had a moderately enlarged ovary of 7.5 mm (*cf*. 3.0–5.5 mm in the others). The April and two July birds were in early to middle stages of wing-moult (primaries 3 to 6 growing), and two July, the August and an October male were in advanced stages of wing-moult with the outer primaries growing.

HABITAT. Mainly secondary lowland forest but may ascend occasionally to about 800 m.

Bias musicus   Black and White Flycatcher

SPECIMENS. 1 ♂, 1 ♀, Aug. 1968. — *B. m. musicus* (Guinea Bissau to Zaire).

IMPERMANENT COLOURS. Legs yellow in male, pale grey in female. Iris bright yellow. Bill black.

STOMACH CONTENTS. Insects, including small black hymenoptera and beetles.

ANNUAL CYCLE. Neither bird was in breeding condition (gonads 2 mm). The male was in an early stage of wing-moult (inner primaries growing).

HABITAT AND HABITS. Due perhaps to its conspicuousness and frequent vocalization this species appears to be common at Nimba in both lowland and montane primary and secondary forests, where it prefers the higher trees, but it does not avoid lower trees in clearings and at forest edges. On Mount Nimba it occurs up to about 900 m. It is usually found in pairs, sometimes in small groups of 3–5 birds which mingle with other species.

Batis (poensis) occultus   White-browed Puff-back Flycatcher

SPECIMENS. 2 ♂♂, Jul. 1967, Oct. 1968. 1 imm. ♂, Mar. 1968. 2 ♀♀, Oct. 1968 (2).

IMPERMANENT COLOURS. Legs black. Iris yellow. Bill black.

STOMACH CONTENTS. Insects, including black flying ants and small beetles.

ANNUAL CYCLE. No evidence of breeding (ovaries 4–5 mm, testes 1.0–1.5 mm). One October female was in an advanced stage of wing-moult (9th primary growing), and the remainder were in fresh plumage.

GEOGRAPHICAL VARIATION. Lawson (1984) has recently demonstrated that the West African mainland populations of this forest dwelling *Batis* flycatcher are specifically distinct from those inhabiting the island of Fernando Po (with which they were once linked), both in size and colour. Males differ from *B. poensis* in having the head top and mantle blue black with a considerable admixture of grey and white, giving the bird a quite different appearance. The supra loral spot is large and white. There is also a conspicuous white supercilium, while the white edge to the tertials is broad, as is the white edge to the outer tail feathers and the breast band is narrower. Females are similar in colouration to those of *B. poensis* with the exception of the breast band, which is similar in colour (a dark vinous chestnut) but it is clearly defined and delineated with white flanks and no suffusion onto the upper abdomen.

STATUS AND DISTRIBUTION. Although this small, shy forest flycatcher is considered to be rather rare in West Africa it may be not uncommon. It is so closely similar to other flycatchers that it may have been overlooked in the past. It is known from a few localities in the Ivory Coast, Ghana, south-west Nigeria and southern Cameroon. This is a new species for Liberia.

Platysteira cyanea Scarlet-spectacled Wattle-eye

SPECIMENS. 3 ♂♂, Jul. 1968, Sept. 1967, Oct. 1968. — *P. c. cyanea* (Senegal to Cameroon and Ubangi-Shari).

IMPERMANENT COLOURS. Legs purplish-black. Iris blue-grey. Eye wattle red. Bill black.

STOMACH CONTENTS. Insects.

ANNUAL CYCLE. The July female had an enlarged ovary of 8 mm and the October bird was noted as having laid. The July female was in rather worn condition and the other two females were in fresh plumage.

HABITAT. Locally a common species at Nimba, frequenting lowland and montane forest clearings and outskirts, also forest-grassland and mosaics, gardens and trees around human settlement. Found up to about 700 m, occasionally higher.

Platysteira castanea Chestnut Wattle-eye

SPECIMENS. 15 ♂♂, Jan., Feb. (2), Mar. 1968, Jul. 1967 (2), 1970, Aug. 1967 (3), 1970, Oct. 1964, 1968, Nov.1968, 1970. 6 imm. ♂♂, Jun. 1968, Aug. 1967 (3), Sept., Oct. 1968. 16 ♀♀, Jan. 1966, Feb., Mar., Apr. 1968, Jul. 1965, 1967 (3), Aug. 1967, 1970, Sept., Oct. 1964, 1968 (2), Nov. 1964, 1968. — *P. c. hormorphora* (Sierra Leone to Togo).

IMPERMANENT COLOURS. Legs dark purple. Iris purple-brown. Eye-wattle dark liver or purplish-black. Bill black.

STOMACH CONTENTS. Insects, including small beetles and a grasshopper.

ANNUAL CYCLE. Gonad data incomplete, especially for August–November. The April female (ovary 10 mm) and a July female (ovary 7 mm, ova enlarging; both birds in fresh plumage) were probably nearing breeding condition, but the March female (ovary 7 mm, in middle stage of wing-moult) was presumably not ready to breed. Males had testes measuring 4–9 mm in January–July, *cf.* 3–5 mm (only 5 measured) in August–November. Single January and October birds were in early stages, and single February and March birds in middle stages of wing-moult. All April–August birds were in fresh plumage. The September–October imm. males were the more advanced of the young birds, and acquiring the black adult breast-band.

HABITAT. A wide variation of biotopes, ranging from primary and secondary lowland forest to forest-grassland mosaics, isolated tree clumps and gardens.

Platysteira blissetti Red-cheeked Wattle-eye

SPECIMENS. 14 ♂♂, Jan. 1971, Mar. (2), Apr. (4), Aug. 1968 (2), Sept. 1967, 1968, Nov. 1968, 1970 (2). 1 imm. ♂, Jul. 1968. 8 ♀♀,, Feb. 1971, Mar., Apr. (2), Sept., Nov. 1968. 1 o imm., Mar. 1968. — *P. b. blissetti* (Sierra Leone to Cameroon).

IMPERMANENT COLOURS. Legs dull grey. Iris chestnut brown. Bill black. Eye-wattle turquoise-blue.

STOMACH CONTENTS. Insects, including small beetles.

ANNUAL CYCLE. Two April females had enlarged ovaries (9–10 mm with ova to *c.* 1 mm) and single March, April, August and November females had moderately enlarged ovaries of 5–6 mm. Two April, one August and both September males had enlarged testes (6–8 mm). No gonad data available for January–February birds, or two November males. Single March and April birds were in middle stages of wing-moult (primaries 4–5 growing) and three August birds were completing wing-moult (outer primaries growing).

HABITAT. Usually heard (voice, and also wing-snapping), and seen around dense undergrowth in primary and secondary lowland forest.

Platysteira concreta Chestnut- or Golden-bellied Wattle-eye

SPECIMENS. 23 ♂♂, Jan., Feb. (4), Mar., Apr. 1968, May 1965, Jun. 1967 (4), 1968 (2), Jul. 1967, 1968, Aug. 1967 (4), 1968, 1970, Sept. 1967. 5 imm. ♂♂, Jun. 1967, 1968, Jul. 1967, 1968, Oct. 1965. 22 ♀♀, Jan. 1966, 1968 (2), Feb. (2), Mar. 1968, May 1965, Jun. 1966, 1967 (4), 1968, Jul. 1967 (3), Aug. 1967 (5), 1968. 2 imm. ♀♀, Jun., Jul. 1968. 1 juv. o, Feb. 1968. — *P. c. concreta* (Sierra Leone to Ghana).

IMPERMANENT COLOURS. Legs black. Iris red-brown or purplish-brown. Eye-wattle lime green. Bill black.

STOMACH CONTENTS. Small insects.

ANNUAL CYCLE. The juvenile of 5 February is the only definite indication of breeding activity. Three females had moderately enlarged ovaries in January, March and August (7–8 mm), cf. eight females June–July, with ovaries of 2–5 mm. Males in January, February (2), March and June (1) had testes measuring 4–6 mm. Single April, May and four June birds were in middle stages of wing-moult (primaries 3–7 growing). Three June, two July and an August bird were completing wing-moult (outer primaries growing). August–September birds were in fresh plumage.

PLUMAGE. The juvenile plumage does not appear to have been described. It differs from the immature in having nearly all the upper parts speckled brown with some paler olive edgings confined to the lower back. The underpats are whitish with a grey suffusion across the breast and there are a few buff-tipped feathers on the sides of the white throat. The wing-covers are broadly edged with buff, forming a double wing bar. In the later immature stages the bird is distinctly yellowish below and greenish above, with some chestnut on the throat.

DISTRIBUTION. Nominate *concreta* is rare in collections and was previously not represented in the BM(NH) collection. This is a new record for Liberia. It is known to occur on the Ivory Coast side of Nimba.

HABITAT. In 1964 and 1966 Curry-Lindahl made his first acquaintance with this species in habitats which were totally different from the descriptions available in the literature at that time, '. . . must be a bird of the undergrowth of primitive forest' (Bannermann, 1953), or '. . . lives in pairs or family groups in the leafy undergrowth of primary forest' (Chapin, 1953). The observations at Nimba were made in the forest-grassland mosaic at Grassfield, where the species was and still is rather common. Juveniles as well as adults feeding young have also been seen there, so apparently the birds breed there. However, this bird has also been observed in pure forest habitats mainly in the lowland.

Erythrocercus mccalli Chestnut-cap Flycatcher

SPECIMENS. 6 ♂♂, Jan. 1970, Jun. 1967, Sept. 1968 (2), Oct. 1967, 1968. 1 ♀, Sept. 1968. — *E. m. nigeriae* (Sierra Leone to southwest Nigeria).

IMPERMANENT COLOURS. Legs pale brown. Iris pale yellow. Bill brown, whitish-horn below.

STOMACH CONTENTS. Insects, including small beetles and naked caterpillars.

ANNUAL CYCLE. No evidence of breeding activity (testes 1.0–2.5 mm in June–October males, no data for the January male; ovary of the September female 3 mm). Single June and October birds were in advanced stages of wing-moult (outer primaries growing), and the September birds were in early to mid-stages (primaries 3–6 growing).

HABITAT. Three individuals were found in the ridge forest of Mount Nimba at about 1200 m on 25 February 1980. This is the only observation Curry-Lindahl has made of this bird at Nimba. Presumably this habitat is not representative for the Chestnut-cap Flycatcher. In the Ituri Forest of Zaire, where it is locally common, it is met with in primary lowland forest.

Trochocercus nitens Blue-headed Crested Flycatcher

SPECIMENS. 6 ♂♂, Feb. 1971, Sept. 1967, 1968, Oct. 1968, 1970, Dec. 1968. — *T. n. reichenowi* (Sierra Leone to Togo).

IMPERMANENT COLOURS. Legs blue-grey. Iris brown. Bill black.

STOMACH CONTENTS. Insects.

ANNUAL CYCLE. The December male had enlarged gonads (7 mm; cf. 1–2 mm in three September–October males, no data for the February and one October male). The February bird was in worn condition. Single September and October males were completing wing-moult, outer primaries growing, and another September bird had primaries 4 and 5 growing.

HABITAT. Lowland forest.

Trochocercus nigromitratus Dusky Crested Flycatcher

SPECIMENS. 12 ♂♂, Jan. 1968 (2), 1969, Jun. 1967 (3), Jul. 1967 (2), 1968, Aug. 1967, Sept. 1965, 1967. 12 ♀♀, Jan. 1966, 1969, Apr. 1968, Jun. 1966, 1967 (4), Jul. (3), Aug. 1967.

IMPERMANENT COLOURS. Legs dark grey. Iris brown. Bill black.

STOMACH CONTENTS. Insects.

ANNUAL CYCLE. No definite evidence of breeding activity. Three June and a July female had moderately enlarged ovaries of 5–6 mm. The males' gonads were small, not exceeding 2.5 mm. Two August birds were in early stages of wing-moult, the 4th primary growing.

DISTRIBUTION. The discovery of this small flycatcher at Nimba is interesting in that it extends the known range of this species by some 1700 km westwards. This is a new record for Liberia. In addition it is now recorded from south-west Nigeria to Gabon, east to Sankuru and upper Zaire, Uganda and at Kakamega in west Kenya.

HABITAT. Swamp forest or damp undergrowth in primary and secondary forests, but also observed several times in forest-grassland mosaics close to water courses.

Terpsiphone rufiventer   Red-bellied Paradise Flycatcher

SPECIMENS. 25 ♂♂, Jan., Feb., Apr. 1968 (2), Jun. (10), Jul. 1967 (2), Aug. 1967 (4), 1970, Sept. 1967, Oct. 1968, 1970, Nov. 1964. 11 ♀♀, Feb. 1970, Jun. 1967 (3), Jul. 1965, 1967 (2), 1970, Sept. 1964, Oct. 1970, Nov. 1964. — *T. r. nigriceps* (Sierra Leone to Ghana).

IMPERMANENT COLOURS. Legs dark blue-grey. Iris brown. Bill dark grey to blue-black.

STOMACH CONTENTS. Insects.

ANNUAL CYCLE. A June female was in breeding condition with an enlarged ovary and a yolk of 10 mm. Two other June females had moderately enlarged ovaries of 7 mm. Seven males had enlarged testes in January (7.5 mm), February (10 mm), April (8, 9 mm) and June males (8, 10, 11.5 mm), cf. 1–3 mm for July–October birds. Single June and July birds were commencing wing-moult (inner primaries growing), and two June and single July and September birds were in mid wing-moult (5th primary growing).

HABITAT. Undergrowth and middle layers of primary lowland and montane forests up to about 700 m, but also found in forest-grassland mosaics as at Grassfield and Yekepa.

Terpsiphone viridis   Paradise Flycatcher

SPECIMENS. 2 ♂♂, Jan., Mar. 1968. 2 imm. ♂♂, Apr. 1969, May 1971. 1 ♀, Nov. 1964. — *T. v. speciosa* (Liberia to Sudan).

IMPERMANENT COLOURS. Legs black. Iris brown. Bill blue-grey.

STOMACH CONTENTS. Insects.

ANNUAL CYCLE. None of the adults examined was in breeding condition (testes, 1–2 mm). The males were white-phase birds and the March males had the white tail streamers fully developed. No wing-moult.

HABITAT AND STATUS. In 1963–66 this species was observed in the newly opened up forest-grassland mosaic at Grassfield. In later years it appeared in similar habitat at Yekepa, and in plantations of *Gmelina* and other exotic deciduous trees. A new record for Liberia.

Family Remizidae

Anthoscopus flavifrons   Forest Penduline Tit

This species was observed at Nimba (AF-W, JK & SK) in 1971. It was later seen by Curry-Lindahl in 1973–74 and 1976. These are the first records for Liberia. They represent an important extension of range some 700 km west from the species' nearest known locality in Ghana. In western Africa it is also found in forest clearings in Nigeria, Cameroon and Gabon.

Family Paridae

Parus funereus   Dusky Tit

SPECIMENS. 6 ♂♂, Apr. 1969, Jun. 1970, Jul. 1967, Aug. 1968, Oct., Nov. 1967. 5 imm. ♂♂, Jul. 1967 (4), Oct. 1967. 5 ♀♀, May 1971, Jul. (2), Oct. 1967 (2). 1 imm. ♀, Jun. 1970. — *P. f. funereus* (Liberia to Gabon).

IMPERMANENT COLOURS. Legs greyish-black. Iris red. Bill black.

STOMACH CONTENTS. Insects.

ANNUAL CYCLE. Gonad data incomplete. The November male had enlarged testes of 9.5 mm, cf. 2–3 mm in single July and August males. July and October females had small ovaries measuring 6–7 mm. Single April, May and July birds were in advanced stages of wing-moult (7th and 8th primaries growing), and two July birds were completing (outer primaries growing).

HABITAT AND STATUS. Observed in 1964–65 and later in small groups visiting tree-tops, and higher layers of primary and secondary forest up to about 800 m; also, when in mixed bird flocks, visiting other types of habitats such as clearings and forest outskirts, and once the forest-grassland mosaic at Grassfield. Dusky Tits were almost invariably conspicuous members of mixed bird parties at Nimba. This is a new record for Liberia and represents an extension of range some 800 km west.

Family Nectariniidae

Anthreptes fraseri   Scarlet-tufted Sunbird

SPECIMENS. 8 ♂♂, Apr. 1968, Jun. (3), Aug. 1967, Oct. 1968 (2), Nov. 1964. 12 ♀♀, Jun. 1967, Jul. 1967 (3), 1968, Aug. (3), Sept. 1967 (2), Oct. 1968, Nov. 1964. — *A. f. idius* (Sierra Leone to Ghana).

IMPERMANENT COLOURS. Legs olive-green. Iris brown. Bill brown.

STOMACH CONTENTS. Insects, including caterpillars; also some spiders.

ANNUAL CYCLE. Little evidence of breeding activity. The females' ovaries were rather small, 2–4 mm for June–July birds, 2–5 mm for August–September and 3 mm for the October female. Testes were moderately enlarged in June males (3–5 mm) and one August male (6 mm), cf. 1–2 mm in other males (except November male, for which no data). No wing-moult.

HABITAT AND HABITS. This sunbird occurs in flocks high up in the foliage of primary forest and is sometimes a member of insect-hunting bird parties. At Nimba in both lowland and montane forests.

Anthreptes rectirostris   Yellow-chinned Sunbird

SPECIMENS. 6 ♂♂, Jun. 1967, Aug., Sept. (2), Oct. 1965, 1968. 2 imm. ♂♂, Aug. 1967, Oct. 1965. 1 ♀, Oct. 1968. — *A. r. rectirostris* (Sierra Leone to Ghana).

IMPERMANENT COLOURS. Legs black. Iris red-brown. Bill black.

STOMACH CONTENTS. Many small fruits 4 mm in diameter. No insects found.

ANNUAL CYCLE. The October female was noted as having laid, and its ovary contained a yolk measuring 4 mm. The males' testes measured 3–4 mm for June to September birds and 2 mm for the October male. No wing-moult.

HABITAT. Lowland secondary forest, at all heights from the undershrubs to the high tree-tops, up to 700 m.

Anthreptes collaris   Collared Sunbird

SPECIMENS. 10 ♂♂, Apr. 1968, Jun. 1967, Sept. 1968 (2), Oct. 1968 (2), 1970 (2), Nov. 1964, Dec. 1965. 5 imm. ♂♂, Mar., Apr. (2), Jun., Oct. 1968. 10 ♀♀, Mar., Apr., May 1968, Jun. 1967, 1968, Jul., Aug., Sept. 1968, Oct., Nov. 1968. 3 juv. ♀♀, Jul. 1967, May, Nov. 1968. — *A. c. subcollaris* (Senegal to west of the lower Niger).

IMPERMANENT COLOURS. Legs black. Iris brown. Bill black.

STOMACH CONTENTS. Insects, including caterpillars; also small seeds and fruit-pulp.

ANNUAL CYCLE. Single June and September females were noted as having recently laid, and an August female had an enlarged ovary of 6 mm. Single June, September and two October males had enlarged testes, 6–8 mm. The March, May and one November bird were in middle stages of wing-moult (5–7th primaries growing).

HABITAT. Mainly secondary lowland forests and the edges of montane forests up to about 1200 m.

Nectarinia seimundi   Little Green Sunbird

SPECIMENS. 4 ♂♂, Apr., Jul., Sept., Oct. 1968. 10 ♀♀, Jun., Jul. 1967 (2), Sept. (3), Oct. 1968 (4). 1 o, Jul. 1968. — *N. s. kruensis* (Sierra Leone to Ghana).

IMPERMANENT COLOURS. Legs black. Iris brown. Bill black, yellowish below.

STOMACH CONTENTS. Insects, including small beetles and caterpillars.

ANNUAL CYCLE. An October female was noted as having laid and one July, the three September and one other October female had moderately enlarged ovaries of 4–5 mm. July to October males' testes measured 3–5 mm, cf. 1 mm in the April male, which was in an early stage of wing-moult (inner primaries growing).

HABITAT. Lowland forest and shrub.

Nectarinia olivacea   Olive Sunbird

SPECIMENS. 13 ♂♂, Feb., Jun. 1966, 1967 (5), Jul. 1965, Aug. 1967, Sept. 1964, Nov. 1964, 1965, 1970. 3 imm. ♂♂, Jun. 1967, 1968, Aug. 1967. 12 ♀♀, Mar. 1975, Jun. 1967 (5), 1970, Jul. 1965, Nov. 64 (2), 1970, Dec. 1965. 2 imm. ♀♀, Jun. 1970, Oct. 1968. 2 o, Jan. 1966, Mar. 1968. — *N. o. guineensis*, (Guinea Bissau to Ghana).

IMPERMANENT COLOURS. Legs brown. Iris brown. Bill black.

STOMACH CONTENTS. Insects, including flying termites; also spiders and many small yellow seeds.

ANNUAL CYCLE. No evidence of breeding activity, but gonad data only available for ten June birds and one August male (testes 2 mm). Three females had ovaries measuring 5–6 mm and two males had testes of 3.5 and 5.5 mm. The remaining birds' gonads did not exceed 2 mm. A November male was in an early stage of wing-moult (2nd primary growing), and a November female in a late stage (7th primary growing).

HABITAT. Practically ubiquitous at Nimba. It is found in the interior of primary and old secondary forest growth, both in the lowland and the highland up to about 1000 m, as well as in the forest-shrub-grassland mosaics and in gardens.

Nectarinia verticalis   Olive-backed Sunbird

SPECIMENS. 5 ♂♂, Feb., Mar. 1968, Jun. 1966, 1970, Nov. 1968. 2 imm. ♂♂, Jun., Nov. 1968. 1 ♀, Nov. 1968. — *N. v. verticalis* (Senegal to Nigeria).

IMPERMANENT COLOURS. Legs black. Iris brown. Bill black.

STOMACH CONTENTS. Insects and one large hard seed.

ANNUAL CYCLE. Gonad data not available for June birds.

The March male had enlarged testes of 6 mm, *cf.* February (1 mm) and November (4 mm). The ovary of the November female was small (3 mm). February and March birds were in fresh plumage and the remainder were in worn condition.

HABITAT. This is a savanna species, inhabiting forest clearings and more open spaces.

Nectarinia cyanolaema Blue-throated Brown Sunbird

SPECIMENS. 13 ♂♂, Jun. 1970, Jul. 1967, 1968 (3), Aug. 1967 (3), Sept. (4), Oct. 1967. 3 imm. ♂♂, Sept. 1967, Oct. 1968, Dec. 1967. 5 ♀♀, Jul. 1967, 1968 (2), Aug. 1968 (2). — *N. c. magnirostrata* (Sierra Leone to Liberia).

IMPERMANENT COLOURS. Legs black. Iris brown. Bill black.

STOMACH CONTENTS. Insects and small spiders.

ANNUAL CYCLE. An August female had an enlarged ovary of 8 mm with ova of 1 mm, and was probably in breeding condition. Single July, August and three September males had moderately enlarged testes of 5–6 mm, and the October male had enlarged testes measuring 8 mm. Single June and July birds were in advanced stages of wing-moult (7th primary growing), and single July and August birds were completing (outer primaries growing).

HABITAT. Secondary lowland and montane forests, often along edges and in glades, up to about 1200 m.

Nectarinia fuliginosa Carmelite Sunbird

This sunbird was observed at Nimba by Forbes-Watson in 1967 or 1968. It occurs in forest clearings or gardens with flowering shrubs, avoiding densely forested regions, and is found mainly in coastal areas from Liberia to Gabon and Angola (PRC).

Nectarinia venusta Variable Sunbird

SPECIMENS. 6 ♂♂, Jan. 1966, 1968, Sept. 1967 (2), Oct. 1968 (2). 1 ♀, Nov. 1968. — *N. v. venusta* (Senegal to north Cameroon and Ubangi-Shari).

IMPERMANENT COLOURS. Legs black. Iris brown. Bill black.

STOMACH CONTENTS. Insects.

ANNUAL CYCLE. The November female had a moderately enlarged ovary of 5 mm. The two October males had enlarged testes of 5 mm, *cf.* 1 mm for January and 2–3 mm for September birds. January birds were worn and September–November birds in fresh plumage.

HABITAT. Open country with scattered trees, gardens and forest-grassland mosaics. At Mount Nimba up to about 1200 m.

Nectarinia adelberti Buff-throated Sunbird

SPECIMENS. 10 ♂♂, Jun., Jul. (3), Aug. 1968 (3), Oct. 1965, 1967, Nov. 1968. 5 juv. ♂♂, Jun. (2), Jul. (3) 1968. 2 imm. ♂♂, Aug., Oct. 1967. 5 ♀♀, Jun. (2), Jul. 1968, Aug., Oct. 1967. — *N. a. adelberti* (Sierra Leone to Ghana).

IMPERMANENT COLOURS. Legs black. Iris brown. Bill black.

STOMACH CONTENTS. Insects, including small caterpillars.

ANNUAL CYCLE. The five juveniles gave evidence of egg laying in May–June, even though June to August females' ovaries did not exceed 4.5 mm (no data for October female). Two August males had enlarged testes of 4 and 7 mm, and single October and November birds of 5 mm. June to August birds were in fresh plumage and October–November birds in worn condition.

HABITAT. Lowland primary and secondary forests, but often makes excursions into flowering trees outside the forest in order to feed.

Nectarinia chloropygia Olive-bellied Sunbird

SPECIMENS. 5 ♂♂, Jan. 1970, Feb., Mar., Aug. 1968, 1971. 2 imm. ♂♂, Jun. 1968 (2). 3 ♀♀, Mar. 1968 (2), Aug. 1971. — *N. c. kempi* (Sierra Leone to south-west Nigeria).

IMPERMANENT COLOURS. Legs black. Iris brown. Bill black.

STOMACH CONTENTS. Insects and some seeds.

ANNUAL CYCLE. Gonad data incomplete; no data for January and two August birds. Single February and August males had enlarged testes of 5 and 7 mm respectively and a March female had an enlarged ovary measuring 7 mm and was probably in breeding condition. The remaining March female and the March male were in wing-moult (primaries 6 and 9 growing).

HABITAT. A wide vertical and ecological range, from gardens, bush, the forest-grassland mosaic and clearings in lowland secondary forest at the foot of Nimba, to well lighted edges of montane forest up to about 1200 m.

Nectarinia minulla — Tiny Sunbird

SPECIMENS. 1 ♂, Oct. 1968. 1 ♀, Sept. 1967.

IMPERMANENT COLOURS. Legs black. Iris brown. Bill black.

STOMACH CONTENTS. Small insects.

ANNUAL CYCLE. Gonad data available for male only, testes 3 mm. Both birds were in fresh plumage.

DISTRIBUTION. This is a new record for Liberia and it represents an important extension of range some 800 km west. The species is now known from Liberia to southern Cameroon and Fernando Po, Zaire and east to western Uganda.

HABITAT. Netted in July–September 1978 in the grassland-forest mosaic at Grassfield (RW).

Nectarinia cuprea — Copper Sunbird

SPECIMENS. 5 ♂♂, Mar., Jun (2), Aug. 1968 (2). 1 imm. ♂, Jun. 1968. 1 ♀, Jun. 1968. — *N. c. cuprea* (Senegal to Ethiopia and Tanzania).

IMPERMANENT COLOURS. Legs black. Iris brown. Bill black.

STOMACH CONTENTS. Insects, including small beetles.

ANNUAL CYCLE. The March and two August males had enlarged gonads of 6 mm, *cf.* 2 mm in the June males. The female's ovary was small (4 mm). No wing-moult.

HABITAT AND STATUS. Grassy and bushy sites close to lowland forest as well as similar clearings. May occasionally visit gardens when trees there are in flower. This is a new record for Liberia.

Nectarinia coccinigaster — Splendid Sunbird

SPECIMENS. 2 ♂♂, Oct. 1968 (2).

IMPERMANENT COLOURS. Legs black. Iris brown. Bill black.

STOMACH CONTENTS. Insects.

ANNUAL CYCLE. Testes of the males were small (1.0–1.5 mm). Both were in early to mid stages of wing-moult (3rd to 5th primaries growing).

HABITAT AND STATUS. Open country with bush, scattered trees and the forest-grassland mosaic. Visits flowering trees in gardens. This species is migratory, although the pattern is not as yet understood. In nearby Sierra Leone it is only present in May–December.

Nectarinia johannae — Johanna's Sunbird

SPECIMENS. 12 ♂♂, Jan. 1970, Feb. 1968 (5), Jun. 1967, Jul. 1968, Oct. 1967, 1968 (2), Dec. 1968. 5 ♀♀, Feb. 1968, 1969, Jul. 1968, Oct., Nov. 1967. — *N. j. fasciata* (Sierra Leone to Dahomey).

IMPERMANENT COLOURS. Legs black. Iris brown. Bill black.

STOMACH CONTENTS. Insects, including caterpillars; also some spiders.

ANNUAL CYCLE. Little evidence of breeding activity. The males' testes were small (1–3 mm) and single females in February, October and November had slightly enlarged ovaries of 5 mm. A February male was in an advanced stage of wing-moult (8th primary growing), three October birds were in middle stages (4th to 6th primaries growing), and the December male was completing wing-moult (outer primaries growing).

HABITAT. Mainly observed along edges and in clearings of primary and lowland forest, but it does certainly live inside the forest as well.

Nectarinia superba — Superb Sunbird

SPECIMENS. 3 ♂♂, Apr. 1974, Jun., Nov. 1968. 1 imm. ♂ Jun. 1968. 1 ♀, Jun. 1968. — *N. s. ashantiensis* (Sierra Leone to Ghana).

IMPERMANENT COLOURS. Legs black. Iris brown. Bill black.

STOMACH CONTENTS. Insects and a few small green seeds.

ANNUAL CYCLE. The June female had an enlarged ovary of 8 mm and was probably in breeding condition. Males' testes measured 2 mm in June and 5 mm in November. The April male (no gonad data) was in an advanced stage of wing-moult (outer primaries growing), and the November male was in the middle of stage (5th primary growing).

HABITAT. Primary and secondary lowland and montane forests, including clearings and edges up to 1200 m.

Family Zosteropidae

Zosterops senegalensis — Yellow White-eye

SPECIMENS. 8 ♂♂, May 1968 (2), Jun. 1967 (2), Aug. (2),

Oct., Nov. 1968. 1 ♀, Jun. 1967. — *Z. s. demeryi* (Sierra Leone to Ivory Coast).

IMPERMANENT COLOURS. Legs blue-grey. Iris brown. Bill black.

STOMACH CONTENTS. Insects; fruit pulp, including small hard seeds.

ANNUAL CYCLE. Single May, June, August and October males had enlarged gonads (6–7 mm), and were probably in breeding condition. The ovary of the female was small (5.5 mm). The two May and a November male were in advanced stages of wing-moult (8th primary growing), and the June female was completing (outer primaries growing).

HABITAT AND HABITS. At Nimba this species frequents a wide range of habitats. It is common even in the dry season in the parkland and gardens at Yekepa, and in March often sings vigorously from isolated trees standing in the middle of the dry, brown lawns. It has also been seen and heard in the deciduous *Gmelina* plantations during the dry season when there is hardly a leaf on the trees. Other habitats are clearings and farms in the lowland and montane forests up to about 800 m.

Family Emberizidae

Emberiza tahapisi Cinnamon-breasted Rock-Bunting

A flock of about eight birds was observed (KC-L) in the bare rocky mine area of Mount Nimba at about 1200 m on 4 March 1980. This is a new record for Liberia. It is migratory, but its movements in West Africa are so far little understood (Curry-Lindahl, 1981).

Family Fringillidae

Serinus mozambicus Yellow-fronted Canary

SPECIMEN. 1 imm. ♂, Jan. 1968 (gonads small). — *S. m. caniceps* (Senegal to Nigeria).

IMPERMANENT COLOURS. Legs dull grey. Iris brown. Bill pinkish-brown.

STOMACH CONTENTS. Grass seeds.

HABITAT AND STATUS. This species was first observed in 1965 at Nimba. As it generally inhabits cultivated ground and gardens the lack of records in 1963–64 suggests that it was absent from Nimba prior to 1965. It increased considerably during the late 1960s and even more so in the following decade, after the expansion of cultivation and gardens at Yekepa. This is a new record for Liberia.

Family Estrildidae

Mandingoa nitidula Green-backed Twin-spot

SPECIMENS. 12 ♂♂, Mar. 1966, Apr. 1968, Jun. 1967 (5), 1968, Jul. 1967, Aug. 1971 (2), Sept. 1967. 2 imm. ♂♂, Jan., Feb. 1968. 2 juv. ♂♂, Sept. 1967, 1968. 8 ♀♀, Feb. 1971, May 1968, Jun. (2), Jul. (2), Sept. 1967, Dec. 1965. 1 imm. ♀, Jan. 1968. — *M. n. schlegeli* (Sierra Leone to Uganda).

IMPERMANENT COLOURS. Legs pale brown. Iris brown. Bill red, black towards the base.

STOMACH CONTENTS. Seeds and vegetable matter.

ANNUAL CYCLE. The two September juveniles indicate egg-laying in August. The September female had an enlarged ovary with ova to 10 mm, *cf*. ovaries of 4–6 mm in the May and four June–July females. (No gonad data for February or December birds.) Five June males and the September male had moderately enlarged testes of 4–6 mm (no gonad data for March, July and August males). No wing-moult.

HABITAT. Dense thickets and secondary forest, often near cultivated areas; also the forest-grassland mosaics at Grassfield and Yekepa.

Pirenestes sanguineus Crimson Seed-Cracker

SPECIMENS. 10 ♂♂, Feb. (2), Mar., Apr., May, Jun., Jul. 1968, Sept. 1965, 1968, 1970. 12 imm. ♂♂, Feb. 1967, 1968 (8), Mar. (2), May 1968. 7 ♀♀, Feb. (3), Apr., May 1968 (3). 1 imm. ♀, Feb. 1968.

IMPERMANENT COLOURS. Legs brown slightly tinged yellow. Iris brown. Bill blackish-blue.

STOMACH CONTENTS. Seeds and vegetable matter.

ANNUAL CYCLE. No evidence of breeding activity, but no gonad data for a third of the specimens. Two February, the April and the May females had ovaries of 4–7 mm and single February and March males had testes of 4–5 mm, *cf*. single April, May, July and September birds with testes of 1–4 mm. A March male was in an early stage of wing-moult, inner primaries growing, three February birds were in advanced stages, 6th and 7th primaries growing, and four April–May birds were completing wing-moult, outer primaries growing.

DISTRIBUTION AND GEOGRAPHICAL VARIATION. Two adult males had larger and more massive bills (breadth of lower mandible at base, 17.5 mm) than the rest and agree with B.M.(N.H.) specimens of the nominate form collected in Gambia, Guinea Bissau and a single male from Sierra Leone. The remainder which have a distinctly less robust bill (Nimba birds average 13 mm) are *P. s. coccineus*, which is found in Sierra Leone and

Liberia. While formerly the smaller-billed and larger-billed birds presumably occupied different geographical areas, the clearing of forest may have influenced their distribution, and now different types are found together and may interbreed (see Hall & Moreau, 1970).

HABITAT. The lowland bush and cultivated area below Mount Nimba, but also swampy bush areas and the vicinity of forest streams and thickets in old forest clearings.

Nigrita canicapilla Grey-headed Negro-Finch

SPECIMENS. 8 ♂♂, Feb. 1971, Apr. 1968 (2), Jun. 1966, Jul., Aug. 1968, Oct. 1967 (2). 8 ♀♀, Jun., Jul. 1967, Aug. 1968, Sept. 1968 (2), 1970, Oct. 1967 (2). — *N. c. emiliae* (Guinea to Ghana and Togo).

IMPERMANENT COLOURS. Legs dark brown. Iris bright red, yellow after death. Bill black.

STOMACH CONTENTS. Seeds, vegetable matter, pink fruit pulp and some insects.

ANNUAL CYCLE. Single July and October females had enlarged ovaries (11, 9 mm) and the August female was noted as having recently laid. Males had enlarged testes for April (6, 8 mm), July (10 mm), August (8 mm) and one October male (6.5 mm). Two June, two September and one October female were in advanced stages of wing-moult (7th to 10th primaries growing).

HABITAT. Tall bush with scattered trees; clearings and edges of secondary lowland forest; also tree plantations and gardens.

Nigrita bicolor Chestnut-breasted Negro-Finch

SPECIMENS. 7 ♂♂, Jan. 1968, Jun., Jul. (2), Aug., Sept. 1967 (2). 5 imm. ♂♂, Feb., Jun. 1968, Sept. 1967, 1970 (2), Oct. 1967. 5 ♀♀, Feb. 1968, Jun., Aug., Sept., Oct. 1967. 1 imm. ♀, Jun. 1968. — *N. b. bicolor* (Sierra Leone to Ghana).

IMPERMANENT COLOURS. Legs brown. Iris red. Bill black.

STOMACH CONTENTS. Insects and seeds.

ANNUAL CYCLE. No evidence of breeding activity. The females' ovaries measured 5–6 mm (no data for February female). Males had enlarged testes (5.0–6.5 mm) in June, July and September, *cf.* 1 mm for the January male. The June female was commencing wing-moult (1st primary growing), the August female and January male were in the later stages (4th and 7th primaries growing, resp.).

HABITAT. Lowland and montane primary and secondary forests, along their edges. On Mount Nimba it occurs in pairs at many localities between 700 and 1000 m.

Nigrita fusconota White-breasted Negro-Finch

SPECIMENS. 3 ♂♂, Aug. 1968, Oct. 1967, 1968. 1 ♀, Jul. 1967. 1 o, Aug. 1968. — *N. f. uropygialis* (Guinea to southern Nigeria).

IMPERMANENT COLOURS. Legs dark brown. Iris brown. Bill black.

STOMACH CONTENTS. Insects and grass seeds.

ANNUAL CYCLE. No evidence of breeding activity. The July female had an ovary measuring 5 mm, the August male had testes of 5 mm, and the October males had testes of 1.5 and 4 mm. One October male was completing wing-moult (outer primary growing).

STATUS AND HABITAT. This is a new record for Liberia. It is found in forest clearings and along forest edges.

Parmoptila jamesoni Red-fronted Ant-pecker

SPECIMENS. 19 ♂♂, Jan. 1966, 1968 (2), Feb., Apr. 1968, Jun. 1967 (2), 1968, Jul. 1967 (2), 1968 (3), Aug. 1967, 1968 (2), Sept. 1967, Oct. 1968, Nov. 1970. 3 imm. ♂♂, Aug., Nov. 1968 (2). 13 ♀♀, Jan., Apr. 1968 (2), Jun. 1967 (3), 1968, Jul. 1967 (2), 1968, Sept. 1967, Oct. 1968 (2).

IMPERMANENT COLOURS. Legs pale brown. Iris chestnut-brown. Bill black.

STOMACH CONTENTS. Insects, including small beetles and ants; also small seeds.

ANNUAL CYCLE. An April female had a soft-shelled egg (0.6 g) in the oviduct. Single April, June and two July females (both in wing-moult) had moderately enlarged ovaries of 6 mm. A September female had an enlarged ovary of 10 mm and was possibly in breeding condition. Single males had enlarged testes in January, February and April (4–6 mm), and seven males (four of them in wing-moult) had testes of 4.5–6.0 mm in June, July and August. Six June–July birds were in middle stages of wing-moult (4th to 7th primaries growing). A single October female was in early wing-moult (inner primaries growing), and another October female was just completing wing-moult (outer primaries growing).

DISTRIBUTION AND STATUS. *Parmoptila jamesoni* was long known from West Africa only by old specimens collected in 'Denkera', an area of Ghana south of Kumasi. In 1966 it was rediscovered on Mount Nimba. It has not been found in Cameroon, where its place is taken by *P. woodhousei*, but reappears in central Zaire. The Nimba birds are *P. j. rubrifrons*. This is the first record of this species for Liberia and it represents an extension of range from Ghana of some 800 km west. They are birds of primary forest or forest edge, occasionally accompanying mixed bird parties.

Spermophaga haematina — Blue-bill

SPECIMENS. 12 ♂♂, Feb. (2), Apr. 1968, Jun. (5), Jul. 1967, Oct. 1964, Nov. 1970 (2). 2 imm. ♂♂, Jan., Oct. 1968. 12 ♀♀, Jan. 1971, Jun. (6), Jul. 1967, Oct. 1965, 1970 (2), Nov. 1970. 1 imm. ♀, Oct. 1968. — *S. h. haematina* (Gambia to Ghana).

IMPERMANENT COLOURS. Legs blackish-brown. Iris red-brown. Bill steel-blue, tipped pink.

STOMACH CONTENTS. Insects and seeds.

ANNUAL CYCLE. No evidence of breeding activity, but no gonad data for January, October and November birds. The females' ovaries were small (3–6 mm) and the males' testes did not exceed 4 mm. The April male was completing wing-moult (outer primaries growing).

HABITAT. Thickets and bushes, especially near stagnant water, rivers surrounded by forest, and old farms; also the forest-grassland mosaic at the foot of Mount Nimba.

Estrilda melpoda — Orange-cheeked Waxbill

SPECIMENS. 8 ♂♂, Mar., Jun., Aug. 1968 (3), Sept. 1968 (2), Oct. 1969. 2 imm. ♂♂, Sept., Nov. 1968. 1 juv. ♂, Jun. 1967. 8 ♀♀, Jun. 1966, 1968, Aug. 1968 (5), Sept. 1967. — *E. m. melpoda* (Gambia to N. Zaire etc.).

IMPERMANENT COLOURS. Legs brown. Iris brown. Bill pinkish-red.

STOMACH CONTENTS. Seeds.

ANNUAL CYCLE. The juvenile, with tail-feathers less than half-grown on 16 June, indicates egg-laying in May. A September female, with an enlarged ovary of 7 mm, may have been approaching breeding condition; *cf.* five August females with ovaries of 2 mm (no data for March or June females). Single June and August males had enlarged testes of 6 mm, and the two September males had testes of 4 and 5 mm, no data for the March and October males. No wing-moult.

HABITAT AND HABITS. Found wherever there are patches of medium to tall grasses growing in a range of habitats, particularly along paths, in clearings and just beside the forest edge from lowland areas up to 1200 m; also in the forest-grassland mosaics. Usually seen feeding in flocks of about 10 birds but sometimes gathering in flocks of hundreds.

Estrilda astrild — Common Waxbill

SPECIMENS. 9 ♂♂, Mar., Apr. 1968, Jun. 1966, Aug. 1968 (6). 1 imm. ♂, Sept. 1968. 2 ♀♀, Aug. 1968 (2). 1 juv. o, Aug. 1968. — *E. a. kempi* (Sierra Leone and Liberia).

IMPERMANENT COLOURS. Legs grey-black. Iris brown. Bill red.

STOMACH CONTENTS. Seeds.

ANNUAL CYCLE. The August juvenile indicates egg-laying probably in late July. Two August males had enlarged ovaries of 5 and 6 mm. Five August males had moderately enlarged gonads of 3–6 mm, *cf.* 1.0–1.5 mm in March and April males. No wing-moult.

HABITAT AND HABITS. A common bird at Nimba in grassy habitats and cultivations particularly at lower levels, but occasionally found up to about 1000 m. They spend much of their time travelling in flocks of 15–30 birds seeking seeds from the grasses, which are usually harvested from the grass tops before the seeds have been released.

Estrilda caerulescens — Lavender Firefinch

This firefinch was observed at Nimba (AF-W) in 1967 or 1968. This is the first record of this species for Liberia. It is generally found in comparatively arid areas, but also frequents the edges of thickets, grass verges of roads and open places where the grass is short. It is found from Senegal and Mali east to southern Chad and the Central African Republic (PRC).

Lagonosticta senegala — Red-billed Firefinch

This species was observed at Nimba (KC-L & AF-W). It is very common in grassy areas, where it is particularly attracted to gardens and human settlements.

Lagonosticta rubricata — Dark Firefinch

SPECIMENS. 3 ♂♂, Apr. (2), Aug. 1968. 3 imm. ♂♂, Feb. (2), Apr. 1968. 1 ♀, Feb. 1968. — *L. r. polionota* (Guinea Bissau to Ghana and Nigeria).

IMPERMANENT COLOURS. Legs grey. Iris brown. Bill blue-grey.

STOMACH CONTENTS. Seeds.

ANNUAL CYCLE. Gonad data only available for the August male which was in fresh plumage with testes of 5 mm. One April male was completing wing-moult (outer primaries growing).

HABITAT. Bush and open grassy areas and thickets by streams.

Lagonosticta rara   Black-bellied Firefinch

This firefinch was observed at Nimba (AF-W) in 1967 or 1968. This is the first record for Liberia. In West Africa it is found in savanna from Senegal to Cameroon.

Amandava subflava   Orange-breasted Waxbill

SPECIMEN. 1 ♀, Jun. 1966. — *A. s. subflava* (Senegal to Ethiopia).

IMPERMANENT COLOURS. Legs pale brown. Iris red. Bill blackish with some red at the sides.

STOMACH CONTENTS. Seeds.

ANNUAL CYCLE. The size of the ovary of the female was not recorded. It was in an early stage of wing-moult (4th primary growing).

HABITAT AND STATUS. This species was observed (KC-L) at Nimba in 1963, 1966 and subsequent years in and close to the lowland grassland bordering Guinea as well as in the opened up areas of Yekepa and Grassfield. It is fond of the vicinity of water, even where the vegetation mostly consists of dry broken branches and twigs from earlier clearings. This is a new record for Liberia.

Lonchura bicolor   Black and White Mannikin

SPECIMENS. 8 ♂♂, Feb. (3), Jun. 1968 (4), Sept. 1967. 2 imm. ♂♂, Feb. 1968 (2). 1 juv. ♂, Nov. 1968. 8 ♀♀, Feb. 1968, Jun. 1967, 1968 (3), Aug. 1965, 1967, Sept. 1965. 2 imm. ♀♀, Feb. 1968 (2). 2 juv. ♀♀, Oct. 1967, Nov. 1964. 2 juv. o, Feb., Nov. 1968. — *L. b. bicolor* (Guinea Bissau to Cameroon).

IMPERMANENT COLOURS. Legs grey-brown. Iris brown. Bill blue-black.

STOMACH CONTENTS. Seeds and vegetable matter.

ANNUAL CYCLE. The five juveniles indicate egg-laying in September–October and December. Gonad data lacking for two February and single August and September birds. Three June females had moderately enlarged ovaries of 6–8 mm, and four June males had testes of 4–6 mm. Single February and August birds were in mid wing-moult (5th and 6th primaries growing), and single February and June birds were completing wing-moult (outer primaries growing).

HABITAT. Cultivation, abandoned farms, forest clearings and young secondary growth.

Lonchura fringilloides   Magpie Mannikin

SPECIMENS. 6 ♂, Jul. 1968 (2), Aug. (2), Sept. 1967, Dec. 1964. 3 imm. ♂♂, Feb. (2), Dec. 1968. 3 ♀♀, Feb. 1968, Aug., Oct. 1967. 2 imm. ♀♀, Feb., Oct. 1968. 1 o, Feb. 1968.

IMPERMANENT COLOURS. Legs black. Iris brown. Bill black.

STOMACH CONTENTS. Seeds and insects.

ANNUAL CYCLE. No evidence of breeding activity, but gonad data incomplete. Single August and October females had ovaries of 4.5 and 6.5 mm respectively. The two July and single August and September males had testes of 4.5–5.0 mm. Two February birds were in middle stages of wing-moult (5th primary growing).

HABITAT. Locally common at Nimba in cultivated areas and in gardens.

Lonchura cucullata   Bronze Mannikin

SPECIMENS. 2 ♂♂, Feb. 1968 (2). 1 imm. ♂, Jul. 1965. 1 ♀, Feb. 1968. 1 imm. ♀, Feb. 1968. — *L. c. cucullata* (Senegal to western Kenya).

IMPERMANENT COLOURS. Legs grey-brown. Iris brown. Bill black.

STOMACH CONTENTS. Seeds.

ANNUAL CYCLE. No evidence of breeding activity. The three February adults had small gonads (1–3 mm), and were in advanced stages of wing-moult (6th, 8th and 9th primaries growing).

HABITAT. Villages, gardens, cultivation, and any areas of open country or bush up to the edge of the forest.

Pholidornis rushiae   Tit-Hylia

SPECIMENS. 9 ♂♂, Feb., Apr. 1968, Jun., Jul. 1967 (2), Sept. 1967 (2), 1968, 1970. 7 ♀♀, Apr. 1968, Jun. 1970, Aug. 1968, 1971, Sept. 1967 (2), Oct. 1968. 1 imm. ♀, Apr. 1968. 1 o, Aug. 1968. 1 juv., Feb. 1968. — *P. r. ussheri* (Sierra Leone to Ghana).

IMPERMANENT COLOURS. Legs waxy-yellow. Iris dark orange, grey in imm. Bill black, lower mandible yellow-orange.

STOMACH CONTENTS. Insects.

ANNUAL CYCLE. The juveniles, collected on 15 February, indicates egg-laying in January. Gonad data incomplete. Single females had moderately enlarged ovaries (4–5 mm) in April, August, September and October. Two September males had testes of 3.5 and 4.0 mm, *cf.* 1–2 mm for the remainder. Two July males were in middle stages of wing-moult (4th and 7th primaries growing), and single June and September males were completing (outer primaries growing).

SYSTEMATIC STATUS. This species has variously been placed with the Nectariniidae, Estrildidae or Ploceidae. Hall & Moreau (1970) did not place it in a family and 'purely for convenience' put it between the Sittidae and the Nectariniidae. It was left in a genus *incertae sedis* by Traylor (1968), who was equally doubtful. A recent appraisal of the species by Vernon & Dean (1975) shows it to be closely similar to the penduline-tits *Anthoscopus caroli* and *A. minutus* in call, social behaviour, feeding habits, size and juvenile plumage, nest structure and breeding behaviour. They suggest that *P. rushiae* be regarded either as a member of the Remizidae or as a remarkable case of convergence with that family.

HABITAT AND HABITS. The Tit-Hylia shows a preference for secondary forest and trees in clearings, feeding high up in the tree tops. It is found in both lowland and montane forests, and has been recorded up to 1200 m on Nimba (1 March 1980).

Family Ploceidae

Amblyospiza albifrons — Grosbeak Weaver

SPECIMENS. 11 ♂♂, Jan. 1970, Jul., Aug. 1968, Sept. 1968 (2), 1970, 1975, Oct. 1967 (2), 1969, Nov. 1970. 3 imm. ♂♂, Sept. 1968 (3). 3 ♀♀, Sept. 1968, Oct. 1969, Nov. 1970. 1 imm. ♀, Jan. 1970. — *A. a. capitalba* (Sierra Leone to Ghana).

IMPERMANENT COLOURS. Legs grey. Iris brown. Bill black, light greyish-horn in the female.

STOMACH CONTENTS. Hard brown seeds.

ANNUAL CYCLE. A September female was noted as having recently laid. Single July, August and two September males had enlarged testes of 9–11 mm and were probably in breeding condition. Two October males had testes of 6 and 7 mm (gonad data incomplete for the remaining adults). No wing-moult. January, October and November birds were in very worn condition.

HABITAT AND STATUS. In 1966 this species was observed in dry reeds in the Yah Valley. In later years it was mostly seen in forest clearings and in dry aquatic vegetation. This is a new record for Liberia.

Ploceus aurantius — Orange Weaver

A flock of about 8 birds, comprising both sexes, was seen (KC-L) on 25 February 1980 between Grassfield and the airstrip at Nimba, in riverside trees in the forest-grassland mosaic. A year later he searched the same area for signs of a colony, but no old nests which could be attributed to Orange Weavers were found.

Ploceus cucullatus — Black-headed Village Weaver

SPECIMENS. 4 ♂♂, Feb., Mar., Apr. 1968, Nov. 1970. 4 imm. ♂♂, Feb. 1968, Jul. 1965, Sept. 1964, 1967. 11 ♀♀, Jul. 1966, Aug. 1967 (3), 1970, Sept. 1964, 1967 (4), 1970. 3 imm. ♀♀, Sept. 1967 (2), Nov. 1970. 1 o, Aug. 1967. — *P. c. cucullatus* (Senegal to Zaire).

IMPERMANENT COLOURS. Legs brownish-flesh. Iris red, orange in the female. Bill black, dark horn in the female.

STOMACH CONTENTS. Seeds and insects.

ANNUAL CYCLE. Of the four September females with gonad data, one had recently laid (1 Sept.), one had a yolk of 8 mm, one had ova to 5.5 mm, and one had an ovary of 8 mm. Three August females had ovaries of 7 mm (gonad data incomplete for the remaining females). The males had testes of 8.5 mm in February, 8 mm in March and 4 mm in April (no data for November male). The November male was in an early stage of wing-moult (inner primaries growing), and the February male and November female were completing (outer primaries growing).

HABITAT. Forest clearings and savanna, showing a preference for towns, villages and cultivation, but can also breed in high forest.

Ploceus castaneofuscus x *cucullatus* — hybrid Weaver

SPECIMEN. 1 ♂, Feb. 1968; enlarged testes (8 mm), fresh plumage.

IMPERMANENT COLOURS. Legs brownish-pink. Iris pale yellow-orange. Bill black.

STOMACH CONTENTS. Oil palm fruits.

PLUMAGE. The head, chin and throat of this hybrid *Ploceus* are black as in *P. cucullatus*. The underparts are like *castaneofuscus*, but are a paler chestnut with the belly, vent and undertail coverts tinged yellowish. The back is dull yellow with a few feathers edged pale chestnut. The wings are black and broadly edged like *cucullatus*, but with a duller buffish-yellow. The tail is intermediate between the two species and is blackish with a hint of yellow, and the rump (also intermediate) is a mixture of yellow and pale chestnut. The iris colour was also noted as a mixture of the two species.

There are previous records of hybrids between the closely allied *P. nigerrimus* and *P. cucullatus* (Mackworth-Praed & Grant, 1970), and between *P. nigerrimus* and *P. castaneofuscus* (Serle, 1957).

Ploceus castaneofuscus — Black and Chestnut Weaver

SPECIMENS. 15 ♂♂, Mar. 1968, Aug. (6), Sept. 1967 (3), 1968, Oct. 1965, 1969, 1970, Nov. 1970. 10 imm. ♂♂, Mar. 1968, Aug. (5), Sept. 1964, 1967 (3). 1 juv. ♂, Aug. 1967. 13 ♀♀, Jun., Aug. (8), Sept. (3), Oct. 1967.

IMPERMANENT COLOURS. Legs brown. Iris yellow. Bill black, dark horn below in the female.

STOMACH CONTENTS. Seeds and fruit remains.

ANNUAL CYCLE. Egg-laying in July is indicated by the August juvenile, and a September female had an enlarged ovary with yolks to 10 mm. Another August female had a moderately enlarged ovary of 8.5 mm. A March male had testes of 8 mm, five August males had enlarged testes of 8–11 mm and two September males also had enlarged testes of 10.0 and 10.5 mm, and were probably in breeding condition (no data for October–November males). However, breeding also occurs in February–March (see below under Breeding). September to November birds were in worn condition. No wing-moult.

BREEDING. On 27 February 1980 a colony was found (KC-L) in all stages of breeding activity near Bossou in Guinea, a few km from the Liberian border at Nimba. Four days later another colony was observed on the Liberian side. Both colonies comprised some 20 nests. The Guinean one was located above a pond-like stretch of river with almost stagnant water. The nests were built in a low tree of which a large branch stretched almost horizontally out over the water, and were hanging over the water only 1–2 m above the surface. The colony in Liberia was located at about 6–8 m in a medium-sized tree standing beside a swamp in the Seka Valley.

HABITAT. Vicinity of swamps, secondary forest clearings, outskirts of farmlands and villages, and the forest-grassland-river mosaic at Grassfield. Breeding colonies have been found (KC-L) in a forest clearing close to a swamp and over a river 'lagoon' in secondary forest.

Ploceus superciliosus — Compact Weaver

SPECIMENS. 4 ♂♂, Apr. 1968 (3), Sept. 1971. 1 imm. ♂, Apr. 1968. 1 ♀, Dec. 1968.

IMPERMANENT COLOURS. Legs pale brown. Iris brown. Bill black.

STOMACH CONTENTS. Seeds, fibres and insects.

ANNUAL CYCLE. Gonad data incomplete; no evidence of breeding activity. The December female had an ovary of 3 mm, and two April males had small testes of 1 mm. The female was in wing-moult (5th primary growing).

HABITAT AND STATUS. Cultivated land, opened-up areas, gardens, forest-grassland mosaics and forest edges. In West Africa it is found in the grass savanna belt next to the forest from Senegal to Gabon and Zaire. This is a new record for Liberia.

Ploceus tricolor — Yellow-mantled Weaver

SPECIMENS. 5 ♂♂, Mar., Aug. 1968, Sept. 1967, 1968, Nov. 1964. 3 imm. ♂♂, Jun. 1967, Jul. 1968, Aug. 1967. 2 ♀♀, Aug. 1967, Sept. 1968. 1 imm. ♀, Sept. 1968. — *P. t. tricolor* (Sierra Leone to Cameroon).

IMPERMANENT COLOURS. Legs dark grey-brown. Iris brown. Bill black.

STOMACH CONTENTS. Insects, including beetles, grasshoppers and caterpillars; also some vegetable matter.

ANNUAL CYCLE. No evidence of breeding activity. August and September females' ovaries were not enlarged (7 mm). The two September males had testes of 8 and 10 mm, cf. March and August males with testes of 5 mm (no gonad data for November male). The September female was in an advanced stage of wing-moult (7th primary growing).

HABITAT. Heavy forest; usually found in the tree tops in the interior, or on the edge of primary forest.

Ploceus albinucha — Maxwell's Black Weaver

SPECIMEN. 1 ♀, March 1968; ovary 4 mm, in worn plumage. — *P. a. albinucha* (Sierra Leone to Ghana).

IMPERMANENT COLOURS. Legs brown. Iris greenish-white. Bill brown.

STOMACH CONTENTS. Insects.

HABITAT. The vicinity of villages surrounded by secondary forest.

Ploceus nigricollis — Black-necked Weaver

SPECIMENS. 9 ♂♂, Feb. (2), Mar., Jul. 1968 (3), Sept. 1967, Oct. 1969, Nov. 1965. 2 imm. ♂♂, Mar., Aug. 1968. 15 ♀♀, Feb. (3), Apr., May (4), Jun. (2), Jul. 1965, 1968 (2), Sept. 1967, Oct. 1969. 1 imm. ♀., Jul. 1968. 1 juv. ♀, Apr. 1968. — *P. n. brachypterus* (Senegal to Cameroon).

IMPERMANENT COLOURS. Legs blue-grey. Iris creamy-yellow. Bill black, paler horn in younger birds.

STOMACH CONTENTS. Insects and seeds.

ANNUAL CYCLE. Egg-laying in early February is indicated by the juvenile, collected on 7 April. A July female, with an ovary of 12 mm and ova to 1 mm, was probably in breeding condition. Three February, two May and two June females had moderately enlarged ovaries of 8–9 mm. The males mainly had small testes (2–4 mm), except for two July males with testes of 5 and 6 mm. Single May, September and October birds were in early stages of wing-moult (inner primaries growing), and single February and July birds were in mid to late stages (5th to 7th primaries growing).

HABITAT. Common at Nimba in lowland secondary forests, but may occasionally ascend in montane forests.

Ploceus preussi — Golden-backed Weaver

SPECIMENS. 1 ♂, 1 ♀, Apr. 1968.

IMPERMANENT COLOURS. Legs pinkish-flesh. Iris brown. Bill black.

STOMACH CONTENTS. Insects, including beetles.

ANNUAL CYCLE. No evidence of breeding activity. Gonads of both birds measured 6 mm. The April female was in the middle of wing-moult (5th primary growing), and the male was in worn plumage.

DISTRIBUTION AND STATUS. This is a new record for Liberia. It is found in Sierra Leone, southern Cameroon and Zaire.

Malimbus nitens — Blue-billed Malimbe

SPECIMENS. 10 ♂♂, Jan. 1969, May 1965, Aug. 1967, 1968, Sept. 1973, Oct. 1968, 1970, Nov. 1967, 1968, Dec. 1969. 2 imm. ♂♂, Jun. 1967, Dec. 1968. 12 ♀♀, Mar. 1974, 1975, Jun. 1967 (2), Aug. 1967, 1968, Sept. 1973, Oct. 1968, 1970, Nov., Dec. 1968 (2). 1 imm. ♀, Mar. 1974. 1 juv. o, Nov. 1968.

IMPERMANENT COLOURS. Legs grey. Iris red. Bill blue-grey.

STOMACH CONTENTS. Insects, including grasshoppers, and seeds.

ANNUAL CYCLE. The juvenile, collected on 15 November, indicated egg-laying in early October. Gonad data lacking for January–May and September birds, and two October females. Seven females' ovaries (June–December) measured 6.5–8.0 mm. Single August and October males had testes of 6.0–6.5 mm and the two November males had more enlarged testes of 7 and 9 mm. Single March, May and June birds were in early stages of wing-moult (inner primaries growing), and single March, June and August females were completing wing-moult (8th to 9th primaries growing). November–December birds were in very worn condition.

HABITAT. Dense primary and secondary lowland forest.

Malimbus scutatus — Red-vented Malimbe

SPECIMENS. 3 ♂♂, Aug. 1968, Oct., Nov. 1967. 3 ♀♀, Sept., Nov. 1967 (2). — *M. s. scutatus* (Sierra Leone to Ghana).

IMPERMANENT COLOURS. Legs black. Iris brown. Bill black.

STOMACH CONTENTS. Insects, including caterpillars.

ANNUAL CYCLE. No evidence of breeding activity. A September female had a small ovary of 5.5 mm and two November females had ovaries of 4.5 and 7.5 mm. The males had testes measuring 2 mm in August and 5.5–6.0 mm in October–November. A November female (ovary 7.5 mm) was in an early stage of wing-moult (4th primary growing).

HABITAT. Clearings in secondary lowland forest, cultivated areas and villages.

Malimbus rubricollis — Red-headed Malimbe

SPECIMENS. 1 ♂, Nov. 1967. 2 ♀♀, Aug. 1967 (2). — *M. r. bartletti* (Sierra Leone to Ghana).

IMPERMANENT COLOURS. Legs black. Iris brown. Bill black.

STOMACH CONTENTS. Insects, including beetles; also spiders.

ANNUAL CYCLE. No evidence of breeding activity. The females' ovaries measured 3.0 and 6.5 mm and the testes of the male, 4.5 mm. No wing-moult.

HABITAT. Primary forest.

Malimbus malimbicus — Crested Malimbe

SPECIMENS. 3 ♂♂, Mar. 1974, Jul. 1965, Nov. 1970. 1 imm. ♂, Nov. 1970. 5 ♀♀, Jan. 1970, 1971, Jun. 1967, Sept. 1967, 1968. 2 imm. ♀♀, Feb. 1968, Apr. 1969. — *M. m. nigrifrons* (Sierra Leone to southern Nigeria).

IMPERMANENT COLOURS. Legs black. Iris brown. Bill black.

STOMACH CONTENTS. Insects, including caterpillars and beetles.

ANNUAL CYCLE. Gonad data only available for four females. Two September females had moderately enlarged ovaries of 7.0–7.5 mm, *cf.* 4 and 6 mm for February and June females respectively. January–February females were in early to mid stages of wing-moult (2nd to 6th primaries growing) and the June and July birds were completing wing-moult (outer primaries growing).

HABITAT. Primary and secondary lowland and montane forest up to the ridge of Mount Nimba.

Quelea erythrops   Red-headed Quelea

SPECIMENS. 11 ♂♂, Sept. 1968 (2), Oct. 1967 (4), 1969, Nov. 1967 (2), 1968, 1970. 5 imm. ♂♂, Feb. (2), Mar. 1968, Oct. 1967 (2). 10 ♀♀, Mar. 1968, Oct. 1967 (7), 1969, Nov. 1967. 1 juv., Nov. 1967. — *Q. e. erythrops* (West Africa).

IMPERMANENT COLOURS. Legs brownish-flesh. Iris brown. Bill brown.

STOMACH CONTENTS. Mostly rice and other seeds.

ANNUAL CYCLE. Egg-laying in October is indicated by the juvenile collected on 7 November. Three October females and the November female had enlarged ovaries of 8.5–11.5 mm, *cf.* 3 mm in the March female and 5.5 mm in three other October females. September and October males had enlarged testes (8–9 mm, one 5 mm). No wing-moult. Many of the October birds were in worn plumage.

HABITAT. Edges and clearings close to the edges of secondary lowland and montane forest up to about 800 m. Also forest-grassland mosaics.

Euplectes macrourus Yellow-mantled Whydah

SPECIMENS. 12 ♂♂, Feb., Jun. 1968 (2), Jul. 1965 (4), 1966, 1968, Aug. 1968, Oct. 1969, Nov. 1967. 1 ♀, Mar. 1968. — *E. m. macrourus* (Senegal to Tanzania).

IMPERMANENT COLOURS. Legs black. Iris brown. Bill black with a paler horn tip.

STOMACH CONTENTS. Seeds and other vegetable matter.

ANNUAL CYCLE. Gonad data only available for the two June males (1.5, 2.0 mm) and the November male which had enlarged testes of 9.5 mm. No wing-moult.

HABITAT. Locally common in swamp areas of tall grass or other thick vegetation.

Euplectes ardens   Long-tailed Black Whydah

SPECIMENS. 16 ♂♂, Aug. 1967, Sept. 1964 (2), 1968 (5), 1970, Oct. 1967 (2), 1968, 1969 (2), 1970, Nov. 1965. 2 imm. ♂♂, Sept., Nov. 1968. 4 ♀♀, Feb., Mar. 1968, Oct. 1967, Nov. 1968. — *E. a. concolor* (Senegal to Sudan).

IMPERMANENT COLOURS. Legs black. Iris brown. Bill black.

STOMACH CONTENTS. Seeds and other vegetable matter.

ANNUAL CYCLE. Gonad data incomplete. The August, three September and three October males had enlarged testes of 7–9 mm. No wing moult.

HABITAT. Locally common at Nimba where there are grasslands or beds of *Pennisetum*.

Euplectes hordeaceus   Fire-crowned Bishop

SPECIMENS. 9 ♂♂, Aug. 1968, Sept. 1967, 1968 (2), 1969, Oct. 1967, 1969, Nov. 1967, 1968. 1 imm. o, Nov. 1970. — *E. h. hordeaceus* (Senegal to Angola and Kenya).

IMPERMANENT COLOURS. Legs brown. Iris brown. Bill black.

STOMACH CONTENTS. Seeds and vegetable matter.

ANNUAL CYCLE. Gonad data incomplete. The August, three September and a November male had enlarged testes of 8.5–11.0 mm. No wing-moult. October and November birds were in worn plumage.

HABITAT. Grassland and adjacent forest clearings.

Vidua macroura   Pin-tailed Whydah

SPECIMENS. 7 ♂♂, Jul. 1965, 1968, Aug. 1968 (2), 1970, Sept., Nov. 1969. 2 imm. ♂♂, Mar., Jul. 1968. 2 juv. ♂♂, Sept. 1967, Nov. 1968. 6 ♀♀, Mar., May 1968, Jul. 1965, 1968 (2), Aug. 1967.

IMPERMANENT COLOURS. Legs dark grey. Iris brown. Bill red, dull pink in ♀.

STOMACH CONTENTS. Seeds of various grasses.

ANNUAL CYCLE. The two juveniles, collected on 3 September and 1 November, indicate egg-laying in August–September. Gonad data incomplete. Single July and August females had moderately enlarged ovaries of 7 mm, *cf.* March and May females with ovaries of 3–4 mm. One July and two August males had testes of 5–8 mm. No wing-moult.

HABITAT. Cultivated land and gardens.

Passer griseus   Grey-headed Sparrow

This widespread species was observed at Nimba (KC-L, AF-W, DT & RW). It occurs in towns and villages in savanna and forest, but is absent from closed forest.

Family Sturnidae

Poeoptera lugubris   Narrow-tailed Starling

SPECIMENS. 5 ♂♂, Jul. 1967, 1968, Sept. (2), Oct. 1968. 3 ♀♀, Apr. 1968, Oct. 1967, 1968.

IMPERMANENT COLOURS. Legs black. Iris yellow. Bill black.

STOMACH CONTENTS. Various fruits.

ANNUAL CYCLE. No evidence of breeding activity. The females' ovaries measured 6 mm in April, 6 and 8.5 mm in October. The males' testes were small 2.5–4.5 mm. An October female was in an early stage of wing-moult (3rd primary growing), and the April female was completing wing-moult (8th primary growing).

HABITAT AND STATUS. Lowland forest. The species is found from Sierra Leone to southern Cameroon, northwest Angola, Zaire and Bwamba in Uganda. This is a new record for Liberia.

Onychognathus fulgidus Chestnut-wing Starling

SPECIMENS. 1 ♂, Sept. 1968. 4 ♀♀, Aug. (3), Sept. 1968. — *O. f. hartlaubii* (Sierra Leone to Uganda).

IMPERMANENT COLOURS. Legs black. Iris red. Bill black.

STOMACH CONTENTS. Fruit pulp and seeds.

ANNUAL CYCLE. Two August and the September female had enlarged ovaries of 10–12 mm, and the September male had testes of 6 mm. An August female was completing wing-moult (outer primaries growing), and had an ovary of 10 mm.

HABITAT. Lowland and montane forests up to about 1200 m.

Lamprotornis cupreocauda Copper-tailed Glossy Starling

SPECIMENS. 9 ♂♂, Jan. 1970, Apr. 1968 (2), 1972, Jul. 1967, Aug. 1968, Oct. 1967 (3). 2 imm. ♂♂, Mar. 1968, May 1971. 3 ♀♀, Apr. 1968, Oct. 1967 (2).

IMPERMANENT COLOURS. Legs black. Iris yellow. Bill black.

STOMACH CONTENTS. Mostly small fruits and a few insects.

ANNUAL CYCLE. No evidence of breeding activity. The females had moderately enlarged ovaries measuring 10 mm in April, and 8.5–9.0 mm in October. Gonad data for males incomplete, but three October males had enlarged testes of 9.0–10.5 mm, *cf*. 3–4 mm in single April, July and August birds. A January male was in an early stage of wing-moult (3rd primary growing), an April male was in mid wing-moult (6th primary growing), and another April male was completing (outer primaries growing).

HABITAT. At Nimba this species seems to prefer secondary swamp forests.

Cinnyricinclus leucogaster Violet-backed Starling

SPECIMEN. 1 imm. ♂, Sept. 1968. — *C. l. leucogaster* (Senegal to northwest Tanzania).

IMPERMANENT COLOURS. Legs black. Iris brown. Bill black. Gape yellow.

STOMACH CONTENTS. Fruit pulp.

HABITAT AND STATUS. The only observation made by Curry-Lindahl on this species was of a flock of six females in a mosaic of trees, bushes and grassy glades at Nimba in January 1982.

Cinnyricinclus l. leucogaster is migratory in Nigeria (Elgood *et al.*, 1973), migrating south in the dry season and north, to the northern Guinea and Sudan zones, in the wet season. In Sierra Leone it is present December–May, in the southern Ivory Coast November–April. The January observation at Nimba fits this schedule but not the September record.

Family Oriolidae

Oriolus oriolus Golden Oriole

This Palaearctic migrant to tropical and southern Africa was observed in primary lowland high forest at Nimba in 1964 and March 1976 (KC-L). These are the first records for Liberia. In West Africa it is an uncommon spring and autumn migrant, widely recorded from Senegal to Cameroon.

Oriolus auratus African Golden Oriole

Three individuals of this species visited a garden in Grassfield on 6 March 1979 (KC-L). The northern race (*O. a. auratus*) of the African Golden Oriole is migratory from the Sudanese savannas, where it breeds, southwards. It visits the southern Ivory Coast in November–April. The birds at Nimba were apparently on migration. This is a new record for Liberia.

Oriolus brachyrhynchus Western Black-headed Oriole

SPECIMENS. 9 ♂♂, Jun. 1967, Jul. 1967, 1970, Aug. (2), Sept. 1967, Oct. 1968, 1974. Nov. 1964. 4 imm. ♂♂, Mar. 1968, Sept. 1969, Oct. 1970, Nov. 1968. 9 ♀♀, Jan., Mar. 1968 (2), May 1971, Jun., Aug. (2), Sept 1967, Oct. 1968. 2 imm. ♀♀, Feb. 1966, Jul. 1968. — *O. b. brachyrhynchus* (Sierra Leone to Togo).

IMPERMANENT COLOURS. Legs blue-grey. Iris red, chestnut-brown in ♀. Bill pinkish-brown.

STOMACH CONTENTS. Mainly hairy caterpillars; also flying ants and some beetles.

ANNUAL CYCLE. No evidence of breeding activity. An August female had a moderately enlarged ovary measuring 10 mm and single September and October birds had ovaries of 8.0–8.5 mm; the remainder were 2–7 mm. The males' testes were small, 2.0–4.5 mm. The two March females and an October male were in wing-moult, 4th to 6th primaries growing.

HABITAT. Mostly observed in clearings with shrubs and tall trees in lowland forest.

Oriolus nigripennis — Black-winged Oriole

SPECIMENS. 2 ♂♂, Jul., Sept. 1968. 1 ♀, Sept. 1968.

IMPERMANENT COLOURS. Legs blue-grey. Iris red. Bill pinkish-brown.

STOMACH CONTENTS. Insects, including beetles and flying ants; also small fruits.

ANNUAL CYCLE. No evidence of breeding activity. The female had a moderately enlarged ovary of 9 mm, and the July and September males' testes measured 3 and 5 mm respectively. No wing-moult.

HABITAT. Primary and secondary lowland and montane forests up to about 900 m.

Family Dicruridae

Dicrurus ludwigii — Square-tailed Drongo

SPECIMENS. 1 ♂, Jan. 1968. 1 ♀, May 1968. — *D. l. sharpei* (Senegal to Kenya).

IMPERMANENT COLOURS. Legs black. Iris red. Bill black.

STOMACH CONTENTS. Insects, including beetles.

ANNUAL CYCLE. The May female had an enlarged ovary of 12 mm and was probably in breeding condition. The male had testes of 7 mm and was in worn plumage.

HABITAT. Edges, clearings and glades of both primary and secondary, lowland and montane forests up to about 1000 m.

Dicrurus atripennis — Shining Drongo

SPECIMENS. 11 ♂♂, Feb. 1969, Jun. 1967 (6), Jul. 1965, 1968, 1970 (2). 8 ♀♀, Jun. (3), Aug. (2), Sept. 1967, Oct. 1968, Nov. 1967. 1 o, Jul. 1967.

IMPERMANENT COLOURS. Legs black. Iris red. Bill black.

STOMACH CONTENTS. Insects, including beetles, ants and grasshoppers.

ANNUAL CYCLE. The females' ovaries measured 6.5–7.0 mm in June, 7 and 8 mm in August, 8.5 mm in September, 3 mm in October, and 10 mm in November. Gonad data lacking for the February male and three July males. Two June males had enlarged testes (6.5 & 9.5 mm) and the remainder were small (1.0–3.5 mm). Two June females were in advanced stages of wing-moult (outer primaries growing).

HABITAT. Lowland secondary forest and forest-grassland mosaics.

Dicrurus adsimilis — African Drongo

SPECIMENS. 3 ♀♀, Jun. 1967, Jul. 1967 (2). — *D. a. atactus* (Sierra Leone to southwest Nigeria).

IMPERMANENT COLOURS. Legs black. Iris red. Bill black.

STOMACH CONTENTS. Insects and beetles.

ANNUAL CYCLE. No evidence of breeding activity (ovaries 5 mm June; 8.0 and 8.5 mm July). One July female was in an advanced stage of wing-moult (7th primary growing).

HABITAT. A wide range of habitats from glades and clearings in both lowland and montane forests up to about 1100 m. Also in forest-grassland mosaics, gardens and parkland country as well as grasslands with scattered trees.

Family Corvidae

Corvus albus — Pied Crow

This widespread species was observed at Nimba (AF-W) in 1967 or 1968. It occurs around towns and farmland but is absent from closed forest (PRC).

References

Adam, J. G. 1971–1983. Flore descriptive des Monts Nimba. Vols 1–6. *Mém. Mus. Nat. Hist.* Nat. Sér. B, **20**: 1–528; **22**: 529–908; **24**: 909–1378; **25**: 1379–1588; **CNRS**: 1589–2054; **CNRS**: 2055–2183.

Aellen, V. 1963. La Réserve Intégrale du Mont Nimba. 29. Chiroptères. *Mém. Inst. fr. Afr. noire* **66**: 629–638.

Allen. G. M. 1930. The birds of Liberia. In: 'The African Republic of Liberia etc.' *Contr. Dept. trop. Med. and Inst. trop. Biol. Med.* Cambridge, Mass. **5**: 636–748.

Angel, F., Guibé, J. & Lamotte, M. 1954. La Rèserve Intégrale du Mont Nimba. 31. Lézards. *Mém. Inst. fr. Afr. noire* **40**: 371–380.

Angel, F., Guibé, J., Lamotte, M. & Roy, R. 1954. La Réserve du Mont Nimba. 32. Serpents. *Mém. Inst. fr. Afr. noire* **40**: 381–402.

Aubréville, A. 1962. Position chorologique du Gabon. In: *Flora du Gabon* **3**: 3–11.

Bannermann, D. A. 1930–1951. *The Birds of Tropical West Africa*, 1–8. Crown Agents, London.

Bannerman, D. A. 1953. *The Birds of West and Equatorial Africa*. 2 vols. Oliver and Boyd, London.

Bigot, L. 1963. Note ornithologique sur les monts Nimba, avec analyses de contenus stomacaux. *O.R.f.O.* **33**: 283–285.

Booth, A. H. 1958. The zoogeography of West African Primates: A review. *Bull. de l'IFAN* **20**(2): 587–622.

Bouet, G. 1931. Contribution à la Repartition des Oiseaux en Afrique Occidentale. *Oiseau* **1**: 363–377, 426–437, 487–502.

Bouet, G. 1955–1961. *Oiseaux de l'Afrique tropicale* (Faune de l'Union française **XVI** & **XVII**). Paris.

Britton, P.L. (Ed.) 1980. Birds of East Africa their habitat, status and distribution. *E. Afr. Nat. Hist. Soc.*, Nairobi.

Brooke, R.K. 1971. Taxonomic and distributional notes on the African Chaeturini. *Bull. Br. Orn. Club* **91**: 76–79.

Brosset, A. 1984. Chiroptères d'altitude du Mont Nimba (Guinée). Description d'une espèce nouvelle, *Hipposideros lamottei*. *Mammalia* **48**: 545–555.

Brown, L. H., & Amadon, D. 1968. *Eagles, hawks and falcons of the world.* Hamlyn for Country Life Books, Feltham.

Brunel, J. & Thiollay, J. 1969. Liste préliminaire des oiseaux de Côte d'Ivoire. *Alauda* **37**: 230–254, 315–337.

Carcasson, R. H. 1964. A preliminary survey of the zoogeography of African butterflies. *E. Afr. Wildl. J.* **2**: 122–157.

Carcasson, R. H. 1971. New species of African Geometrinae (Geometridae). *J. Lepid. Soc.* **25**: 169–176.

Chapin, J. P. 1932–54. The Birds of the Belgian Congo. 4 vols. *Bull. Am. Mus. Nat. Hist.* **65**: 1–756; **75**: 1–632; **75A**: 1–826; **75B**: 1–846.

Coe, M. J. 1975. Mammalian ecological studies on Mount Nimba, Liberia. *Mammalia* **39**: 523–587.

Coe, M. J. & Curry-Lindahl, K. 1965. Ecology of a Mountain: First Report on Liberian Nimba. *Oryx* **8**: 177–184.

Coetzee, J. A. 1964. Evidence for a considerable depression of the vegetation belts during the upper Pleistocene of the E. African mountains. *Nature* **204**: 564–566.

Colston, P. R. 1981. A newly described species of *Melignomon* (Indicatoridae) from Liberia, West Africa. *Bull. Br. Orn. Club* **101**: 291–294.

Curry-Lindahl, K. 1960. Ecological Studies on Mammals, Birds, Reptiles and Amphibians in the Eastern Belgian Congo. Part 2. *Annls Mus. r. Congo Belge. Sci. Zool.* **87**: 1–250.

Curry-Lindahl, K. 1961. *Contribution à l'Étude des Vertébrés Terrestres en Afrique Tropicale.* Vol. 1. Exploration du Parc National Albert et du Parc National de la Kagera. Mission K. Curry-Lindahl (1951–1952, 1958–1959). 420 pp. Bruxelles.

Curry-Lindahl, K. 1964. Yellow Wagtails, *Motacilla flava flavissima,* found in great numbers at Mount Nimba, Liberia. *Ibis* **106**: 255–256.

Curry-Lindahl, K. 1965. Biological investigations of the Nimba Range, Liberia. *IUCN Bull.* New Ser. **17**: 7.

Curry-Lindahl, K. 1968. Activities of the Nimba Research Committee. *IUCN Bull.* **2**: 1.

Curry-Lindahl, K. 1969a. Report to the Government of Liberia on Conservation, Management and Utilization of Wildlife Resources. *IUCN Publs.* New Ser. Suppl. Paper **24**: 1–31.

Curry-Lindahl, K. 1969b. Research and conservation of wildlife in Liberia. *LAMCO News* No. 3: 5–8.

Curry-Lindahl, K. 1972. *Let Them Live.* A Worldwide Survey of Animals Threatened with Extinction. 394 pp. New York.

Curry-Lindahl, K. 1974. Jentink's Duiker (*Cephalophus jentinki*) in Liberia. *Mammalia* **38**: 187.

Curry-Lindahl, K. 1979. *A conservation plan for Liberia with special emphasis on wildlife resources and the Nimba area.* Memorandum to the Government. 10 pp. Monrovia.

Curry-Lindahl, K. 1981. *Bird Migration in Africa*: Movements between six continents. 2 vols. London, New York, Toronto, Sydney & San Francisco.

Curry-Lindahl, K. & Harroy, J. P. 1972. *National Parks of the World.* Vol. 2. 241 pp. New York.

Curry-Lindahl, K. & Lamotte, M. 1964. Milieu montagnard tropical. In: *The Ecology of Man in the Tropical Environment.* IUCN Publs. New ser. **4**: 146–162.

De Roo, A., Huselmans, J., Verheyen, W. 1971. Contribution à l'Ornithologie de la République du Togo. *Rev. Zool. Bot. Afr.* **83**: 84–94.

Eisentraut, M. 1963. *Die Wirbeltiere des Kamerungebirges.* Hamburg & Berlin.

Elgood, J. H. 1975. The new Nigerian check-list. *Bull. Nigerian Orn. Soc.* **11**: 68–73.

Elgood, J. H. 1977. Forest birds of southwest Nigeria. *Ibis* **119**: 462–480.

Elgood, J. H. 1982. The birds of Nigeria (An annotated check-list). *B.O.U. Check-list* No. 4, p. 246.

Elgood, J. H., Fry, C. H. & Dowsett, J. R. 1973. African migrants in Nigeria. *Ibis* **115**: 1–45, 375–411.

Elgood, J. H., Sharland, R. E. & Ward, P. 1966. Palaeartic migrants in Nigeria. *Ibis* **108**: 84–116.

Field, G. D. 1973. Ortolan and Blue Rock Thrush in Sierra Leone. *Bull. Br. Orn. Club* **93**: 81–82.

Forbes-Watson, A. D. 1969. Ornithological results of the I.U.C.N. Survey of Mt. Nimba, Liberia. *Bull. Br. Orn. Club* **89**: 2–3.

Forbes-Watson, A. D. 1970. A new species of *Melaenornis* (Muscicapinae) from Liberia. *Bull. Br. Orn. Club* **90**: 145–148.

Friedmann, H. & Williams, J. G. 1975. The birds of Budongo forest, Bunyoro district Uganda. *J. E.Afr. Nat. Hist. Soc. and Nat. Mus.* **141**: 18p.

Goodwin, D. 1967. *Pigeons and doves of the world*. Br. Mus. (Nat. His.), London.

Grandison, A. G. C. 1978. The occurrence of Nectophrynoides (Anura: Bufonidae) in Ethiopia. A new concept of the genus with a description of a new species. *Monit. Zool. Ital.* N.S. Suppl. **XI**(6): 115–172.

Grandison, A. G. C. 1981. Morphology and phylogenetic position of the West African *Didynamipus sjoestedti* Anderson 1903 (Anura: Bufonidae). *Monit. Zool. Ital.* N.S. Suppl. **XV**(11): 187–215.

Grubb, P. 1979. Patterns of speciation in African mammals. *Bull. Carn. Mus. Nat. Hist.* **6**: 152–167.

Guibé, J. & Lamotte, M. 1958. La Réserve Intégrale du Mont Nimba. 12. Batraciens. *Mém. Inst. fr. Afr. noire* **53**: 241–273.

Guibé, J. & Lamotte, M. 1963. La Réserve Intégrale du Mont Nimba. 27. Batraciens du genre *Phrynobatrachus*. *Mém. Inst. fr. Afr. noire* **66**: 601–627.

Haftorn, S. 1971. *Norges Fugler*. 862 pp. Oslo, Bergen & Trondheim.

Hald-Mortensen, P. 1971. A collection of Birds from Liberia and Guinea. *Steenstrupia* **1**: 115–125.

Hall, B. P. & Moreau, R. E. 1970. *An Atlas of speciation in African Passerine Birds*. Br. Mus. (Nat. Hist.), London.

Hamilton, A. C. 1970. The interpretation of pollen diagrams from highland East Africa. *Paeleoecol. of Afr.* **7**: 45–149.

Hamilton, A. C. 1974. The history of vegetation. *In*: E. M. Lind & M. E. S. Morrison *East African Vegetation* pp. 188–209. Longman, London.

Heim de Balsac, H. 1958. La Réserve Intégrale du Mont Nimba. 14. Mammifères Insectivores. *Mém. Inst. fr. Afr. noire* **53**: 301–337.

Heim de Balsac, H. & Lamotte, M. 1958. La Réserve Intégrale du Mont Nimba. 15. Mammifères rongeurs (Muscardinidés et Muridés). *Mém. Inst. fr. Afr. noire* **53**: 339–357.

Hill, J. E. 1982. Records of bats from Mount Nimba, Liberia. *Mammalia* **46**: 116–120.

Karr, J. R. 1975. Production, Energy Pathways and Community Diversity in Forest Birds. *In*: F. B. Golley & E. Medina (Eds), 'Tropical Ecological Systems: Trends in Terrestrial and Aquatic Research'. *Ecological Studies* **11**: 161–176.

Karr, J. R. 1976a. On the relative abundance of migrants from the north temperate zone in tropical habitats. *Wilson Bull.* **88**: 433–458.

Karr, J. R. 1976b. Within – and between – habitat avian diversity in African and neotropical lowland habitats. *Ecological Monographs* **46**: 457–481.

Karr, J. R. 1980. Geographical variation in the avifaunas of tropical forest undergrowth. *Auk* **97**: 283–298.

Karr, J. R. & James, F. C. 1975. Eco-Morphological Configurations and Convergent Evolution in Species and Communities. *In*: M. L. Cody & J. M. Diamond (Eds), *Ecology and Evolution of Communities*, pp. 258–291. Cambridge, Mass.

Keith, S., Benson, C. W. & Irwin, M. P. S. 1970. The genus *Sarothura* (Aves, Rallidae). *Bull. Am. Mus. Nat. Hist.* **143**: 1–84.

Kendall, R. L. 1969. An ecological history of the Lake Victoria Basin. *Ecol. Monog.* **39**: 121–76.

Kingdon, J. 1981. Where have all the colonists come from? A zoogeographical examination of some mammalian isolates in eastern Africa. *Afr. J. Ecol.* **19**: 115–124.

Kukla, G. J. 1977. Pleistocene land-sea correlations. 1. Europe. *Earth Science Review* **13**: 307–374.

Lack, P. C., Leuthold, W. & Smeenk, C. 1980. Check list of birds of the Tsavo (East) National Park, Kenya. *J. E.Afr. Nat. Hist. Soc. and Nat. Mus.* **170**: 1–25.

Lamotte, M. 1959. Observations écologiques sur les populations naturelles de *Nectophrynoides occidentalis* (Fam. Bufonidés). *Bull. biol. Fr. Belg.* **93**: 355–413.

Lamotte, M. 1983. The undermining of Mount Nimba. *Ambio* **12**(2–3), 174–179.

Lamotte, M. & Xavier, F. 1972. Recherches sur le développement embryonnaire de *Nectophrynoides occidentalis* Angel, amphibian anoure vivipare. 1. *Anns. Embryol. Morphogen.* **5**: 315–340.

Lawson, W. J. 1984. The West African mainland forest dwelling population of *Batis*; a new species. *Bull. Brit. Orn. Club* **104**: 144–146.

Laurent, R. 1958. La Réserve Intégrale du Mont Nimba. 13. Les rainettes du genre *Hyperolius*. *Mém. Inst. fr. Afr. noire* **53**: 275–299.

Lebrun, J. 1961. Les deux flores d'Afrique tropicale. *Acad. Roy. Belg., Cl. Sc., Mem* 8°, **32**(6): 81 pp.

Leclerc, J. C., Lamotte, M., Richard-Molard, J., Rougerie, G. & Portères, P. 1955. La Réserve Naturelle Intégrale du Mont Nimba. La chaine du Nimba: essai géographique. *Mém. Inst. fr. Afr. noire* **43**: 1–256.

Leonard, J. 1965. Contribution à la sub division phytogéographique de la Region Guineo-Congolaise d'aprés la repartition géographique d'Euphorbiacees d'Afrique tropicale. *Webbia* **19**: 627–649.

Livingstone, D. A. 1962. Age of deglaciation in the Ruwenzori Range, Uganda. *Nature* **194**: 589–590.

Louette, M. 1974. Contribution to the Ornithology of Liberia (Pt.3). *Revue Zool. afr.* **88**: 741–748.

Louette, M. 1981a. A new species of Honeyguide from West Africa (Aves, Indicatoridae). *Revue Zool. afr.* **95**: 131–135.

Louette, M. 1981b. Contribution to the Ornithology of Liberia. *Revue Zool. afr.* **95**: 342–355.

Macdonald, M. A. 1980. Further notes on uncommon forest birds in Ghana. *Bull. Br. Orn. Club* **100**: 170–172.

Macdonald, M. A. & Taylor, I. R. 1977. Notes on some uncommon forest birds in Ghana. *Bull. Br. Orn. Club* **97**: 116–120.

Mackworth-Praed, C. W. & Grant, C. H. B. 1970. *The birds of Central and Western Africa*, 2 vols. Longman, London.

McGregor, I. A. & Thomson, A.L. 1965. Blue Rock-Thrush *Monticola solitaria* in the Gambia. *Ibis* **107**: 401.

Misonne, X. & Verschuren, J. 1976. Les rongeurs du Mont Nimba. *Acta zool. path. antverp.* **66**: 199–220.

Monod, T. 1957. Les grandes divisions chorologiques de l'Afrique. *Publ. C.C.T.A./C.S.A.* **24**: 146 pp.

Monod, T. 1966. The late Tertiary and Pleistocene in the Sahara. *In*: F. C. Howell & F. Bourlière (Eds), *African Ecology and Human Evolution* 2nd ed. pp. 117–229. Methuen and Co. Ltd., London.

Moreau, R. E. 1936. Breeding seasons of birds in East African evergreen forest. *Proc. Zool. Soc. Lond.* **1936**: 631–653.

Moreau, R. E. 1966. *The bird faunas of Africa and its islands*. Academic Press, London & New York.

Moreau, R. E. 1972. *The Palaearctic-African Bird Migration Systems*. Academic Press, London & New York.

Morel, G. J. & Browne, P. W. P. 1981. Les *Buteo* Paléarctiques en Mauritanie et au Sénégal. *Malimbus* 3: 2–6.

Morony, J. J. Jr., Bock, W. H. & Farrand, J. Jr. 1975. *Reference list of the birds of the world*. Amer. Mus. Nat. Hist., New York.

Morrison, M. E. S. 1968. Vegetation and climate in the uplands of South-West Uganda during the later Pleistocene period. 1. Muchoya swamp, Kigezi district. *J. Ecol.* **156**: 363–384.

Rand, A. L. 1951. Birds from Liberia, with a discussion on barriers between Upper and Lower Guinea subspecies. *Fieldiana, Zool.* 32: 561–653.

Ripley, D. S. & Bond, G. M. 1971. Systematic notes on a collection of birds from Kenya. *Smiths. Contrib. to Zool.* **11**: 21 pp.

Rougeot, P. C. 1950. Contribution à l'étude des indicatoridés de la forêt Gabonaise. *L'Oiseau* 20: 51–63.

Rougeot, P. C. 1951. Nouvelle observations sur le *Melichneutes robustus*. Bates. *L'Oiseau* 21: 127–134.

Roux, F. 1983. A new race of *Glaucidium capense, G. c. etchécopari*. *L'Oiseau et R.F.O.* 53: 99–104.

Schnell, R. 1952. Végétation et Flore de la région montagneuse du Nimba. *Mém. Inst. fr. Afr. noire* 22: 1–604.

Schouteden, H. 1970. Quelques oiseaux du Libéria – *Rev. zool. Bot. Afr.* 82: 187–192.

Schouteden, H. 1971. Quelques oiseaux du Libéria – *Rev. zool. Bot. Afr.* 84: 297–300.

Serle, W. 1957. A contribution to the ornithology of the eastern region of Nigeria. *Ibis* 99: 371–418, 628–685.

Serle, W. 1959. Note on the immature plumage of the Honey-guide *Melignomon zenkeri*. Reichenow. *Bull. Br. Orn. Club* 79: 65.

Serle, W. 1981. The breeding season of birds in the lowland rainforest and in the montane forest of West Cameroon. *Ibis* 123: 62–74.

Serle, W., Morel, G. J. & Hartwig, H. 1977. *A field guide to the Birds of West Africa*. Collins, London.

Snow, D. W. 1976. The relationship between climate and annual cycles in the Cotingidae. *Ibis* 118: 366–401.

Snow, D. W. (Ed.) 1978. *An Atlas of speciation in African Non-passerine birds*. Br. Mus. (Nat. Hist.), London.

Snow, D. W. & Snow, B. K. 1964. Breeding seasons and annual cycles of Trinidad land-birds. *Zoologica*, N.Y. **49**: 1–39.

Thiollay, J. M. 1977. Distribution saisonnière des rapaces diurnes en Afrique occidentale. *L'Oiseau* 47: 25–85.

Traylor, M. A. 1968. *In*: R. A. Paynter, Jr. (Ed.), *Check-list of birds in the World* 14. Mus. Comp. Zool., Cambridge, Mass.

Traylor, M. A. 1970. Two new birds from the Ivory Coast. *Bull. Br. Orn. Club* 90: 78–80.

Troupin, G. 1966. Etude phytocenologique du Parc National d'Akagera et du Rwanda Oriental. *Inst. Nat. Rech. Scient., Butare. Publ.* **2**: 293 p.

Vernon, C. J. & Dean, W. R. J. 1975. On the systematic position of *Pholidornis rushiae*. *Bull. Br. Orn. Club* 95: 20.

Verschuren, J. 1976. Les chiroptères du Mont Nimba (Liberia). *Mammalia* 40: 615–632.

Verschuren, J. 1979. Note sur les oiseaux du Liberia. *Gerfaut* 69: 379–391.

Verschuren, J. & Meester, J. 1977. Notes sur les *Soricidae* (Insectivora) du Nimba Libérien. *Mammalia* 41: 291–299.

Walsh, J. F. & Grimes, L. G. 1981. Observations on some Palaearctic land birds in Ghana. *Bull. Br. Orn. Club* 101: 327–334.

White, C. M. N. 1960–63. *A revised checklist of African passerine birds*. Gov. Printer, Lusaka.

White, C. M. N. 1965. A revised checklist of African non-passerine birds. Gov. Printer, Lusaka.

White, F. 1928. The Afromontane region. *In*: M. J. A. Werger (Ed.), *Biogeography and Ecology of Southern Africa* pp. 463–513. Junk, Hague.

White, F. 1979. The Guineo-Congolian region and its relationships to other phytochoria. *Bull. Jard. Bot. Nat. Belg.* **49**(172): 11–55.

Wolton, R. J., Arak, P. A., Godfray, H. C. J. & Wilson, R. P. 1982a. Oxford Expedition to Liberia, 1978. *Bull. of the Oxford University Exploration Club*. New Series. 5: 2–8.

Wolton, R. J., Arak, P. A., Godfray, H. C. J. & Wilson, R. P. 1982b. Megachiroptera at Mount Nimba, Liberia, with notes on Microchiroptera. *Mammalia* 46: 419–448.

Xavier, F. 1978. Une espèce nouvelle de *Nectophrynoides* (Anoure, Bufonide) des Mont. Nimba, *N. liberiensis* n.sp. 1. *Bull. Soc. zool. Fr.* **103**: 431–441.

Appendix
Biometrics of Nimba Birds
Measurements are in millimetres, weights in grams.
O = unsexed; M = male; F = female; ad = adult; imm = immature; juv = juvenile.

Species	Sex	Age	No	WEIGHT Individual measurement	WEIGHT Mean	WING Individual measurement	WING Mean	TAIL Individual measurement	TAIL Mean	BILL Individual measurement	BILL Mean
ARDEIDAE											
Ixobrychus sturmii	F	ad	1	138		155		46		38	
Butorides striatus	M	ad	1	203		165		54		66	
	F	ad	1	191		165		54		70	
ANATIDAE											
Anas querquedula	M	ad	1	303.4		190		63		44	
ACCIPITRIDAE											
Polyboroides typus	F	ad	1	871		415		255		39	
	F	imm	1	716		385		220		38	
Dryotriorchis spectablis	F	ad	2	653,702	685.5	300,300	300	235,240	237.5	40,41	40.5
	F	imm	1	650		285		230		33	
Accipiter tachiro	M	ad	5		157.6 ± 5.3		180.4 ± 5		148.2 ± 7.3		25.3 ± 1.7
	M	imm	4	134,139.3, 141,161	143.8	174,178, 180,185	179.3	146,150(2), 155	150.3	22,24,25, 26	24.3
	F	ad	3	255,260.5, 316	277.2	205(2),213	207.6	145,166, 173	161.3	27,28(2)	27.7
	F	imm	2	249,262	255.5	204(2)	204	168,178	173	28(2)	28
	O	imm	1	174.5		180		152		25	
A. badius	F	ad	1	143		185		142		23	
A. erythropus	M	ad	3	60,78.2, 87.3	75.2	140(2),145	141.7	98,100,106	101.3	18,19(2)	18.7
	M	imm	1	71.5		145		86		17	
	M	juv	1	79.4		122		62		15	
Urotriorchis macrourus	M	ad	4	468,481, 491,500	485	270,275(3)	273.8	325,330, 335,350	335	31,33(2), 34	32.8
	F	ad	2	725,761	743	300,301	300.5	365,370	367.5	32,36	34
	F	imm	1	650		289		345		36	
Kaupifalco monogrammicus	M	ad	2	217,263	240	210,215	212.5	130(2)	130	25,27	26
	F	ad	3	267,280, 291	279.3	208,214, 220	214	135,138, 142	138.3	28(3)	28
Buteo buteo	M	ad	3	633,696, 720	683	360,368, 375	367.7	185,186, 191	187.3	34(3)	34
Spizaetus africanus	F	ad	2	1119,1161	1140	365(2)	365	260,270	265	40,43	41.5
Hieraaetus ayresii	M	ad	1	615		315		195		31	
Pernis apivorus	M	ad	2	816,870	843	393,395	394	215,230	222.5	35,39	37
	F	ad	2	902,1053	977.5	410,415	412.5	215,225	220	35(2)	35
Macheirhamphus alcinus	M	ad	1	492		330		150		13	
FALCONIDAE											
Falco tinnunculus	F	ad	2	190,219	204.5	255,258	256.5	166,170	168	23(2)	23

Species	Sex	Age	No	WEIGHT		WING		TAIL		BILL	
				Individual measurement	Mean	Individual measurement	Mean	Individual measurement	Mean	Individual measurement	Mean
PHASIANIDAE											
Francolinus lathami	M	ad	4	243,264, 266,270	260.8	134,137, 140,150	140.3	45,51,56, 59	52.7	21(4)	21
	F	ad	3	211,227, 228	222	133,135(2)	134.3	43,50,54	49	20(2),21	20.3
	O	juv	1	98.4		–		–		–	
	O	chick	1	9.8		–		–		–	
F. bicalcaratus	F	ad	1	437		160		58		33	
F. ahantensis	M	ad	3	504,522, 594	540	185(2),190	186.7	73,80,84	79	30,31,33	31.3
	F	ad	6		469 ± 57.9		173 ± 7.6		65.6 ± 3.6		29 ± 1
RALLIDAE											
Canirallus oculeus	M	ad	1	278		166		67		40	
	F	ad	2	273,279	276	170,175	172.5	58,80	69	40(2)	40
Amaurornis flavirostris	F	ad	1	91		103		42		30	
Sarothrura pulchra	M	ad	4	47.9,49,50, 53.2	50	78,80,81(2)	80	41,42,43, 44	42.5	16,17(3)	16.8
	F	ad	4	33,46,47.9 50.6	44.4	78,79,85(2)	81.8	35,37,38 40	37.5	16.5,17(3)	16.9
Himantornis haematopus	M	ad	3	504.5,509 595	536.2	210,220, 226	218.7	81(2),83	81.7	40,45,46	43.7
	F	ad	1	870		220		75		47	
HELIORNITHIDAE											
Podica senegalensis	M	ad	2	320,357	338.5	140,168	154	123,145	134	38,43	40.5
	F	imm	1	163.4		98		89		36	
	O	juv	1	–		65		45		28	
JACANIDAE											
Actophilornis africanus	F	ad	1	290		175		45		40	
CHARADRIIDAE											
Vanellus senegallus	M	ad	1	228		225		87		37	
Charadrius forbesi	M	ad	1	46.4		130		60		20	
	F	ad	3	47,48,49	48	117,126, 128	123.7	55,57,61	57.7	19(3)	19
Tringa ochropus	F	ad	2	76.4,78.7	77.5	140,142	141	58(2)	58	38(2)	38
T. hypoleucos	M	ad	2	43.4,45	44.2	103,105	104	50(2)	50	27,28	27.5
	F	ad	2	41,42.2	41.6	103,108	105.5	50(2)	50	29,30	29.5
COLUMBIDAE											
Columba unicincta	M	ad	2	372,405	388.5	210,215	212.5	104,106	105	26,27	26.5
	F	ad	1	390		210		115		25	
C. iriditorques	M	ad	15		130.3 ± 8.4		160.2 ± 5.4		90 ± 7.6		20.6 ± 1
	F	ad	18		122.1 ± 10.3		152.9 ± 3.5		83.2 ± 4.3		20.2 ± 1.2
	F	juv	1	90.1		121		63		22	
Streptopelia semitorquata	F	ad	1	190.5		175		103		23	

Appendix

Species	Sex	Age	No	WEIGHT Individual measurement	Mean	WING Individual measurement	Mean	TAIL Individual measurement	Mean	BILL Individual measurement	Mean
Turtur tympanistria	M	ad	9		64.6 ± 7.3		110.5 ± 4.3		69.7 ± 1.7		17.8 ± 1
	F	ad	6		60.2 ± 2.8		109.5 ± 2.1		66.8 ± 2.5		17.2 ± 0.8
	F	juv	2	50,56.9	53.4	106,110	108	61,62	61.5	16,17	16.5
T. afer	M	ad	2	53.3,60.3	56.8	104,110	107	70,71	70.5	15(2)	15
	F	ad	2	53.7,56.4	55.1	103,106	104.5	64(2)	64	15(2)	15
T. brehmeri	M	ad	7		106.6 ± 12.3		133 ± 2.2		100 ± 3.2		20.8 ± 0.9
	F	ad	4	92.2,93.4, 109,112	101.7	130(2), 132(2)	131	94,96, 103(2)	99	19,20(3)	19.8
Aplopelia larvata	M	ad	2	130,164.5	147.3	150,152	151	89,100	94.5	22(2)	22
	F	ad	1	85		140		90		21	
Treron calva	M	ad	4	–,195.6, 209,212	205.5	150,155(2), 156	154	73,75,78, 80	76.5	21,22(3)	21.8
	F	ad	4	–,193.4, 206,213.2	204.2	150,152, 155,156	153.3	67,72,78, 79	74	20,22(3)	21.5

MUSOPHAGIDAE

Species	Sex	Age	No	Individual measurement	Mean	Individual measurement	Mean	Individual measurement	Mean	Individual measurement	Mean
Tauraco persa	M	ad	1	284		190		200		30	
	F	ad	3	–,255, 263.4	259.2	183,185, 187	185	180(2),185	181.7	27(2),29	27.7
T. macrorhynchus	M	ad	3	261,272(2)	268.3	167,170, 182	173	180,190, 195	188.3	29(2),30	29.3
	F	ad	8		225.3 ± 8.9		168.5 ± 6.6		177 ± 9.9		29 ± 0
Corythaeola cristata	F	ad	1	849		320		390		42	

CUCULIDAE

Species	Sex	Age	No	Individual measurement	Mean	Individual measurement	Mean	Individual measurement	Mean	Individual measurement	Mean
Clamator levaillantii	M	ad	5		104.6 ± 9.2		168.4 ± 3.2		215 ± 10.8		29.5 ± 0.6
	F	ad	1	112		170		215		30	
Cuculus solitarius	F	ad	1	84		167		133		27	
	O	ad	1	60.1		165		123		26	
C. canorus	M	ad	3	–,89,95	92	196,205, 206	202.3	150,155, 158	154.3	26(2),27	26.3
	F	ad	3	79,85,97	87	193,195, 203	197	135,140, 150	141.7	26(2),28	26.7
Cercococcyx mechowi	M	ad	1	54.2		137		152		23	
	F	imm	1	43.4		131		142		24	
C. olivinus	M	ad	2	64.66	65	146,147	146.5	155,163	159	25(2)	25
Chrysococcyx klaas	M	imm	3	20,25,25.6	23.5	90(2),101	93.7	63,68,70	67	15,17,19	17
	F	ad	1	24.7		95		75		19	
	F	imm	3	22.2,22.3, 26.4	23.6	94,96,97	95.7	67,70,73	70	18(3)	18
C. caprius	M	ad	7		26.1 ± 4.4		108.3 ± 3.5		71.3 ± 4.6		19.7 ± 1.5
	F	ad	3	27.3,31, 31.5	29.9	109,110, 117	112	70,74,75	73	18(2),20	18.7
	O	imm	1	30.1		103		70		20	
C. cupreus	M	ad	7		35.5 ± 2.6		108.3 ± 2.7		105.5 ± 4.8		20.5 ± 1.2
	F	ad	7		35.1 ± 3.7		101.9 ± 2		74.1 ± 3.2		20.1 ± 0.9
	O	imm	1	32.3		100		70		19	
Ceuthmochares aereus	M	ad	6		55 ± 8.2		120.2 ± 6.3		184.6 ± 5.1		29.2 ± 1.1
	M	juv	1	37		110		153		21	
	F	ad	2	60,67	63.5	115,120	117.5	180,200	190	28,30	29

Species	Sex	Age	No	WEIGHT Individual measurement	Mean	WING Individual measurement	Mean	TAIL Individual measurement	Mean	BILL Individual measurement	Mean
Centropus leucogaster	M	ad	1	293.5		200		300		41	
	M	juv	1	204		175		100		38	
	F	ad	2	327,346	336.5	192,200	196.5	300,310	305	44,46	45
C. senegalensis	M	ad	2	150,157	153.5	150(2)	150	160,180	170	30,32	31
STRIGIDAE											
Tyto alba	F	ad	1	340		290		110		35	
Otus icterorhynchus	M	ad	2	66.9,78.8	72.8	127,135	131	62,72	67	20,21	20.5
	F	ad	2	67,79.3	73.2	125,127	126	62,65	63.5	20(2)	20
O. s. scops	M	ad	1	48		152		62		18	
	F	ad	4	58.6,63.5, 81,122	81.3	148,150(2),152 160		63,65,66, 68	65.5	17,18(3)	17.8
O. leucotis	F	ad	1	222.5		185		93		24	
Jubula lettii	F	ad	1	183.4		242		155		26	
Bubo africanus	F	ad	1	680		305		158		37	
B. poensis	F	ad	3	685,797, 815	765.7	320,325(2)	323.3	160,165, 178	167.7	40,44(2)	42.7
	F	juv	2	641,653	647	295,310	302.5	88,120	104	40,44	42
B. shelleyi	F	ad	1	1257		430		240		58	
B. leucostictus	M	ad	2	486,536	511	320,335	327.5	190,193	191.5	31,34	32.5
	F	ad	2	535,601	568	330,333	331.5	185,198	191.5	34,35	34.5
	F	juv	1	524		330		190		31	
	O	imm	1	–		330		195		28	
Scotopelia ussheri	M	juv	1	743		340		195		46	
Glaucidium tephronotum	M	ad	3	–,79.6,85.3	82.4	102,103, 105	103.3	61,62,70	64.3	15(2),16	15.3
	F	ad	1	75.3		105		60		16	
G. capense	M	ad	1	82.5		118		66		17	
	F	ad	2	93.4,119	106.2	128(2)	128	70,77	73.5	17,18	17.5
Strix woodfordi	M	ad	4	242,246.5, 248 249,254.5		235,238, 245,246	241	115,117, 120,126	119.5	28,30,31(2)	30
	M	juv	1	182		230		120		26	
	F	ad	1	300		240		130		28	
CAPRIMULGIDAE											
Caprimulgus binotatus	M	ad	1	63.2		163		97		20	
	O	ad	1	–		155		95		19	
C. inornatus	M	ad	2	33,51.1	42.1	153,156	154.5	115(2)	115	17,19	18
	M	juv	1	35.2		114		55		16	
	F	ad	5		47 ± 9.9		156.6 ± 3.1		111.2 ± 2.7		20.2 ± 0.7
C. climacurus	M	ad	1	42		147		223		19	
	F	ad	2	35,49.1	42.1	136,145	140.5	115,205	160	16(2)	16
Macrodipteryx longipennis	M	ad	5		40.7 ± 8.5		171.5 ± 4.8		97.5 ± 8.5		18.3 ± 1.7
	F	ad	7		48.5 ± 9		166.3 ± 1.5		101 ± 5.6		19 ± 1.5
APODIDAE											
Apus apus	M	ad	2	36.7,39	37.8	163,166	164.5	62,69	65.5	10(2)	10
	F	ad	4	39.2,40, 40.6,41.2	40.3	167(2), 173(2)	170	68(2),70(2)	69	10(3),11	10.3

Appendix 111

				WEIGHT		WING		TAIL		BILL	
Species	Sex	Age	No	Individual measurement	Mean	Individual measurement	Mean	Individual measurement	Mean	Individual measurement	Mean
Cypsiurus parvus	O	ad	1	12.2		125		86		6	
Raphidura sabini	M	ad	5		19.9 ± 1.6		123.3 ± 0.9		45 ± 1.3		7.6 ± 0.5
	F	ad	5		19.2 ± 0.8		126.8 ± 5.4		45.7 ± 2.8		8.4 ± 0.7
	O	ad	1	19.8		130		46		8	
Neafrapus cassini	M	ad	1	41.5		155		29		10	
	F	ad	1	40.1		163		30		8	
TROGONIDAE											
Apaloderma narina	M	ad	5		68.8 ± 3.7		120.8 ± 4		150.5 ± 4.2		21.2 ± 0.9
	F	ad	1	70.3		123		148		20	
ALCEDINIDAE											
Ceryle maxima	M	ad	1	321		190		112		94	
	F	ad	2	281,383.7	333.4	193,198	195.5	110(2)	110	90,95	92.5
C. rudis	F	ad	1	63		139		70		62	
Alcedo quadribrachys	M	ad	6		34.3 ± 2.6		78.4 ± 1.6		33.4 ± 2.2		50.6 ± 1.3
	F	ad	4	32.3,36.9, 37.9,40	36.8	80(3),82	80.5	33,36,37, 38	36	49,50(2), 52	50.3
A. cristata	M	ad	2	11.5,13.5	12.5	53,54	53.5	24,26	25	30,32	31
A. leucogaster	M	ad	12		14.5 ± 1.4		54.1 ± 1.7		22.3 ± 1.7		29.6 ± 1.7
	F	ad	14		14.7 ± 1.9		55.5 ± 1.1		21.7 ± 1.6		32.2 ± 2.2
	O	ad	1	13.2		55		22		31	
Ispidina picta	M	ad	8		9.7 ± 1.1		53.4 ± 1.1		22.7 ± 2.1		26 ± 2.1
	F	ad	6		11.1 ± 0.8		52.5 ± 0.6		22.5 ± 1.3		25.8 ± 1.7
	O	ad	1	10		50		23		17	
I. lecontei	M	ad	1	9.5		46		18		30	
	M	imm	1	10		45		18		28	
Halcyon senegalensis	M	ad	2	50.9,53.3	52.1	92,104	98	65,82	73.5	42,45	43.5
	F	ad	3	–,51.7,56.4	54.2	95,97,100	98.5	60,62,76	68	42,45(2)	44
H. malimbica	M	ad	12		74.4 ± 10.1		113.7 ± 3.5		76.8 ± 4.3		56.6 ± 2.9
	F	ad	6		83.9 ± 6.4		114.2 ± 2.3		77 ± 2		55.3 ± 2.3
	F	imm	1	75.3		117		80		56	
H. badia	M	ad	2	47.4,58	52.7	92,94	93	50,67	58.5	43,44	43.5
	M	juv	1	37		83		27		30	
	F	ad	2	50.5,57	53.8	90,93	91.5	53(2)	53	42,45	43.5
	O	ad	1	54.7		90		53		47	
H. leucocephala	M	ad	4	37,38,40, 41	39	95,100, 102,105	100.5	54,55,59(2)	56.8	43,44,45(2)	44.3
	F	ad	2	47.4,48	47.7	99,100	99.5	55,60	57.5	43,46	44.5
MEROPIDAE											
Merops apiaster	M	ad	3	51.2,53.4, 56.7	53.8	133,142, 153	142.7	105,110(2)	108.3	43,44,45	44
	F	ad	2	51.2,54	52.6	130,147	138.5	98,100	99	40,42	41
M. albicollis	M	ad	7		21.4 ± 2.7		97.5 ± 1.5		110.3 ± 45.4		35 ± 0.9
	F	ad	1	17		94		85		31	
M. pusillus	M	ad	3	10,14.2, 14.8	13	74(2),75	74.3	56,57,58	57	26,30(2)	28.7
	M	imm	1	14.5		67		51		26	
	F	ad	2	11,14.6	12.8	73,78	75.5	51,60	55.5	28,30	29

Species	Sex	Age	No	WEIGHT Individual measurement	Mean	WING Individual measurement	Mean	TAIL Individual measurement	Mean	BILL Individual measurement	Mean
M. gularis	M	ad	9		25.5 ± 3.5		92.6 ± 1.6		67.7 ± 2.6		39.2 ± 1.6
	M	juv	1	28.8		81		62		28	
	F	ad	5		26.4 ± 3.6		91.3 ± 2.3		69.8 ± 3.3		37.4 ± 0.9
M. muelleri	M	ad	5		22.1 ± 1.7		83.3 ± 1.5		75.2 ± 2.2		35.8 ± 1.6
	M	imm	2	17.4,22.5	20	82,83	82.5	65,74	69.5	33(2)	33
	F	ad	3	21,22.4, 24.6	22.7	80,85(2)	83.3	70,74,76	73.3	35(2),36	35.3
CORACIIDAE											
Coracias abyssinica	M	ad	2	91.4	–	157,158	157.5	195,260	227.5	38,40	39
	F	ad	1	92.3		155		215		35	
Eurystomus glaucurus	M	ad	1	103.3		172		85		27	
	F	ad	2	86.6,121.2	103.9	167,180	173.5	87,88	87.5	27,29	28
E. gularis	M	ad	3	91,99, 104.3	98.1	151,154, 155	153.3	84,85,92	87	26(2),29	27
	M	imm	2	91.7,92.8	92.3	150,152	151	80,88	84	28,29	28.5
	F	ad	3	92,93.4, 103.3	96.2	145,150, 153	149.3	80,90,95	88.3	26(2),27	26.3
PHOENICULIDAE											
Phoeniculus bollei	M	ad	2	60.1,69.8	64.9	133,135	134	210,220	215	50,51	50.5
	F	ad	1	47.6		128		220		38	
P. castaneiceps	M	ad	5		23.6 ± 1.2		108.8 ± 4.2		163.8 ± 18.9		32 ± 2
	F	ad	1	22.6		95		145		29	
	O	ad	1	23		100		170		30	
BUCEROTIDAE											
Tockus camurus	M	ad	5		105.9 ± 5.3		148.2 ± 3.6		157.4 ± 8.4		63.8 ± 2.2
	F	ad	2	84.4,93.3	88.9	145,146	145.5	160(2)	160	55,60	57.5
	O	ad	1	84.5		141		147		58	
T. hartlaubi	M	ad	4	96.6,100.8,100.7 102.3,103		145,150, 155(2)	151.3	165,175, 180,190	177.5	60,65(2),66	64
	F	ad	3	–,83.4(2)	83.4	132,145, 157	144.7	140,160, 165	155	55,60(2)	58.3
T. fasciatus	M	ad	1	271		260		250		95	
	F	ad	3	220,221, 228	223	230,235, 245	236.7	220,230, 235	228.3	75,80,87	80.7
	O	ad	2	191(1)	–	245,255	250	230,265	247.5	90,100	95
Tropicranus albocristatus	M	ad	7		292.4 ± 17.3		235.5 ± 6.4		439 ± 18.2		93.5 ± 2.8
Ceratogymna atrata	M	ad	2	1096,1183	1139.5	360,380	370	300,330	315	177,180	178.5
	F	ad	2	907,1087	997	333,350	341.5	290,300	295	135,137	136
Bycanistes cylindricus	F	ad	1	921		290		260		134	
CAPITONIDAE											
Lybius hirsutus	M	ad	4	59,59.7, 62,68.4	62.3	90,92,93, 94	92.3	50(3),58	52.7	26,27,30(2)	28.3
	F	ad	6		59.7 ± 4.7		92.2 ± 2.6		50.6 ± 5.6		27.6 ± 0.5
Gymnobucco calvus	M	ad	9		52.6 ± 4.8		91.6 ± 2.2		46 ± 2.1		21.5 ± 0.5
	F	ad	6		56.5 ± 3.9		92.5 ± 1.5		48.2 ± 3.1		21.8 ± 0.4

				WEIGHT		WING		TAIL		BILL	
Species	Sex	Age	No	Individual measurement	Mean	Individual measurement	Mean	Individual measurement	Mean	Individual measurement	Mean
Pogoniulus duchaillui	M	ad	15		40 ± 2.8		78.8 ± 1.8		41.6 ± 2.8		17.7 ± 0.6
	M	imm	1	29.4		78		37		16	
	F	ad	6		40.2 ± 2.9		77 ± 2.5		40.4 ± 0.9		17.6 ± 0.5
	F	juv	1	37.9		77		40		15	
P. scolopaceus	M	ad	11		12.9 ± 1.6		54.3 ± 1.4		31.2 ± 1.7		15.7 ± 0.6
	F	ad	7		14.1 ± 0.9		54.3 ± 1.4		31.2 ± 1.1		15.5 ± 0.4
	F	juv	1	9		50		25		13	
P. subsulphureus	M	ad	15		8.9 ± 0.9		48.3 ± 1.1		23 ± 0.8		12.5 ± 0.5
	M	imm	2	8,9.6	8.8	48(2)	48	22(2)	22	11,12	11.5
	F	ad	9		9.4 ± 0.9		47.8 ± 1		22.9 ± 0.6		12.4 ± 0.3
P. atroflavus	M	ad	6		14.7 ± 1.7		58.8 ± 1.1		27.6 ± 1.1		13.6 ± 0.9
	M	juv	2	15,15.5	15.3	56,58	57	26(2)	26	13,14	13.5
	F	ad	3	13.7,16.1,17.5	15.8	56,57,58	57	26(2),28	26.7	13,14(2)	13.7
Trachyphonus purpuratus	M	ad	1	82.2		109		100		25	
	F	ad	1	83.2		101		100		26	

INDICATORIDAE

				WEIGHT		WING		TAIL		BILL	
Species	Sex	Age	No	Individual measurement	Mean	Individual measurement	Mean	Individual measurement	Mean	Individual measurement	Mean
Indicator maculatus	M	ad	11		45.9 ± 3.1		101.4 ± 2.6		62.4 ± 3.9		14.6 ± 0.5
	F	ad	12		48.3 ± 2.9		100.5 ± 2		56.8 ± 1.8		14.3 ± 0.6
	O	ad	2	49,52	50.5	97,100	98.5	57,64	60.5	13(2)	13
I. conirostris	M	ad	12		31.5 ± 1.6		92.5 ± 1.4		55.9 ± 1.7		12.4 ± 0.3
	F	ad	5		30.8 ± 1.8		89 ± 1.9		55.8 ± 3		12.3 ± 0.4
I. exilis	M	ad	12		19.9 ± 1.2		77.7 ± 3.1		45.5 ± 2.5		10.6 ± 0.5
	F	ad	9		20.1 ± 1.2		75.3 ± 0.5		43.4 ± 1.6		10.3 ± 0.4
I. willcocksi	M	ad	2	19.5,20.2	19.9	74,75	74.5	45,47	46	10(2)	10
	F	ad	5		16.3 ± 0.4		70.8 ± 0.5		44 ± 4.9		9.8 ± 0.5
Melichneutes robustus	M	ad	4	51,52.3,52.9,54.9	52.8	94(2),96,98	95.5	54,59,64(2)	60.3	15,16(3)	15.8
	F	ad	2	46.9,47.1	47	93,97	95	54(2)	54	16(2)	16
Melignomon eisentrauti	M	ad	6		25.5 ± 3.5		83.2 ± 2.9		49.8 ± 1.7		12.8 ± 0.4
	F	ad	5		22.4 ± 2.6		80.6 ± 1.7		47.4 ± 1.5		12.4 ± 0.5
Prodotiscus insignis	M	ad	3	9.4,10.7,11	10.4	63,67,68	66	38,40,42	40	9(2),10	9.3
	F	ad	3	9.1,9.8,11.4	10.1	61,63,66	63.3	43(2),45	43.6	9,10(2)	9.6
	O	ad	1	9.2		64		45		8	
P. regulus	O	imm	1	11		80		58		9	

PICIDAE

				WEIGHT		WING		TAIL		BILL	
Species	Sex	Age	No	Individual measurement	Mean	Individual measurement	Mean	Individual measurement	Mean	Individual measurement	Mean
Jynx torquilla	M	ad	1	36.4		88		63		21	
Campethera maculosa	M	ad	3	46,55.3,60.2	53.8	100(2),103	101	54,57,62	57.7	21(3)	21
	F	ad	1	57.8		103		54		20	
C. caroli	M	ad	7		64.9 ± 3.2		103.7 ± 2.6		53.5 ± 2.2		29.4 ± 0.9
	F	ad	8		62.5 ± 5.6		106.7 ± 2.9		57.3 ± 4.4		29.5 ± 0.8
C. nivosa	M	ad	12		38.6 ± 3.6		91.1 ± 2.4		43.9 ± 2.8		20.4 ± 0.8
	F	ad	11		39.9 ± 3		90.5 ± 2.8		42.6 ± 3.2		20.4 ± 0.6
	O	ad	1	36		90		45		19	

Species	Sex	Age	No	WEIGHT Individual measurement	Mean	WING Individual measurement	Mean	TAIL Individual measurement	Mean	BILL Individual measurement	Mean
Dendropicos gabonensis	M	ad	4	26.8,28.6, 30,31.4	29.2	83,85(2),86	84.8	38(2),40,42	39.5	19,20(2),21	20
	F	ad	6		26.1 ± 3.2		85 ± 1.4		40.1 ± 0.4		19.8 ± 0.3
D. pyrrhogaster	M	ad	6		69.3 ± 4.8		116.2 ± 1.6		63.6 ± 2.6		32.4 ± 2.3
	F	ad	1	63.3		113		60		30	
EURYLAEMIDAE											
Smithornis capensis	M	ad	1	25.3		72		49		15	
S. rufolateralis	M	ad	12		20.5 ± 2.7		66.7 ± 1.8		41.8 ± 2.6		15.7 ± 1.1
	M	imm	9		18.2 ± 2.7		61.4 ± 1.3		43.6 ± 3		14.7 ± 0.8
	F	ad	2	19.6,23.1	21.4	62(2)	62	39,40	39.5	16(2)	16
	F	imm	4	10,16.9, 17.7,19	15.9	60,62(2),64	62	39,40,42(2)	40.8	14,15,16(2)	15.3
PITTIDAE											
Pitta angolensis	M	ad	2	45.2,48.2	46.7	103,108	105.5	32,33	32.5	22,23	22.5
ALAUDIDAE											
Mirafra africana	F	ad	1	33.6		83		51		17	
Pinarocorys erythropygia	M	ad	1	30.1		103		54		16	
HIRUNDINIDAE											
Riparia riparia	M	ad	1	11.1		106		50		8	
Hirundo rustica	M	ad	10		17.5 ± 1.5		120 ± 3.1		75.2 ± 16.5	11	± 0
	F	ad	1	19		118		60		11	
H. nigrita	M	ad	1	16.6		106		40		12	
	F	ad	1	18.5		108		40		12	
H. abyssinica	M	ad	5		15.2 ± 1.5		98 ± 2.5		60.3 ± 12.3		9.2 ± 0.5
H. griseopyga	M	ad	1	10		93		55		8	
	F	ad	1	9.6		80		52		7	
	O	ad	1	10.3		90		54		7	
H. fuligula	M	ad	1	16.1		108		44		10	
	F	ad	1	17.8		113		43		11	
Psalidoprocne nitens	M	ad	7		9.6 ± 0.8		94.2 ± 1.3		42.5 ± 0.6	8	± 0.5
	F	ad	13		10 ± 0.7		89.5 ± 3.8		42 ± 0.4	8	± 0.5
MOTACILLIDAE											
Motacilla flava	M	ad	18		13.7 ± 1.7		83 ± 2.5		66.8 ± 2.5	16	± 0.5
	F	ad	31		12.3 ± 0.4		80.1 ± 2.4		65.4 ± 2.5		16.1 ± 0.4
	O	ad	42		15.7 ± 1.3		81.3 ± 2.5		66.6 ± 1.9		16.2 ± 0.7
M. clara	M	ad	3	17.7,19.4, 20.8	19.3	71(2),74	72	86,87,89	87.3	17(2),18	17.3
	M	imm	1	22.3		78		80		15	
	O	ad	2	19.5,20.4	20	75(2)	75	80,81	80.5	18(2)	18
Anthus similis	M	ad	2	25.8,27.2	26.5	80,87	83.5	59,62	60.5	17(2)	17
	F	ad	2	25.8,28.9	27.4	77,83	80	58,62	60	17(2)	17

Appendix 115

Species	Sex	Age	No	WEIGHT Individual measurement	Mean	WING Individual measurement	Mean	TAIL Individual measurement	Mean	BILL Individual measurement	Mean
A. trivialis	M	ad	3	19,24.8, 31.8	25.2	85,87,90	87.3	54,57,60	57	15(3)	15
	F	ad	1	13		81		60		14	
	O	ad	1	20.8		85		56		15	
Macronyx croceus	M	imm	1	45.3		97		80		20	

CAMPEPHAGIDAE

Species	Sex	Age	No	WEIGHT Individual measurement	Mean	WING Individual measurement	Mean	TAIL Individual measurement	Mean	BILL Individual measurement	Mean
Coracina azurea	M	ad	10		46 ± 4.6		108.4 ± 2.7		71.1 ± 3.9		20.1 ± 1.4
	F	ad	3	42.6,46, 51.3	46.6	102,107, 110	106.3	68(2),70	68.6	17,21(2)	19.7
	O	ad	1	48.6		105		68		19	
C. quiscalina	M	ad	9		39.7 ± 4.2		99.2 ± 2.8		66.3 ± 2.4		20.2 ± 0.8
	M	imm	1	40		97		64		19	
	F	ad	4	32.5,37.7, 41.4,42	38.3	97,98,100, 103	99.5	63,65,68, 70	66.5	20(3),21	20.3
C. phoenicea	M	imm	1	26		100		83		21	
C. lobata	M	ad	15		33.3 ± 1.3		98 ± 2.9		66.6 ± 3.6		17.5 ± 0.8
	M	imm	3	32.3,33.4, 36.9	34.2	94,97(2)	96	65,70(2)	68.3	17,18(2)	17.6
	F	ad	2	32.4,32.7	32.5	95,98	96.5	64,73	68.5	18(2)	18
	F	imm	1	29.4		94		67		18	

PYCNONOTIDAE

Species	Sex	Age	No	WEIGHT Individual measurement	Mean	WING Individual measurement	Mean	TAIL Individual measurement	Mean	BILL Individual measurement	Mean
Pycnonotus barbatus	M	ad	9		36.2 ± 3.3		93.9 ± 1.9		74 ± 2.1		18.8 ± 0.4
	F	ad	4	32.8,34.5, 36.8,38.8	35.7	85,89,91, 92	89.3	68,72,73, 75	72	18(2),19(2)	18.5
Andropadus curvirostris	M	ad	8		23.2 ± 2.9		75 ± 2.7		67 ± 2.5		15.8 ± 0.5
	F	ad	7		21.7 ± 0.8		72.2 ± 1.7		66.7 ± 2		15.5 ± 0.6
	O	ad	1	24.1		78		68		16	
A. gracilis	M	ad	2	16.9,17.1	17	66,68	67	52,60	56	14(2)	14
	F	ad	2	15,17.1	16.1	63,65	64	53,54	53.5	14(2)	14
A. ansorgei	M	ad	5		19.9 ± 0.8		72 ± 1.4		62.4 ± 2.3		15.2 ± 0.8
	F	ad	1	20.1		72		66		15	
A. gracilirostris	M	ad	9		29.2 ± 3.8		80.6 ± 3.4		70.5 ± 2.7		20 ± 0.9
	F	ad	4	26,26.8, 27.8,30	27.7	80(2),81, 85	81.5	68,70,73, 74	71.3	19,20(2),21	20
A. virens	M	ad	9		23.9 ± 8		74.9 ± 2.1		65.1 ± 3.6		15.2 ± 0.7
	F	ad	11		21.2 ± 1.5		70.5 ± 3		61.1 ± 2.9		15.1 ± 0.6
A. latirostris	M	ad	10		26.3 ± 2.7		80 ± 3.5		70.8 ± 3.5		16.3 ± 1
	M	imm	4	21.9,22.3, 25.1,27	24.1	74,75(2),77	75.3	67,68,70, 72	69.3	15,16,17(2)	16.3
	F	ad	12		22.4 ± 1.5		74.2 ± 2.7		66.1 ± 2.3		15.2 ± 0.4
	F	imm	1	22		72		68		13	
Calyptocichla serina	M	ad	3	36.4,39.5, 39.8	38.6	85,88,90	87.7	70,71,72	71	18,19,20	19
	F	ad	9		38.8 ± 3.4		89.1 ± 2.3		72.8 ± 1.5		20 ± 0
Baeopogon indicator	M	ad	12		43.6 ± 3.5		97.9 ± 3.8		64.9 ± 1.9		20.2 ± 0.4
	F	ad	8		40.3 ± 4.9		96.8 ± 1.9		62.5 ± 2.3		19.1 ± 0.7

116 Birds of Mount Nimba

Species	Sex	Age	No	WEIGHT Individual measurement	Mean	WING Individual measurement	Mean	TAIL Individual measurement	Mean	BILL Individual measurement	Mean
Ixonotus guttatus	M	ad	3	35.2,36.1, 36.2	35.8	88(2),90	88.7	68(2),70	68.7	15,16,17	16
	F	ad	3	31.4,35.4, 38.6	35.1	83(2),86	84	67,71(2)	69.7	15,17(2)	16.3
	O	ad	1	35.3		91		70		16.5	
Chlorocichla simplex	M	ad	9		48.3 ± 5.5		103.5 ± 3.4		85.3 ± 4.9		21.8 ± 1.8
	F	ad	7		42.4 ± 5.8		100 ± 2.1		81.8 ± 3.8		20.5 ± 1.3
Thescelocichla leucopleura	M	ad	4	60.6,62.3(2) 67.4	63.2	107,110, 111,115	110.8	90,95, 101(2)	96.8	24(2),25,26	24.8
	F	ad	3	53.2,58,59	56.8	102,103, 105	103.3	96,98(2)	95.3	23(2),24	23.3
Phyllastrephus scandens	M	ad	4	–,52.3,59, 64	58.4	107,109, 112,115	110.8	100,103, 108	103.7	21,22(2),23	22
	F	ad	1	51.2		110		98		22	
	O	imm	1	56.4		100		97		22	
P. baumanni	M	ad	5		30.3 ± 2.7		81.8 ± 5.1		73.5 ± 3.7		20.3 ± 0.5
	F	ad	4	23.5,23.7, 25.8,26.5	24.9	69(2),70,74	70.5	63(2),68,70	66	17,18,19(2)	18.3
	O	ad	1	23.4		80		74		21	
P. icterinus	M	ad	18		19.4 ± 2.5		76.7 ± 2.3		67.1 ± 2.7		19.4 ± 0.7
	F	ad	11		17.9 ± 3.9		72 ± 2.6		63.3 ± 2.6		18 ± 0.4
P. albigularis	M	ad	2	26.1,27.3	26.7	82,83	82.5	63,69	66	21,22	21.5
	F	ad	4	16.2,19.3, 19.4,20.2	18.8	66,68(2),70	67.8	55,59(2),66	59.8	18(3),19	18.3
Bleda syndactyla	M	ad	8		46.4 ± 5.8		110 ± 2.9		88.3 ± 3.2		28 ± 1.4
	F	ad	9		44.1 ± 3.6		101.9 ± 1.6		83 ± 2.8		24.4 ± 1.3
B. eximia	M	ad	5		49.2 ± 3.3		111.3 ± 1.7		93.2 ± 3		27.3 ± 0.5
	F	ad	9		44.8 ± 2.7		100.4 ± 3.1		83.7 ± 3.4		23.3 ± 1.3
B. canicapilla	M	ad	6		43.1 ± 4.3		100.2 ± 3.3		86 ± 5.9		21.3 ± 0.9
	F	ad	10		38.4 ± 2.5		98.3 ± 3.4		84 ± 2.3		20.6 ± 0.8
	O	ad	1	43.2		100		85		21	
Criniger barbatus	M	ad	11		44.1 ± 3.6		103.5 ± 3.3		90.4 ± 2.1		23.3 ± 1.1
	M	juv	1	47.2		95		70		20	
	F	ad	8		41.6 ± 3.3		98.1 ± 2		80.3 ± 5		21.8 ± 1
C. calurus	M	ad	10		36.7 ± 3.8		96 ± 3.7		80.2 ± 4.6		22.3 ± 0.8
	M	juv	1	33.4		97		78		23.5	
	F	ad	5		35.5 ± 2.1		92.3 ± 1.5		75.8 ± 1.7		21.5 ± 0.6
C. olivaceus	M	ad	8		29.1 ± 2.3		88.4 ± 2.1		73 ± 2.1		19 ± 0.7
	F	ad	6		26.7 ± 3		82.3 ± 1.5		68.5 ± 3.1		17.9 ± 0.5
Nicator chloris	M	ad	5		52.2 ± 3.7		106.6 ± 3.6		98.8 ± 4.5		23.9 ± 1.1
	F	ad	7		38.3 ± 3.5		90.3 ± 4.9		89.4 ± 5.1		21.1 ± 1.4
	O	ad	2	48,52.6	50.3	101,102	101.5	100,103	101.5	23(2)	23
LANIIDAE											
Prionops caniceps	M	ad	1	55.7		122		76		26	
	M	imm	1	59.4		120		75		26	
	F	ad	5		52.4 ± 7.4		119.4 ± 2.5		74.2 ± 2.4		25.4 ± 0.5
Dryoscopus gambensis	M	ad	1	37.6		95		78		25	
	F	ad	3	30.7,33,34	32.6	87,88,92	89	76,80,82	79.3	23,24,25	24
	F	imm	1	30.4		90		79		24	

				WEIGHT		WING		TAIL		BILL	
Species	Sex	Age	No	Individual measurement	Mean	Individual measurement	Mean	Individual measurement	Mean	Individual measurement	Mean
D. sabini	M	ad	3	31,40.7, 43.9	38.5	80,84,85	83	-,71,75	73	28,29,30	29
	M	imm	2	41.4,42.8	41.9	85,86	85.5	76,82	79	27,29	28
	F	ad	3	32.4,39, 39.2	35.8	85(3)	85	75(2),86	78.7	25(3)	25
Tchagra minuta	M	ad	2	25,32.3	28.7	74,77	75.5	80(2)	80	22,23	22.5
	F	ad	3	30.3,34.2, 34.6	33	75,78(2)	77	74,80,84	79.3	22,23,24	23
T. australis	M	ad	2	31.4,36.3	33.8	75(2)	75	91,95	93	22(2)	22
	F	ad	2	34.4,38	36.2	72,75	73.5	93,94	93.5	20(2)	20
Laniarius leucorhynchus	M	ad	5		57.1 ± 5.1		94.6 ± 2.7		83.6 ± 4.1		27.2 ± 0.4
	F	ad	2	57,62	59.5	90,97	93.5	80(2)	80	27(2)	27
	F	imm	1	56.6		90		80		27	
Malaconotus multicolor	M	ad	21		51 ± 4.4		100.5 ± 3.7		86.8 ± 3.4		22.7 ± 1.4
	M	imm	2	48.1,48.4	48.3	90,95	92.5	83,85	84	20,23	21.5
	F	ad	3	46.2,53.9, 54.8	51.6	90(2),96	92	82,85,86	84.3	20,22,23	21.8
	F	imm	1	42.3		95		86		22	
	O	ad	1	49.6		101		81		22	
M. cruentus	M	ad	7		76.5 ± 6.8		107.6 ± 3.5		99.4 ± 4.8		31.3 ± 1.9
	M	juv	1	70		102		76		26	
	F	ad	4	70.1,71.8, 75,91.2	77	103,106, 108(2)	106.3	96,97,100, 103	99	30,31,32(2)	31.3
M. lagdeni	M	ad	1	97		115		100		35	
	O	ad	1	96		108		96		31	
Lanius collaris	M	ad	4	32,35,37.2, 37.3	35.4	90,91(2),92	91	102,105, 108,109	104.3	18,19,21(2)	19.3
	F	ad	2	30.3,34.6	32.5	87,90	88.5	102,106	104	19,20	19.5
	M	imm	1	47		100		76		21	
	O	ad	1	34.3		98		72		20	

TURDIDAE

Species	Sex	Age	No	Individual measurement	Mean	Individual measurement	Mean	Individual measurement	Mean	Individual measurement	Mean
Saxicola rubetra	M	ad	7		15.1 ± 1.9		78.2 ± 3.3		42.2 ± 1.8		14.8 ± 0.8
	F	ad	2	9,12.3	10.7	74,75	74.5	40(2)	40	15,16	15.5
Monticola saxatilis	M	ad	1	48		116		54		22	
Erythropygia leucosticta	M	ad	11		26.3 ± 2.9		79.4 ± 1.9		60.9 ± 3.8		18.3 ± 0.5
	F	ad	7		23.9 ± 2.8		74.4 ± 1.6		55.9 ± 2.1		18.1 ± 0.4
Alethe diademata	M	ad	13		32.1 ± 2.4		93.9 ± 1.9		75.1 ± 2.4		20.2 ± 0.4
	M	juv	6		30.4 ± 1.9		91 ± 3		70.6 ± 1.8		19.2 ± 0.4
	F	ad	7		31.8 ± 0.9		89.4 ± 1.1		68.3 ± 3.4		19.8 ± 0.5
	F	imm	4	27,29,29.8, 30.1	29	82,88(2),90	87	65,70(3)	68.7	19(2),20(2)	19.5
A. poliocephala	M	ad	9		32.7 ± 2.8		93.9 ± 3		56.5 ± 3.7		20 ± 0.1
	M	juv	7		32.6 ± 3.2		90.1 ± 1.8		54.3 ± 2.3		18.8 ± 0.8
	F	ad	7		31.9 ± 1.6		91.8 ± 3		54 ± 1.8		19.3 ± 0.8
	F	juv	6		27.1 ± 3.4		90 ± 3.6		52.8 ± 1.8		18.8 ± 0.5
Sheppardia cyornithopsis	M	ad	9		19 ± 1.9		73.4 ± 3.1		51.1 ± 3.1		15.4 ± 0.5
	M	imm	4	15,16.8, 17.1,18	16.7	68(2),69,74	69.8	46,48,50, 52	49	14(2),15,16	14.8
	F	ad	3	13,17.2, 17.3	15.8	66,67,70	67.7	44,45,48	45.7	14,15(2)	14.7
	O	ad	2	15.6,16.5	16.1	67,74	70.5	46,52	49	15,16	15.5

Species	Sex	Age	No	WEIGHT Individual measurement	WEIGHT Mean	WING Individual measurement	WING Mean	TAIL Individual measurement	TAIL Mean	BILL Individual measurement	BILL Mean
Stiphrornis erythrothorax	M	ad	17		14.9 ± 1.4		64.2 ± 1.8		33.1 ± 2		14.8 ± 0.4
	M	imm	5		14.7 ± 1.8		63.6 ± 2.2		31.2 ± 1.8		14.2 ± 0.4
	M	juv	3	14,14.1,14.6	14.2	60,62,63	61.7	26,28,30	28	13,15(2)	14.3
	F	ad	7		14.5 ± 1.4		61.8 ± 1.7		30.8 ± 1.6		14.5 ± 0.6
	F	imm	1	13.7		60		30		15	
Cossypha polioptera	M	ad	6		21.6 ± 1.5		81.5 ± 1.8		61.2 ± 2.6		17.5 ± 0.6
	F	ad	4	17.1,18,19,20.3	18.6	75(3),78	75.8	53(2),55	54	17(2),18(2)	17.5
	O	ad	2	20.9,21.2	21.1	75,80	77.5	57,61	59	16,17	16.5
C. cyanocampter	M	ad	3	28,31.6,32.2	30.6	88,90,92	90	71,72,74	72.3	19,20(2)	19.7
	F	ad	1	29		85		66		20	
	O	ad	1	–		93		77		20	
C. niveicapilla	M	ad	1	28		95		78		18	
Neocossyphus poensis	M	ad	10		54.9 ± 4.2		110.7 ± 2.7		81.7 ± 4.3		19.6 ± 0.5
	F	ad	9		54.5 ± 2.4		106.6 ± 3.5		78.8 ± 2.6		19 ± 0.8
N. finschi	M	ad	9		37.7 ± 2.4		100.8 ± 3.2		74 ± 2.1		16.7 ± 0.5
	F	ad	5		36.3 ± 1.8		97 ± 5.3		70.8 ± 1.3		17.2 ± 0.4
Luscinia megarhynchos	M	ad	4	18,19,20.5,22.2	19.9	80,82,84,85	82.8	54,56,58(2)	56.6	18(3),19	18.3
	F	ad	3	17(2),33.5	22.5	80,82,86	82.7	55,56(2)	55.7	17,18(2)	17.7
Turdus pelios	M	ad	3	52.2,62.5,78	64.2	115(2),124	118	75,80,85	80	23(2),24	23.3
	F	ad	2	61.2,63	62.1	111,115	113	80,83	81.5	23(2)	23
	F	imm	1	56		110		80		22	
T. princei	M	ad	2	64.3,69.3	66.8	109,110	109.5	67,68	67.5	22,24	23
	M	imm	1	59.7		109		65		22	
	F	ad	3	59,64.7,69.2	64.3	107,108,110	108.6	65,66,68	66.3	22(3)	22
	O	ad	1	55		103		67		22	
TIMALIIDAE											
Trichastoma fulvescens	M	ad	9		32.7 ± 2.1		79.1 ± 3.2		60.8 ± 2.8		19.7 ± 0.5
	M	juv	2	29.4,34.6	32	70,72	71	59,61	60	18,19	18.5
	F	ad	8		27.6 ± 4.1		74.3 ± 1.5		57.1 ± 1.8		19.8 ± 0.3
T. rufipennis	M	ad	12		25.4 ± 1.2		73.1 ± 2.2		53.9 ± 2.2		17.6 ± 0.5
	F	ad	15		22.2 ± 1.9		68.3 ± 3		50 ± 2.4		17 ± 0.6
T. cleaveri	M	ad	15		26.9 ± 2.2		73.1 ± 2.1		53.3 ± 3.1		17.8 ± 1.1
	M	juv	1	22.3		64		38		14	
	F	ad	6		25.6 ± 2.7		70.7 ± 2.1		52 ± 2		17.5 ± 0.8
T. rufescens	M	ad	10		34.7 ± 2.3		81.2 ± 3.4		63.1 ± 3.8		18.8 ± 0.6
	F	ad	8		34.2 ± 2.5		78.1 ± 2.9		59.4 ± 4.2		18.8 ± 0.5
T. puveli	M	ad	1	43		90		68		20	
	F	ad	2	38.1,39.6	38.9	79,83	81	62,63	62.5	19(2)	19
Phyllanthus atripennis	M	ad	8		83.9 ± 6		117.3 ± 4.3		79.9 ± 3.8		26 ± 0.5
	F	ad	7		86.4 ± 6.3		119.3 ± 3		81.3 ± 3.3		25.6 ± 0.5
PICATHARTIDAE											
Picathartes gymnocephalus	F	ad	2	166,226	196	150,157	153.5	173,174	173.5	33(2)	33

Appendix

				WEIGHT		WING		TAIL		BILL	
Species	Sex	Age	No	Individual measurement	Mean	Individual measurement	Mean	Individual measurement	Mean	Individual measurement	Mean
SYLVIIDAE											
Acrocephalus	M	ad	1	–		56		43		18	
scirpaceus	F	ad	2	10(2)	10	66,69	67.5	43,45	44	18(2)	18
A. arundinaceus	M	ad	1	29.1		96		75		24	
	F	ad	2	20.1,26	23.1	93,95	94	70,72	71	24(2)	24
Melocichla mentalis	M	ad	1	36		80		72		19	
Hippolais polyglotta	M	ad	2	8.9,9	9	65,68	66.5	46,47	46.5	15,17	16
	F	ad	2	–,9.8		66,67	66.5	43,45	44	15,17	16
	O	ad	1	9.8		66		42		15	
Sylvia borin	M	ad	6		17.1 ± 2.8		75.3 ± 1.9		49.5 ± 1.8		14.5 ± 1
	F	ad	1	12		77		–		16	
	O	ad	2	12.4,12.9	12.7	72,77	74.5	47,48	47.5	15(2)	15
S. atricapilla	M	ad	4	14.4,15.2, 15.6,16	15.3	72,76(2),79	75.8	51,55(2),56	54.3	14(2),15(2)	14.5
	F	ad	4	13.5,14, 14.4,15	14.2	70,72,73, 74	72.3	51,52,53, 54	53	14(3),15	14.3
Phylloscopus trochilus	M	ad	6		7.1 ± 1.1		65.6 ± 2.1		44.4 ± 0.9		12.2 ± 0.8
	F	ad	3	5,6,7	6	60,65(2)	63.3	40,42,44	42	13(3)	13
	O	ad	1	6.7		60		42		12	
P. sibilatrix	M	ad	1	8.9		70		41		13	
	F	ad	2	8.8,9	8.9	70(2)	70	40(2)	40	13,14	13.5
Cisticola erythrops	M	ad	8		13.5 ± 1.7		59.1 ± 2.4		50.6 ± 3.8		17 ± 0.8
	M	juv	2	11,17	14	52,62	57	40,52	46	15,16	15.5
	F	ad	4	11.8,12.5, 13,14.2	12.9	53,54,55(2)	54.3	45(2),47,48	46.3	16(4)	16
C. lateralis	M	ad	2	18,23.4	20.7	69,70	69.5	49,50	49.5	16,17	16.5
	F	ad	4	13,14,15, 17	14.8	56(2),64,66	60.5	43,50(3)	48.3	14,15,17(2)	15.8
C. natalensis	M	ad	2	17,22.8	19.9	68,70	69	48,55	51.5	16(2)	16
	F	ad	1	16.1		58		48		14	
C. brachyptera	M	ad	8		7.3 ± 1.2		48.8 ± 3.8		31.5 ± 2.4		12 ± 0
	M	juv	2	7.4,9.1	8.3	44,46	45	20,35	27.5	11(2)	11
	F	ad	4	6,6.6,6.7, 10.2	7.4	43,45,46, 48	45.3	33,35(3)	34.5	12(4)	12
	O	imm	1	8.1		43		37		12	
Prinia subflava	M	ad	8		8.7 ± 0.8		49.5 ± 1.9		42.3 ± 3		13.9 ± 0.3
	M	juv	3	6.2,6.4,8	6.9	47,49,53	49.7	40,43(2)	42	13(3)	13
	F	ad	2	8.6,10	9.3	45,50	47.5	42(2)	42	14(2)	14
P. leontica	M	ad	4	11.9,12.8, 13,13.6	12.8	54(2),55(2)	54.5	46(2),49,50	47.8	14(2),15(2)	14.5
	F	ad	1	12.2		54		42		15	
Apalis nigriceps	M	ad	8		8.4 ± 0.6		49 ± 1.7		42.1 ± 2		12 ± 0
	M	imm	1	7.6		47		40		11	
	F	ad	3	8(3)	8	45,46,49	46.7	40(3)	40	12(3)	12
A. sharpii	M	ad	14		9.1 ± 0.8		50.2 ± 1.4		45.3 ± 2.5		13.9 ± 0.3
	M	imm	4	8.4,9,9.2, 9.3	8.8	47,52(3)	50.6	40,45(2),48	44.8	14(3)	14
	M	juv	2	8.3,9	8.7	50(2)	50	43,46	44.5	13,14	13.5
	F	ad	7		8.3 ± 0.5		46.9 ± 2		41 ± 2.2		14 ± 0
	F	imm	1	6.7		45		40		14	
	F	juv	1	9		50		43		13	

Species	Sex	Age	No	WEIGHT Individual measurement	Mean	WING Individual measurement	Mean	TAIL Individual measurement	Mean	BILL Individual measurement	Mean
Bathmocercus cerviniventris	M	ad	7		15.8 ± 2.1		58.6 ± 1.5		49.6 ± 2.4		16.1 ± 0.4
	F	imm	1	15.7		56		45		16	
Camaroptera superciliaris	M	ad	8		9.1 ± 1.1		49.1 ± 1.5		25.8 ± 1.6		16.6 ± 0.5
	M	imm	1	8.2		50		27		16	
	F	ad	4	7.5,7.8, 8.2,9.5	8.3	46(2),47(2)	46.5	25(2),26,27	25.8	15(3),16	15.3
C. chloronota	M	ad	16		10.7 ± 1		53.8 ± 1.9		21.9 ± 2.6		15 ± 0
	M	imm	11		10.1 ± 0.9		51 ± 9.9		22 ± 7.7		14.9 ± 0.4
	F	ad	9		10.3 ± 1.2		48.3 ± 1.4		18.3 ± 0.8		14.8 ± 0.4
C. brachyura	M	ad	11		10.7 ± 1		52.7 ± 2.1		33.2 ± 1.4		15.7 ± 0.5
	M	imm	2	8.1,10.2	9.1	48,52	50	30,33	31.5	15,16	15.5
	F	ad	3	8.1,9,9.1	8.7	48,52,53	51	30(2),32	30.7	15,16(2)	15.7
Eremomela badiceps	M	ad	7		9.3 ± 0.8		54.6 ± 1		30.1 ± 1.2		13 ± 0
	F	ad	3	10.4,10.6, 10.7	10.6	54,55,56	55	32(2),34	32.7	12,14,15	12.7
Sylvietta virens	M	ad	7		7.4 ± 0.6		46.3 ± 1.1		13 ± 0.3		13 ± 0
	F	ad	9		7.9 ± 0.8		45.9 ± 1.8		12.6 ± 1.1		12.9 ± 0.4
	O	ad	1	6.7		46		13		13	
S. denti	M	ad	1	8.1		51		13		10	
	F	ad	1	8.7		49		13		10	
Macrosphenus concolor	M	ad	9		13.9 ± 0.9		57.8 ± 2.5		38 ± 2.7		18 ± 0
	F	ad	6		13.9 ± 0.8		55.3 ± 1.9		35.1 ± 3		18 ± 0
M. kempi	M	ad	16		13.2 ± 1.1		59.5 ± 1.5		33.6 ± 3		21 ± 0
	M	imm	4	12.3,12.4, 13,16.6	13.6	52,55(3)	54.3	33,38(3)	36.8	20(3),21	20.3
	F	ad	5		11.7 ± 1.7		55.5 ± 2.4		29.8 ± 1		20.7 ± 0.5
	F	imm	3	11.4(2), 12.3	11.7	51,52(2)	51.7	34,35(2)	34.7	20(3)	20
	O	ad	1	14.4		62		36		21	
Hylia prasina	M	ad	10		12.7 ± 1.4		65.4 ± 3		37.9 ± 3.4		13.1 ± 0.3
	M	imm	6		11 ± 0.9		60.7 ± 2.6		35.3 ± 0.8		12.8 ± 0.4
	F	ad	11		10.5 ± 1.3		59.1 ± 1.3		35.3 ± 0.9		13 ± 0.4
	F	imm	2	8,10	9	59,60	59.5	35(2)	35	13(2)	13
	O	ad	2	12,13.3	12.7	60,67	63.5	38,40	39	12,13	12.5

MUSCICAPIDAE

Species	Sex	Age	No	WEIGHT Individual measurement	Mean	WING Individual measurement	Mean	TAIL Individual measurement	Mean	BILL Individual measurement	Mean
Muscicapa striata	M	ad	1	13		88		54		14	
	F	ad	2	13,14	13.5	80,86	83	55(2)	55	14,16	15
	F	imm	1	13		79		50		14	
M. epulata	M	ad	2	9.3,10.7	10	58,61	59.5	32,35	35.5	12(2)	12
	F	ad	1	8.8		60		30		12	
	F	imm	1	9.5		58		34		12	
M. olivascens	M	ad	8		17.6 ± 0.8		74.9 ± 1.7		58.6 ± 1.7		15.4 ± 0.6
	M	juv	1	17.9		71		61		14	
	F	ad	3	12.3,13.4, 14.7	13.5	67,69,70	68.7	55(3)	55	15(3)	15
	O	imm	1	13.2		71		63		14	
M. ussheri	M	ad	3	16.3,17.3, 19	17.5	83,84,86	84.3	43(3)	43	12(3)	12
	F	ad	3	16.8,18, 19.8	18.2	81,82,89	84	40(2),44	41.3	12(3)	12
	O	ad	1	18		85		42		11	

Appendix

				WEIGHT		WING		TAIL		BILL	
Species	Sex	Age	No	Individual measurement	Mean	Individual measurement	Mean	Individual measurement	Mean	Individual measurement	Mean
M. griseigularis	M	ad	1	13.6		56		52		15	
	M	imm	1	11		54		53		15	
	F	ad	4	11(2),11.3, 11.7	11.3	54(2),56(2)	55	52,53(3)	52.8	14(2),15(2)	14.3
Ficedula hypoleuca	M	ad	2	12.5,16.9	14.7	80,82	81	45,48	46.5	12,13	12.5
	F	ad	1	11		78		44		12	
	O	ad	1	9.2		77		42		12	
Fraseria ocreata	M	ad	9		32.2 ± 1.9		93.7 ± 2.1		68.8 ± 4.4		20.6 ± 0.7
	M	imm	2	27.6,28	27.8	90,95	92.5	68,77	72.5	20,21	20.5
	F	ad	8		30.3 ± 2.4		90.4 ± 2.2		67.4 ± 2.8		19.9 ± 1.4
F. cinerascens	M	ad	1	18.5		83		62		18	
	F	ad	3	13.3,17.1, 21	17.1	75(2),81	77	48,51,68	55.7	16(2),17	16.3
Melaenornis annamarulae	M	ad	9		39.7 ± 1.9		106 ± 2.9		74 ± 2.6		18.5 ± 0.9
	F	ad	3	37,42.2, 42.3	40.5	104,106, 107	105.7	68,69,75	70.7	18(2),19	18.3
Hyliota violacea	M	ad	4	−,14,16.2, 17	15.7	76,77,78, 79	77.5	36,37,38(2)	37.3	16(2),17(2)	16.5
	F	ad	5		15.8 ± 1.1		74.2 ± 1.5		35.6 ± 1.1		15.2 ± 1.1
Megabyas flammulatus	M	ad	7		27.6 ± 1.7		88.7 ± 5.2		53.7 ± 2.6		23 ± 1
	M	imm	1	23		86		51		24	
	F	ad	5		25.7 ± 2.2		87.8 ± 0.8		57.8 ± 1.6		23 ± 0.7
Bias musicus	M	ad	1	21.2		91		47		22	
	F	ad	1	19		89		51		20	
Batis (poensis) occultus	M	ad	2	8.8,9.4	9.1	51,53	52	28,29	28.5	14(2)	14
	M	imm	1	9.2		52		30		15	
	F	ad	2	8.7,9	8.9	48,51	49.5	25,26	25.5	13,15	14
Platysteira cyanea	F	ad	3	15(2),15.1	15	65,68(2)	67	44,45,50	46.3	16(2),17	16.3
P. castanea	M	ad	15		11.7 ± 1.3		56.8 ± 1.3		19.6 ± 1.2		15.1 ± 0.3
	M	imm	6		12.1 ± 0.5		55.5 ± 1.2		19.7 ± 0.8		15 ± 0
	F	ad	16		11.4 ± 1		55.8 ± 2.4		19.4 ± 1.9		15 ± 0
P. blissetti	M	ad	14		11 ± 1		53.3 ± 1.4		20.5 ± 0.7		15.2 ± 0.4
	M	imm	1	11.9		54		22		15	
	F	ad	8		11 ± 0.9		53.1 ± 0.8		20.3 ± 0.7		15.1 ± 0.4
	O	imm	1	10.5		52		20		15	
P. concreta	M	ad	23		11.7 ± 1		59.4 ± 1.3		23.3 ± 1.4		15.3 ± 0.4
	M	imm	5		11.5 ± 3.1		58.6 ± 1.3		21.8 ± 1.1		14.8 ± 1.1
	F	ad	22		11.1 ± 1.2		58.6 ± 1.6		22.6 ± 1.7		15.2 ± 0.6
	F	imm	2	8.8,9.8	9.3	57,60	58.5	23(2)	23	14,15	14.5
	O	juv	1	8.8		55		20		12	
Erythrocercus mccalli	M	ad	6		7.3 ± 1		51 ± 1		44 ± 1.6		11 ± 0
	F	ad	1	7.1		50		40		10	
Trochocercus nitens	M	ad	6		10.9 ± 1.4		66.6 ± 1.3		64.2 ± 2.5		16.3 ± 0.5
T. nigromitratus	M	ad	12		9.6 ± 0.9		62.8 ± 2.3		53.5 ± 2.6		15 ± 0
	F	ad	12		8.5 ± 0.9		58.5 ± 1.7		51.2 ± 2.7		14.8 ± 0.4
Terpsiphone rufiventer	M	ad	25		14.4 ± 1.4		76.8 ± 2.6		93 ± 28.9		19.3 ± 0.5
	F	ad	11		13.7 ± 2.1		73.8 ± 2.3		71.8 ± 4.5		19.1 ± 0.3
T. viridis	M	ad	2	15.2,17.3	16.3	88,91	89.5	130,290	210	19,20	19.5
	M	imm	2	12.3(2)	12.3	82,83	82.5	83,84	83.5	20(2)	20
	F	ad	1	12		82		80		20	

				WEIGHT		WING		TAIL		BILL	
Species	Sex	Age	No	Individual measurement	Mean	Individual measurement	Mean	Individual measurement	Mean	Individual measurement	Mean

PARIDAE

Parus funereus
	M	ad	6		25.6 ± 3		87.8 ± 2.7		51.2 ± 2.5		12.9 ± 0.3
	M	imm	5		25.8 ± 1.4		86.2 ± 2.8		50.4 ± 3.3		12.9 ± 0.3
	F	ad	5		25.2 ± 1.7		84.6 ± 1.7		52 ± 1.4		13 ± 0.7
	F	imm	1		23.3		84		45		13

NECTARINIIDAE

Anthreptes fraseri
| | M | ad | 8 | | 10.3 ± 1.1 | | 65.4 ± 1.3 | | 39.5 ± 2.3 | | 17.8 ± 0.5 |
| | F | ad | 13 | | 9.5 ± 1 | | 59.4 ± 2.1 | | 37.2 ± 1.6 | | 16.5 ± 2.8 |

A. rectirostris
	M	ad	6		11 ± 1		59 ± 1.1		28.8 ± 0.9		15.2 ± 0.4
	M	imm	2	10.9,12.5	11.7	59(2)	59	28(2)	28	14,15	14.5
	F	ad	1	9		58		25		15	

A. collaris
	M	ad	10		7.4 ± 0.8		50.8 ± 1.4		30.3 ± 2.4		16 ± 0
	M	imm	5		7.1 ± 0.8		48.5 ± 0.5		26.5 ± 1.4		14 ± 0.5
	F	ad	10		7 ± 0.7		48.8 ± 1.5		27 ± 1.1		15.9 ± 0.3
	F	juv	3	6.6,7,7.8	7.1	46,47,48	47	24,26,29	26.3	15(3)	15

Nectarinia seimundi
	M	ad	4	6.3,6.5(2), 6.8	6.5	50,51,52, 53	51.5	20(2),24(2)	22	16(4)	16
	F	ad	10		5.9 ± 0.7		48.8 ± 1.6		22.4 ± 1.7		15.5 ± 0.5
	O	ad	1	5.5		51		25		16	

N. olivacea
| | M | ad | 13 | | 8.5 ± 1 | | 58.3 ± 2.4 | | 40.3 ± 2.5 | | 25.4 ± 0.8 |
| | F | ad | 12 | | 7.9 ± 1.4 | | 54.7 ± 1.9 | | 38.4 ± 0.9 | | 24.2 ± 0.9 |

N. verticalis
	M	ad	5		12.8 ± 1.3		68 ± 1		42 ± 2		29.4 ± 0.9
	M	imm	2	11.7,14.2	12.9	64,66	65	40,42	41	25,28	26.5
	F	ad	1	10.7		62		35		28	

N. cyanolaema
	M	ad	13		15.5 ± 1.8		70.1 ± 1.4		49.7 ± 1.4		27 ± 0.9
	M	imm	3	14.3,14.8,16	15.1	65,67,68	66.7	44,45(2)	44.7	25,26,28	26.3
	F	ad	5		15.2 ± 1.1		65.8 ± 2.5		45.2 ± 1.8		25.4 ± 0.5

N. adelberti
	M	ad	10		9.9 ± 0.8		64.1 ± 1.2		32.4 ± 2.4		19.8 ± 0.4
	M	imm	7		9.1 ± 0.6		58.7 ± 2.8		28.7 ± 1.6		19.3 ± 0.3
	F	ad	4	8.3,9.2,10.1(2)	9.4	57,59(2),61	59	29,30(2),34	30.8	19(3),20	19.3

N. venusta
| | M | ad | 6 | | 6.5 ± 1 | | 52.3 ± 2.1 | | 30.1 ± 0.4 | | 19.1 ± 0.4 |
| | F | ad | 1 | 5.8 | | 50 | | 27 | | 18 | |

N. chloropygia
	M	ad	5		5.3 ± 0.5		47.4 ± 1.6		25 ± 0.5		18.4 ± 0.4
	M	imm	2	5,5.5	5.3	46,48	47	21,22	21.5	18(2)	18
	F	ad	3	–,5(2)	5	45(2),47	45.7	25(2),28	26	16,17,18	17

N. minulla
| | M | ad | 1 | 6 | | 49 | | 25 | | 18 | |
| | F | ad | 1 | 4.5 | | 44 | | 23 | | 16 | |

N. cuprea
	M	ad	5		8.1 ± 0.4		57.2 ± 1.8		35 ± 1.6		22.2 ± 0.4
	M	imm	1	8.4		55		35		22	
	F	ad	1	7.8		55		30		22	

N. coccinigaster
| | M | ad | 2 | 12.3,15.3 | 13.8 | 72,73 | 72.5 | 39,40 | 39.5 | 28(2) | 28 |

N. johannae
| | M | ad | 12 | | 13.5 ± 1 | | 65.3 ± 1.3 | | 33.5 ± 1.1 | | 32.8 ± 0.9 |
| | F | ad | 5 | | 12 ± 1.9 | | 63.6 ± 2.2 | | 30.6 ± 1.3 | | 32 ± 0.7 |

N. superba
	M	ad	3	13.8,14.5,14.7	14.3	70,71,72	71	40(2),41	40.3	31(3)	3
	M	imm	1	14.7		69		41		31	
	F	ad	1	13.2		67		35		30	

Appendix

				WEIGHT		WING		TAIL		BILL	
Species	Sex	Age	No	Individual measurement	Mean	Individual measurement	Mean	Individual measurement	Mean	Individual measurement	Mean
ZOSTEROPIDAE											
Zosterops senegalensis	M	ad	8		8.4 ± 0.8		54.6 ± 1.7		30.6 ± 1.6		11 ± 0
	F	ad	1		7.6		53		31		11
FRINGILLIDAE											
Serinus mozambicus	M	imm	1		10.1		68		42		11
ESTRILDIDAE											
Mandingoa nitidula	M	ad	12		11.1 ± 0.8		53.9 ± 0.7		30 ± 1		11.8 ± 0.4
	M	imm	4	9.2,10, 11.1,11.2	10.4	50,53(2),55	52.8	20,24(2),28	24	9,10(2),11	10
	F	ad	8		10.8 ± 1.6		52.7 ± 1.8		29.5 ± 0.6		11.5 ± 0.4
	F	imm	2	10,10.5	10.3	53,55	54	27(2)	27	11,12	11.5
Pirenestes sanguineus	M	ad	10		17.8 ± 1.8		62.4 ± 1.4		44.1 ± 1.9		15.3 ± 0.7
	M	imm	12		18.7 ± 1.1		64.2 ± 0.9		47.1 ± 1.7		14.8 ± 0.8
	F	ad	7		18.9 ± 1.2		63.9 ± 1.9		44.4 ± 2.6		15 ± 0
	F	imm	1		18.4		62		45		13
Nigrita canicapilla	M	ad	8		14.5 ± 2.5		65.9 ± 2.1		41.3 ± 2.2		12 ± 0
	F	ad	8		15.2 ± 1.6		65.4 ± 2.2		40.3 ± 0.9		12 ± 0
N. bicolor	M	ad	7		10.7 ± 1.2		57.9 ± 1.7		38.9 ± 0.9		11.3 ± 0.7
	M	imm	5		9.5 ± 0.5		57.2 ± 2		37.6 ± 0.9		11 ± 0.6
	F	ad	5		10.6 ± 0.3		57.2 ± 2		36.8 ± 0.7		10.5 ± 0.4
	F	imm	1		10.9		57		40		10
N. fusconota	M	ad	3	8,8.8,10	8.9	52(2),53	52.3	42,44,45	43.7	10(2),11	10.3
	F	ad	1		10.8		53		39		10	
	O	ad	1		9.2		52		40		10	
Parmoptila jamesoni	M	ad	19		9.2 ± 1.1		52.7 ± 1.6		38.1 ± 0.7		12.1 ± 0.4
	M	imm	3	7.3,7.5,9.3	8	51,52,54	52.3	35,37(2)	36.3	11(2),12	11.3
	F	ad	13		9.8 ± 1.2		52.8 ± 0.8		37.8 ± 0.3		11.9 ± 0.3
Spermophaga haematina	M	ad	12		21.8 ± 1.9		67.9 ± 2.1		51.6 ± 2.5		19.1 ± 0.9
	M	imm	2	19.2,19.8	19.5	69,70	69.5	45,49	47	17(2)	17
	F	ad	12		20.5 ± 2.3		67.7 ± 1.8		50.3 ± 1.8		18 ± 8
	F	imm	1		20.5		65		47		16
Estrilda melpoda	M	ad	8		7.6 ± 0.7		48.3 ± 1.6		42.3 ± 2.2		10 ± 0
	M	imm	3	7.5,7.6,7.8	7.6	44,46,47	45.7	23,35,40	32.7	7,8(2)	7.7
	F	ad	8		7.5 ± 0.7		47.7 ± 0.8		39.5 ± 1.2		10 ± 0
E. astrild	M	ad	9		7.2 ± 0.6		47.1 ± 1.5		43.1 ± 2.4		8.9 ± 0.3
	M	imm	1		7.3		48		39		7.5
	F	ad	2	7,7.7	7.3	45(2)	45	40(2)	40	9(2)	9
	O	juv	1		7.4		43		25		8
Lagonosticta rubricata	M	ad	3	10.3,10.6, 11	10.6	49,50(2)	49.7	37,40(2)	39	13(2),14	13.3
	M	imm	3	10.2(2), 10.4	10.3	50(3)	50	37,38,40	38.3	12(2),13	12.3
	F	ad	1	8.4		48		37		14	
Amandava subflava	F	ad	1	4		44		33		8	
Lonchura fringilloides	M	ad	6		15.9 ± 0.9		61.5 ± 1.5		32.8 ± 1.6		17.3 ± 0.5
	M	imm	3	14.5,16.7, 17.8	16.3	59,60,61	60	30,32(2)	31.3	15(2),16	15.3
	F	ad	3	15.8,16.1, 19	17	60,62,64	62	30,31,32	31	16,17(2)	16.7
	F	imm	2	15,15.2	15.1	58,59	58.5	31,32	31.5	16,17	16.5
	O	ad	1	14		59		33		18	

Species	Sex	Age	No	WEIGHT Individual measurement	Mean	WING Individual measurement	Mean	TAIL Individual measurement	Mean	BILL Individual measurement	Mean
L. bicolor	M	ad	8		9.7 ± 1		51.4 ± 1.8		30 ± 1.1		11.8 ± 0.4
	M	imm	2	9,9.4	9.2	50,51	50.5	30(2)	30	11,12	11.5
	F	ad	8		9.2 ± 1.1		50.8 ± 1.4		29.8 ± 0.7		12 ± 0
	F	imm	2	9.5,10	9.8	46,49	47.5	28(2)	28	10,11	10.5
	–	juv	5		9.7 ± 0.3		52.1 ± 1.3		28.2 ± 0.4		10.5 ± 0.4
L. cucullata	M	ad	2	7.6,10.2	8.9	49,50	49.5	27,30	28.5	10(2)	10
	M	imm	1	7		49		28		10	
	F	ad	1	9.2		49		28		10	
	F	imm	1	8.6		49		27		10	
Pholidornis rushiae	M	ad	9		5 ± 0.4		45.2 ± 1.3		17.3 ± 0.4		8.2 ± 0.3
	F	ad	7		5.3 ± 0.2		44.4 ± 0.8		16.9 ± 0.5		8 ± 0
	F	imm	1	5.3		45		16		8	
	O	ad	1	4.8		46		16		8	
	O	juv	1	4.6		44		16		8	
PLOCEIDAE											
Amblyospiza albifrons	M	ad	11		36.2 ± 4.2		86.3 ± 2.5		53.8 ± 2.3		21.7 ± 0.8
	M	imm	2	31.5,33.8	33.5	85(2)	85	56(2)	56	20(2)	20
	F	ad	3	28.6,30.1,31.2	30	78,79,82	79.7	48,50(2)	49.3	20(3)	20
	F	imm	1	30		80		52		20	
Ploceus cucullatus	M	ad	4	39.7,42.3 44.6,48	43.7	82,90(2),92	88.5	47(2),48(2)	47.5	21,23(3)	22.5
	M	imm	2	39.7,40.5	40.1	85,90	87.5	44,48	46	20,22	21
	F	ad	11		33.3 ± 3.8		79.8 ± 2.2		42.2 ± 1.2		21.5 ± 0.7
P. castaneofuscus x cucullatus	O	ad	1	35.7		80		40		21	
	M	ad	1	43		90		50		22	
P. castaneofuscus	M	ad	15		33.4 ± 4.1		81.7 ± 1.6		48.9 ± 1.8		20.7 ± 0.5
	M	imm	10		35.5 ± 3.8		81.1 ± 1.4		47.1 ± 1.6		20.3 ± 0.5
	F	ad	13		28.5 ± 3.4		76.3 ± 2		44.9 ± 1.9		19.7 ± 0.5
P. superciliosus	M	ad	4	19.6,20.2,20.4,21.3	20.4	64,65,70(2)	67.3	37,38,40,43	39.5	16,17(3)	16.8
	M	imm	1	19.4		64		42		17	
	F	ad	1	20		65		39		17	
P. tricolor	M	ad	5		35.3 ± 2.4		90.8 ± 1.1		45.4 ± 1.9		21.4 ± 0.9
	M	imm	3	23.8,31.3,31.8	29	86(2),88	86.7	43,47,48	46	20,21,22	21
	F	ad	2	29.33	31	85(2)	85	44,47	45.5	21,22	21.5
	F	imm	1	29.7		83		43		20	
P. albinucha	F	ad	1	25.5		77		40		20	
P. nigricollis	M	ad	9		24.1 ± 2.3		75.7 ± 2		50 ± 0		17.9 ± 0.9
	M	imm	2	24.2,25.8	25	75,76	75.5	48(2)	48	16,17	16.5
	F	ad	15		23.4 ± 2.5		73.9 ± 1.3		47.9 ± 2.8		17.9 ± 0.7
	F	imm	2	21.4,23.4	22.4	73,75	74	46,48	47	16,17	16.5
P. preussi	M	ad	1	31.7		85		40		17	
	F	ad	1	31.4		85		38		17	
Malimbus scutatus	M	ad	3	28,29,33	30	86,90(2)	88.7	47(2),50	48.3	19(2),20	19.3
	F	ad	3	29,29.4,32	30	86,89,90	88.3	45(2),48	46	17,18,19	18
M. nitens	M	ad	10		41 ± 3.9		92 ± 2.3		51.3 ± 2.3		21.4 ± 0.7
	M	imm	2	36.4,39	37.7	87,88	87.5	50(2)	50	20(2)	20
	F	ad	12		32.8 ± 2.6		84.2 ± 1.6		50.9 ± 3.1		20.7 ± 0.9
	F	imm	2	31.2,33.2	32.2	85(2)	85	50,53	51.5	20(2)	20

Appendix   125

Species	Sex	Age	No	WEIGHT Individual measurement	Mean	WING Individual measurement	Mean	TAIL Individual measurement	Mean	BILL Individual measurement	Mean
M. rubricollis	M	ad	1	60		103		61		23	
	F	ad	2	51.6,55.8	53.7	101,109	105	56,60	58	23(2)	23
M. malimbicus	M	ad	3	31.2,33.3, 37	33.8	85,90(2)	88.3	52,55,56	55.3	19,20(2)	19.7
	M	imm	1	28		85		50		20	
	F	ad	5		27.5 ± 3.4		84.6 ± 1.6		54.4 ± 1.8		19.3 ± 0.5
	F	imm	2	31.4,33.4	32.4	80,82	81	55,57	56	19,20	19.5
Quelea erythrops	M	ad	11		19.1 ± 1.9		63.4 ± 1.1		29.8 ± 0.6		14.9 ± 0.4
	M	imm	5		16.6 ± 2.5		63 ± 1.3		29.4 ± 1.3		15 ± 0
	F	ad	10		16.5 ± 2.1		61.1 ± 1.9		28.8 ± 1.2		14.7 ± 0.5
	O	juv	1	16		62		29		15	
Euplectes ardens	M	ad	16		19.3 ± 2.7		76.5 ± 1.9		212.5 ± 41.2		15 ± 0
	M	imm	2	19.8,20.9	20.4	68,71	69.5	49,53	51	15(2)	15
E. hordeaceus	M	ad	9		21.4 ± 2.1		75.6 ± 2.2		40 ± 1		16.9 ± 0.3
	O	imm	1	13.4		62		35		16	
E. macrourus	M	ad	12		25.1 ± 2.3		82.8 ± 3.5		103.7 ± 1.5		17.2 ± 0.8
	F	ad	1	18.9		69		46		17	
Vidua macroura	M	ad	7		12.5 ± 1.5		71 ± 1.7		177.7 ± 66.2		11 ± 0
	M	imm	2	13.5,13.9	13.7	66,72	69	38,40	39	11(2)	11
	M	juv	2	11.1,12.8	12	63,70	66.5	35,37	36	9(2)	9
	F	ad	6		11.9 ± 1		65.2 ± 1.8		38.2 ± 3		9.6 ± 0.5
STURNIDAE											
Poeoptera lugubris	M	ad	5		39.1 ± 4.2		96.4 ± 2.2		110.6 ± 10.4		18.6 ± 0.9
	F	ad	3	35.4,37.2, 39	37.2	92,94,98	94.7	80,95,100	91.7	18,19(2)	18.7
Onycognathus fulgidus	M	ad	1	103		134		117		31	
	F	ad	4	81.4,87, 89.7,92.8	87.7	121,125, 126,127	124.8	98,116(2), 118	110.5	30(3),31	30.3
Lamprotornis cupreocauda	M	ad	9		59.8 ± 5.3		122.4 ± 2.1		65.4 ± 4.7		20.6 ± 0.7
	M	imm	2	53.4,61.1	57.3	117,122	119.5	57,62	59.5	20,22	21
	F	ad	3	53,57,64.6	58.2	117,118(2)	117.7	58,60,67	61.7	18(2),21	19
Cinnyricinclus leucogaster	M	imm	1	42.8		101		58		18	
ORIOLIDAE											
Oriolus brachyrhynchus	M	ad	9		50.7 ± 4.5		116.7 ± 3.5		83.2 ± 3.9		23.4 ± 0.7
	M	imm	4	42.2,44.4, 53.7,56.7	49.2	114,115, 116,120	116.3	80(2),81,84	81.3	22(2),23,24	22.8
	F	ad	9		47.4 ± 6.1		113.4 ± 3.2		79.5 ± 3.7		22.5 ± 1
	F	imm	2	43,49.2	46.1	110,115	112.5	76,83	79.5	22(2)	22
O. nigripennis	M	ad	2	55,59.2	57.1	115,122	118.5	70,75	72.5	23,25	24
	F	ad	1	50.2		123		75		25	
DICRURIDAE											
Dicrurus ludwigii	M	ad	1	35.5		105		75		22	
	F	ad	1	33.7		104		70		22	
D. atripennis	M	ad	11		38 ± 2.8		117.6 ± 3		88.5 ± 4.6		23.5 ± 0.8
	F	ad	8		37.8 ± 3.1		114.3 ± 2.3		90.3 ± 5.3		23.5 ± 0.7
	O	ad	1	38.6		120		92		22	
D. adsimilis	F	ad	3	44.2,44.4, 48.3	45.6	118,121, 127	122	100,102, 104	102	24,25(2)	24.7

Index of scientific names

The principal references are given in bold

Accipiter badius, 24, **30**
    erythropus, **30**
    melanoleucus, 24, **30**
    tachiro, **30**
Acrocephalus arundinaceus, **79**
    schoenobaenus, 25, **78**
    scirpaceus, 25, **78–79**
Actophilornis africanus, **36**
Agelastes meleagrides, **35**
Alcedo cristata, **48**
    leucogaster, **49**
    quadribrachys, **48**
Alethe diademata, **73–74**
    poliocephala, **74**
Amandava subflava, 25, **97**
Amaurornis flavirostris, **35**
Amblyospiza albifrons, 25, **98**
Anas querquedula, 24, **28**
Andropadus ansorgei, 17, **66**
    curvirostris, **66**
    gracilirostris, **67**
    gracilis, **66**
    latirostris, **67**
    virens, **66**
Anthoscopus flavifrons, 25, **90**
Anthreptes collaris, **91**
    fraseri, **90–91**
    rectirostris, **91**
Anthus leucophrys, **64**
    similis, 18, 25, **64**
    trivialis, 25, **64**
Apalis nigriceps, 25, **81**
    sharpii, 25, **81–82**
Apaloderma narina, **48**
Aplopelia larvata, 19, **38**
Apus affinis, **47**
    apus, **46**
    batesi, 24, **47**
    melba, 24, **47**
Ardea cinerea, 24, **28**
    goliath, 24, **28**
    melanocephala, **28**
    purpurea, 24, **28**
Ardeola ibis, **27**
Atherurus africanus, 13
Aviceda cuculoides, **32–33**

Baeopogon indicator, **67**
Bathmocercus cerviniventris, 25, **82**
Batis (poensis) occultus, 25, **87–88**
Bias musicus, **87**
Bleda canicapilla, 17, **69**
    eximia, **69**
    syndactyla, **69**
Boocercus euryceros, 13
Bostrichia rara, **28**
Bubo africanus, **43**
    lacteus, 24, **44**
    leucostictus, **44**
    poensis, 24, **43**
    shelleyi, **44**
Buteo auguralis, **31**
    buteo, 24, **31**
Butorides striatus, **27**
Bycanistes cylindricus, **54**
    fistulator, **54**

Calyptocichla, serina, **67**
Camaroptera brachyura, **82–83**
    chloronota, **82**
    superciliaris, **82**
Campephaga lobata, 25, **65**
    phoenicea, **66**
    quiscalina, **65**
Campethera caroli, **59**
    maculosa, **59**
    nivosa, **59–60**
Canirallus oculeus, **35**
Caprimulgus binotatus, 24, **45**
    climacurus, **46**
    inornatus, **45**
    tristigma, 24, **45–46**
Centropus leucogaster, **42**
    senegalensis, **42**
Cephalopus jentinki, 13
Ceratogymna atrata, **54**
    elata, **54**
Cercococcyx mechowi, **41**
    olivinus, 24, **41**
Ceryle maxima, **48**
    rudis, **48**
Ceuthmochares aereus, **42**
Charadrius forbesi, **36**
Chelictinia riocourii, 24, **33**
Chlorocichla simplex, **67–68**
Choeropsis liberiensis, 13
Chrysococcyx caprius, **41**
    cupreus, **41–42**
    klaas, **41**
Ciconia abdimii, 24, **28**
    episcopus, **28**
Cinnyricinclus leucogaster, **102**
Circaetus gallicus, 24, **29**
Circus aeruginosus, 24, **28**
Cisticola brachyptera, **81**
    cantans, 25, **80**
    erythrops, 25, **80**
    lateralis, **80**
    natalensis, 25, **80**
Clamator glandarius, **40**
    levaillantii, **40**
Columba iriditorques, **37–38**
    unicincta, **37**
Coracias abyssinica, 24, **52**
Coracina azurea, **65**
Corvus albus, **103**

Corythaeola cristata, **40**
Cossypha cyanocampter, **74**
    niveicapilla, **75**
    polioptera, 25, **75**
Coturnix delegorguei, 24, **34**
Criniger barbatus, **69**
    calurus, **70**
    olivaceus, 25, **69–70**
Cuculus canorus, **40–41**
    clamosus, **40**
    solitarius, 24, **40**
Cypsiurus parvus, **47**

Dendropicos gabonensis, **60**
    pyrrhogaster, **60**
Dendrohyrax dorsalis, 13
Dicrurus adsimilis, **103**
    atripennis, **103**
    ludwigii, **103**
Didynamipus sjoestedji, 15
Dryoscopus gambensis, **70–71**
    sabini, **71**
Dryotriorchis spectabilis, **29–30**

Egretta garzetta, **27**
    intermedia, 24, **28**
Emberiza tahapisi, 25, **94**
Eremomela badiceps, **83**
Erythrocercus mccalli, **89**
Erythropygia leucosticta, **73**
Estrilda astrild, **96**
    caerulescens, 25, **96**
    melpoda, **96**
Euplectes ardens, 9, **101**
    hordaceus, **101**
    macrourus, **101**
Eurystomus glaucurus, **52**
    gularis, **52**

Falco biarmicus, 24, **33**
    cuvierii, 24, **33**
    naumanni, 24, **34**
    peregrinus, 24, **33**
    subbuteo, 24, **33**
    tinnunculus, 24, **33**
Felis aurata, 13
Ficedula hypoleuca, 25, **86**
Francolinus ahantensis, **34**
    bicalcaratus, **34**
    lathami, **34**
Fraseria cinerascens, **86**
    ocreata, **86**

Glaucidium capense, 24, **45**
    tephronotum, 24, **44–45**
Gorsachius leuconotus, **27**
Guttera edouardi, **35**
Gymnobucco calvus, **55**
Gypohierax angolensis, **28–29**

Halcyon badia, **50**
    leucocephala, **50**
    malimbica, **49–50**
    senegalensis, **49**

Hieraaetus ayresii, 24, **32**
    pennatus, 24, **32**
Himantopus himantopus, **37**
Himantornis haematopus, **35–36**
Hippolais icterina, 25, **79**
    polyglotta, 25, **79**
Hirundo abyssinica, **62**
    fuligula, 25, **62**
    griseopyga, 18, **62–63**
    nigrita, **62**
    rustica, **62**
Hyemoschus aquaticus, 13
Hylia prasina, **84**
Hyliota violacea, 25, **87**

Indicator conirostris, **57**
    exilis, 24, **57**
    maculatus, **56–57**
    willcocksi, 24, **57**
Ispidina lecontei, 24, **49**
    picta, **49**
Ixobrychus sturmii, **27**
Ixonotus guttatus, **67**

Jubula lettii, **43**
Jynx torquilla, 25, **59**

Kaupifalco monogrammicus, **31**

Lagonosticta rara, 25, **97**
    rubricata, **96–97**
    senegala, **96**
Lamprotornis cupreocauda, **102**
Laniarius leucorhynchus, **71**
Lanius collaris, **72**
    senator, **72**
Lonchura bicolor, **97**
    cucullata, **97**
    fringilloides, **97**
Lophaetus occipitalis, 24, **32**
Loxodonota africana, 13
Luscinia megarhynchos, 25, **75**
Lybius bidentatus, **55**
    hirsutus, **55**
    vieilloti, 24, **55**

Macheirhamphus alcinus, 18, **33**
Macrodipteryx longipennis, **46**
Macronyx croceus, **65**
Macrosphenus concolor, **83**
    kempi, **83–84**
Malaconotus cruentus, **71**
    lagdeni, 25, **72**
    multicolor, **72**
Malimbus malimbicus, **100**
    nitens, **100**
    rubricollis, **100**
    scutatus, **100**
Mandingoa nitidula, **94**
Manis tricuspis, 13
Megabyas flammulatus, **87**
Melaenornis annamarulae, 16, 20, 25, **86–87**
Milichneutes robustus, 25, **57–58**
Melignomon eisentrauti, 16, 19, 20, 25, **58–59**

Melocichla mentalis, **79**
Merops albicollis, **50**
    apiaster, 24, **50**
    gularis, 18, **51**
    muelleri, 24, **52**
    pusillus, **51**
Milvus migrans, **32**
Mirafra africana, 25, **61**
Monticola saxatilis, 25, **73**
    solitaria, **73**
Motacilla clara, **64**
    flava, 12, 18, **63–64**
Muscicapa aquatica, 25, **84**
    caerulescens, **85**
    cassini, **84**
    comitata, **85**
    epulata, 25, **84**
    gambagae, 25, **84**
    griseigularis, 25, **86**
    olivascens, 16, 25, **85**
    striata, **84**
    ussheri, **85**
Mycteria ibis, **28**
Myrmecocichla nigra, 25, **73**

Neafrapus cassini, 24, **47**
Nectarinia adelberti, **92**
    chloropygia, **92–93**
    coccinigaster, **93**
    cuprea, 25, **93**
    cyanolaema, **92**
    fuliginosa, **92**
    johannae, **93**
    minulla, 25, **93**
    olivacea, **91**
    seimundi, **91**
    superba, **93**
    venusta, **92**
    verticalis, **91–92**
Nectophrynoides occidentalis, **15**
    liberiensis, **15**
    tornieri, **15**
    viviparus, **15**
    cryptus, **15**
    minutus, **15**
    osgoodi, **15**
    malcolmi, **15**
Neocossyphus finschi, **75**
    poensis, **75**
Neotragus pygmaeus, **13**
Nicator chloris, **70**
Nigrita bicolor, **95**
    canicapilla, **95**
    fusconota, 25, **95**

Onycognathus fulgidus, **102**
Oriolus auratus, 25, **102**
    brachyrhynchus, **102–103**
    nigripennis, **103**
    oriolus, 25, **102**
Otus icterorhynchus, 24, **43**
    leucotis, **43**
    scops, 24, **43**

Pachycoccyx audeberti, 24, **41**
Pan troglodytes, **12**
Panthera pardus, **13**
Parmoptila jamesoni, 25, **95**
Parus funereus, 25, **90**
Passer griseus, **101**
Pernis apivorus, 29, **32**
Phoeniculus castaneiceps, 24, **53**
    bollei, 24, **52–53**
Pholidornis rushiae, **97**
Phyllanthus atripennis, **77**
Phyllastrephus albigularis, **69**
    baumanni, **68**
    icterinus, **68**
    scandens, 25, **68**
Phylloscopus sibilatrix, 25, **80**
    trochilus, **80**
Picathartes gymnocephalus, **77–78**
Pinarocorys erythropygia, 25, **61**
Pirenestes sanguineus, **94–95**
Pitta angolensis, **61**
Platysteira blissetti, **88**
    castanea, **88**
    concreta, 19, 25, **88–89**
    cyanea, **88**
Ploceus albinucha, **99**
    aurantius, **98**
    cucullatus, **98**
    castaneofuscus, 12, **99**
    c. x cucullatus, **98–99**
    nigricollis, **99–100**
    preussi, 25, **100**
    superciliosus, 25, **99**
    tricolor, **99**
Podica senegalensis, **36**
Poeoptera lugubris, 25, **101–102**
Pogoniulus atroflavus, **56**
    duchaillui, **55**
    leucolaima, **56**
    scolopaceus, **55–56**
    subsulphureus, **56**
Polyboroides typus, 28, **29**
Potamochoerus porcus, **13**
Potamogale lamottei, **13**
Prinia leontica, 25, **81**
    subflava, **81**
Prionops caniceps, **70**
Procavia rufescens, **13**
Prodotiscus insignis, **59**
    regulus, 25, **59**
Psalidoprocne nitens, 25, **63**
    obscura, **63**
Psittacus erithacus, **38**
Pteronetta hartlaubi, **28**
Pycnonotus barbatus, 18, **66**

Quelea erythrops, **101**

Rhaphidura sabini, 24, **47**
Riparia riparia, 25, **62**

Sarothrura elegans, **35**
    pulchra, **35**

Saxicola rubetra, 12, **72–73**
    torquata, **73**
Scopus umbretta, 12, 24, **28**
Scotopelia ussheri, **44**
Serinus mozambicus, 25, **94**
Sheppardia cyornithopsis, **74**
Smithornis capensis, **60**
    rufolateralis, **60–61**
Spermophaga haematina, **96**
Spizaetus africanus, 24, **32**
Stephanoaetus coronatus, **32**
Stiphrornis erythrothorax, **74**
Streptopelia semitorquata, **38**
Strix woodfordi, **45**
Sylvia atricapilla, 25, **79**
    borin, **79**
Sylvietta denti, 25, **83**
    virens, **83**
Syncercus nanas, 13

Tachybaptus ruficollis, 24, **27**
Tauraco macrorhynchus, **38**
    persa, **38**
Tchagra australis, **71**
    minuta, 25, **71**
Telacanthura melanopygia, 24, **48**
    ussheri, 24, **48**
Terathopius ecaudatus, **29**
Terpsiphone rufiventer, **90**
    viridis, 25, **90**
Thescelocichla leucopleura, **68**
Tigriornis leucolophus, 12, **27**

Tockus camurus, **53**
    fasciatus, **53–54**
    hartlaubi, **53**
Trachyphonus purpuratus, **56**
Tragelaphus scriptus, 13
Treron calva, **39**
Trichastoma cleaveri, **76–77**
    fulvescens, **76**
    puveli, 25, **77**
    rufescens, **77**
    rufipennis, 25, **76**
Tringa glareola, **37**
    hypoleucos, **37**
    nebularia, **36**
    ochropus, 12, 24, **37**
Trochocercus nigromitratus, 25, **89–90**
    nitens, **89**
Tropicranus albocristatus, **54**
Trudus pelios, **76**
    princei, **76**
Turtur afer, **38**, **64**
    brehmeri, **38**
    tymanistria, **38**
Tyto alba, 13, **42**

Urotriorchis macrourus, **31**

Vanellus senegallus, **36**
Vidua macroura, **101**

Zosterops senegalensis, **93–94.**